Collaborative Teaming

Teachers' Guides
to Inclusive Practices

Collaborative Teaming

Third Edition

by

Margaret E. King-Sears, Ph.D.

Rachel Janney, Ph.D.

and

Martha E. Snell, Ph.D.

·P·A·U·L·H·
BROOKES
PUBLISHING Co ®

Baltimore • London • Sydney

Paul H. Brookes Publishing Co.
Post Office Box 10624
Baltimore, Maryland 21285-0624
www.brookespublishing.com

Typeset by Scribe Inc., Philadelphia, Pennsylvania.
Manufactured in the United States of America
by Sheridan Books, Inc., Chelsea, Michigan.

Library of Congress Cataloging-in-Publication Data
The Library of Congress has cataloged the print edition as follows:
King-Sears, Margaret E.
    Collaborative teaming/by Margaret E. King-Sears, Rachel Janney, and Martha E. Snell.—Third Edition.
        pages   cm.   — (Teachers' Guides to Inclusive Practices)
    Martha E. Snell is listed as the first author on the title page of the previous edition.
    Includes bibliographical references and index.
    ISBN 978-1-59857-656-6 (paper)—ISBN 978-1-59857-789-1 (epub3)
    1. Inclusive education—United States.   2. School support teams—United States.   3. Home and school—
United States.   I. Janney, Rachel.   II. Snell, Martha E.   III. Title.

    LC1201.S64 2015
    371.9'046—dc23   2014031730

British Library Cataloguing in Publication data are available from the British Library.

2019   2018   2017   2016   2015

10   9   8   7   6   5   4   3   2   1

Contents

About the Forms

This book contains eight forms for educational use. Purchasers of this book have permission to photocopy and use the blank forms found in Appendix A (pp. 160–166) and on page 74. Larger, printable versions of these blank forms as well as filled-in examples are also available for download online. Please visit **www.brookespublishing.com/king-sears** to access them.

About the Authors

Margaret E. King-Sears, Ph.D., is Professor in the Division of Special Education and disAbility Research at George Mason University, where she has taught since 2005. Prior to that, she developed and coordinated the inclusive education program at The Johns Hopkins University, where she taught from 1989 to 2005. Her research interests are in co-teaching, self-management, and universal design for learning. She is active in several national organizations, including the Council for Learning Disabilities and the Teacher Education Division of Council for Exceptional Children. She earned her doctorate from the University of Florida.

Rachel Janney, Ph.D., is an independent scholar and consultant who has worked with and on behalf of children and adults with disabilities in a number of capacities, including special education teacher, educational and behavioral consultant, technical assistance provider, teacher educator, researcher, and author. For a number of years, she was a professor in the School of Teacher Education and Leadership at Radford University in Virginia, where she taught courses and supervised student teachers in the special education program, specializing in the inclusion of students with extensive learning and behavioral support needs. Dr. Janney received her master's degree from Syracuse University and her doctorate from the University of Nebraska–Lincoln.

Martha E. Snell, Ph.D., is Professor Emerita in the Curry School of Education at the University of Virginia, where she has taught since 1973 and has directed the graduate program in severe disabilities. Dr. Snell's focus has been on the preparation of teachers, with a particular emphasis on those working with students who have intellectual disabilities and severe disabilities. She has been an active member of the American Association on Developmental and Intellectual Disabilities, TASH, and the National Joint Committee on the Communication Needs of Persons with Severe Disabilities.

CONTRIBUTORS

Melissa Ainsworth, Ph.D., began her career teaching high school English but switched into special education, where she taught middle and high school students with moderate to severe disabilities. She is also the parent of child with severe disabilities. She completed her doctorate in special education and teaches in the Graduate School of Education at George Mason University.

Leighann Alt, M.A., is a special educator who has taught students with a range of disabilities in a variety of educational programs and settings since 1997. For 8 years, she has been a co-teacher in an inclusive elementary class that is focused on meeting the educational needs of students with and without disabilities. She earned her bachelor's degree in child study from St. Joseph's College, and she has a master's degree in liberal studies from Stony Brook University.

Kimberly Avila, Ph.D., is an experienced teacher of students with visual impairments and a Certified Orientation and Mobility Specialist. She has worked with students with blindness and visual impairment from early intervention through senior high school and transition as both a school-based teacher and contracting educational specialist. Dr. Avila is a doctoral fellow with the National Leadership Consortium in Sensory Disabilities.

Colleen Barry, M.Ed., has taught students with autism at the preschool and elementary levels. As a Board Certified Behavior Analyst, she used her behavioral background to blend principles of applied behavior analysis with inclusive practices while in the classroom. She received her master's degree in special education at George Mason University, where she is currently pursuing her doctorate. In addition, she works as a behavior intervention specialist for students along the autism spectrum in a large public school district.

Michelle Dunaway, M.Ed., has taught middle and secondary students with mild to moderate disabilities in both Pennsylvania and Virginia in a variety of educational settings for more than 8 years. She has her bachelor's degree in special education with a concentration in math and science and a master's degree in educational leadership and administration from Holy Family University.

Rachel Hamberger, M.Ed., is a Board Certified Behavior Analyst. She taught preschoolers with autism for 7 years and is now the preschool supervisor of an inclusive preschool. She is working on her Ph.D. in special education at George Mason University.

Catherine Morrison, M.Ed., teaches students with mild to moderate disabilities at the high school level in Hawaii. She holds a master's degree in special education from the University of Hawaii at Mānoa and a bachelor's degree in special education from the University of North Carolina at Wilmington. Her research interests include teaching students how to use self-management and creating inclusive classrooms.

Julia Renberg, M.Ed., has taught general middle school science in Florida and regular, pre–Advanced Placement, and team-taught chemistry in Virginia. She has a B.S. in biochemistry from Belorussian State University and an M.Ed. in English as a second language from George Mason University, where she is currently pursuing a doctoral degree in education leadership with a secondary emphasis on special education.

Karen King Scanlan, B.S.N., RN, CCRN, is a Certified Critical Care Registered Nurse. She is currently a clinical nurse coordinator in an intensive care unit. Her son, Sean Joseph, is a junior at the University of Pittsburgh.

Philip Yovino, M.Ed., is a general education teacher who has been co-teaching a third-grade inclusive class since 2006. He strives to meet the diverse academic, social, and emotional needs of all students. His bachelor's degree is in elementary education, and he has a master's degree in teaching literacy.

Acknowledgments

Many colleagues, parents, and students deserve our recognition and praise for their contributions to what we know about team collaboration. We are particularly grateful to the researchers, practitioners, and family members whose work is featured throughout this book. It is their work that inspires us and helps us learn more about the true meaning of collaboration.

We also extend our gratitude to Christine Burton, Kenna Colley, Johnna Elliott, and Cyndi Pitonyak for their contributions to previous editions of this book—contributions that continue to inform our understanding of the ways educational teams collaborate to support students with a wide array of abilities and needs. Their vast knowledge of inclusive practices, combined with their untiring dedication, have enriched the lives of innumerable students, families, and colleagues.

Finally, we would like to acknowledge and thank our Paul H. Brookes Publishing Co. colleagues, Rebecca Lazo and Stephen Plocher, and Project Manager Janet Wehner, for their excellent support, guidance, editing, and persistence in helping us complete this book and others in the series.

To those who are working to establish meaningful inclusion in schools so that all students have membership, enjoy interactions with peers, and receive the needed supports to learn what is important for them to be successful in life

1

Overview of Collaborative Teaming

FOCUSING QUESTIONS

- What are the characteristics of collaboration and collaborative teaming?
- Why is collaborative teaming important in schools today?
- What are the differences between multidisciplinary and transdisciplinary teaming?
- What are the types of structures teams use?
- How do roles change when professionals collaborate?
- What are the benefits and challenges of collaborative teaming?

Classroom Snapshot

Mrs. Soto, a third-grade teacher, and Ms. O'Brien, a special education teacher who is a member of the third-grade team (which also includes the two other third-grade teachers in the school), are meeting after school to put the final touches on the upcoming unit on simple machines. Mr. Maxwell, a vision specialist who serves the school system on a contractual basis, also is attending this particular meeting to consult with Mrs. Soto and Ms. O'Brien about classroom adaptations for Ava, who has an intellectual disability and is legally blind.

Mrs. Soto and Ms. O'Brien co-teach daily during the language arts block in the morning and 3 days per week during social studies and science lessons in the afternoon. This schedule enables Ms. O'Brien to be in the classroom to provide part of the literacy instruction required by the individualized education programs (IEPs) of three

students in the class (Ava plus Landen and Amelia, who have learning disabilities) and to assist in ensuring that those students' use of literacy skills is supported during content area instruction. Co-teaching during science and social studies also allows Ms. O'Brien to support Ava's active participation in the hands-on activities involved in many content area lessons.

Mrs. Soto and Ms. O'Brien have already decided that they will present the input portion of each lesson in the unit together, using team teaching, with Ms. O'Brien handling visual organizers, showing three-dimensional models, and providing demonstrations, and Mrs. Soto providing oral explanations and showing slides and videos to explain concepts and terms. The team members strive to make their presentations clear and concise because Ava needs verbal descriptions of everything done and shown. This also benefits many students in addition to Ava. The two teachers will use station teaching when students complete their practice activities, with each teacher being responsible for a hands-on activity. The students will rotate through the two teacher-directed stations as well as a third, independent work station in small groups.

The third-grade team worked to incorporate universal design for learning (UDL) features into the unit during their grade-level planning and located many online resources, streaming videos, visual organizers, and hands-on activities in which students will experiment with simple machines and create their own invention that incorporates a simple machine as a culminating activity. The unit was designed from the start to use multimodal methods and differentiated materials, and the two teachers know that Landen and Amelia will need little in the way of further individualization, other than frequently checking their understanding of terms, concepts, and instructions. Ava, however, will need some modified materials and more individualized supports.

Mr. Maxwell, the vision specialist, previously met to consult with Ava's entire team. He gave an overview of the tactile and auditory materials that could assist Ava to be more independent during the school day and demonstrated ways to support the use of her residual vision. The two teachers, however, were keen for Mr. Maxwell to lend his expertise to their problem solving about ways to facilitate Ava's class membership and academic progress within some specific class lessons and activities. Mr. Maxwell shared several resources for accessible sound recordings of materials related to the unit topic, suggested adding braille labels to the hands-on materials used at the learning stations, and stressed the importance of allowing Ava ample time to explore the materials. The two teachers decided to adjust their teaching plans to give Ms. O'Brien time to preview the station materials with Ava during the last part of the whole-class presentation. The team also discussed strategies for facilitating peer support for Ava and decided to talk with Ava's parents about creating a formal peer support network.

⟳ ACTIVITY: *Identify the many aspects of effective collaboration featured in this Classroom Snapshot.*

Classroom Snapshot

Mr. Samson is a high school biology teacher who co-teaches one class with Ms. Franklin, a special education teacher. They have co-taught for several years, so they are familiar with each other's styles and strengths. Routines and procedures (particularly for lab work in science) run smoothly for them and the students; they use guided notes and checklists, and they both agree that scaffolded inquiry provides structure and support while also teaching students how to be scientists. Brad is a student with emotional disabilities and has presented some behavior challenges for the co-teachers and the other students. The co-teachers have a solid classroom management system in place, with individual and group reinforcers available. Brad is not responding well to the reinforcement system, however; he is disruptive and off task, and one of the teachers needs to leave his or her team teaching frequently to talk with him privately. Ms. Franklin suspects Brad's inappropriate behaviors are ways he has learned to get attention from teachers and peers.

Mr. Samson and Ms. Franklin begin noting the number of times Brad is disruptive because that seems to be the main issue right now. After collecting data for several days, they realize the frequency of disruptions is more than they had originally thought. They develop a plan to teach Brad how to use a self-management system to appropriately gain attention. Then, Ms. Franklin figures out when she can meet with Brad to teach him the self-management system. It is difficult to teach self-management during the science class, so she targets several of the study periods that all students have every other day. (The school uses block scheduling.) Brad demonstrates that he knows how to use the self-management system after about three sessions, which include using multiple role-play scenarios that Ms. Franklin developed based on what she had observed during the science class. Now it is time for the real test: Can he use the system during science? Brad begins using self-management in the next science class. The co-teachers continue collecting data on the number of times Brad is disruptive. Wow—what a difference they are seeing! And what a difference Brad must be feeling now that he knows more appropriate ways to gain attention from teachers and peers. The co-teachers also notice that more peers are interacting with Brad in positive and supportive ways.

⏱ ACTIVITY: *If the co-teachers did not already have a strong positive and proactive classroom management system in place, then what effect might this have had on Brad's behavior?*

COLLABORATIVE TEAMS

The teachers in these vignettes engage in multiple types of collaboration as they go about the tasks involved in teaching students with and without disabilities within typical classrooms and shared learning activities. Some students have differentiated learning goals; some need supports for special sensory, physical, or behavioral needs; still others bring with them unique cultural and linguistic characteristics. This book describes how teachers from general and special education backgrounds can collaborate with each other and with other school staff, students, and families to effectively include all students. Their joint work can include several types of teaming efforts, including those designed to 1) prevent students from requiring special education services, 2) develop students' IEPs, and 3) provide ongoing support for those students. Teams also may collaboratively deliver classroom instruction and receive consultative support from other professionals.

The previous edition of this book (Snell & Janney, 2005) primarily focused on student-level teams—groups of people organized to address the learning priorities and related needs of individual students identified to receive special education (York-Barr, 1996). This topic is still addressed in detail in Chapters 2–4. This edition, however, looks more deeply at services indirectly delivered through collaborative consultation (see Chapter 5) and direct services delivered through collaborative teaching (see Chapter 6). This

book is meant to be a guide for educators from general and special education backgrounds who are serving or planning to serve students with a range of abilities and disabilities in inclusive classrooms. In addition, it can be a useful resource for anyone working with an educational team (e.g., related services personnel, administrators, family members). We assume that our readers work in schools where teachers and support staff from general education and special education are jointly responsible for students through various formal and informal types of collaborative teaming—but not necessarily through full-time co-teaching. We also assume that this collaboration is determined by the needs of the students.

The members of collaborative teams apply their complementary skills and knowledge, along with effective teamwork skills, to enhance all students' academic and social success. Collaboration in schools entails joint planning, decision making, and problem solving, and collaboration occurs in a variety of formal and informal group configurations. These collaborative efforts are made possible by belief systems that value shared responsibility for student success, the development of effective team structures and processes, and strong support from administrators who guide the development of a school context that supports those values and processes (Cook & Friend, 2010).

The range of supports that teams can plan for and provide is not limited to establishing success in schoolwork. Team-generated supports can have many different functions, such as

- Reducing barriers to participation in school activities
- Facilitating social interactions among students
- Building peer support
- Encouraging (then using) the contribution of ideas by family members

- Embedding related services into the school day

- Replacing problem behavior with skills

- Designing plans to ease students' transitions between grades and schools and into jobs or college

Likewise, teams take many forms to accomplish these functions.

The ensuing chapters address the essential components of collaborative teaming and the structures within which it occurs. Chapter 2 addresses building a team's organization—its membership, distribution of responsibilities, and ways of operating—and the substantial roles that building administrators play when schools utilize collaborative teaming as they prepare for, initiate, and maintain inclusive education. Chapter 3 delves into the skills and processes team members need to effectively and efficiently work together, including basic communication skills and skills to deal with areas of disagreement and conflict. Chapter 4 describes various problem-solving and action-planning methods that teams use as they plan, implement, and evaluate support plans; make individualized adaptations to general education classwork as needed; and evaluate student progress. Chapter 5 addresses various collaborative consultation arrangements whereby professionals provide indirect services that enable other team members to enhance their skills and knowledge. Chapter 6 details collaborative teaching in which general and special educators join together to teach heterogeneous groups of students.

The students described in this book are composites of student characteristics and personalities we have known over the years. The students are exemplars of the range of special learning and support needs found in inclusive schools in which all students have the opportunity to attend their neighborhood schools and are assigned to age-appropriate classes in natural proportions.

WHY IS COLLABORATION SO IMPORTANT IN SCHOOLS TODAY?

> Quality teaching is not an individual accomplishment; it is the result of a collaborative culture that empowers teachers to team up to improve student learning beyond what any of them can achieve alone. The idea that a single teacher, working alone, can know and do everything to meet the diverse learning needs of 30 students every day throughout the school year has rarely worked, and it certainly won't meet the needs of learners in years to come. (Carroll, 2009, p. 13)

Today's classrooms are filled with students who are diverse in their skills and entry knowledge, their motivation to engage in schoolwork, their home life and past experiences, and their languages. An array of teachers and consultative professionals with complementary talents is needed to promote learning in these classrooms, thereby making collaboration among teachers and other school staff essential.

In addition to this logical rationale for collaboration in schools, special education laws and regulations require collaboration as part of the special education process. Beginning with the earliest version of the Individuals with Disabilities Education Improvement Act (IDEA) of 2004 (PL 108-446)—the Education for All Handicapped Children Act of 1975 (PL 94-142)—the identification process and the development and implementation of IEPs have required teaming among general and special education teachers, administrators, related services providers, and parents. Reauthorizations and amendments to IDEA, along with the rulings in several significant, precedent-setting court cases (e.g., *Daniel R.R. v. State Board of Education*, 1989; *Greer v. Rome City School District*, 1992; *Oberti v. the Board of Education of the Borough of Clementon School District*, 1993; *Sacramento City Unified School District Board of Education v. Rachel H.*, 1994) have bolstered the presumption that the least restrictive environment (LRE) is the general education class in a neighborhood school and more explicitly articulated the multiple supplementary aids and services that should be provided within that general education environment to enable students to progress toward their educational goals. The IDEA also has emphasized general education participation on IEP teams and added the requirement that students with disabilities have access to the general curriculum. All these requirements necessitate additional collaborative teaming.

Collaboration Is Essential to Inclusive Education

Collaborative teaming is not used in schools that strive to practice inclusive education merely because education laws and regulations require it. Collaborative teaming is so central to inclusive schooling that it can be viewed as the glue that holds the school together. It is through collaboration that the educational programs and special education supports for individual students are planned and implemented. Students are not merely placed into general education with collaborative planning, teaching, and consultation; they are actively involved and learning.

The material in this book (and others in the Teachers' Guides to Inclusive Practices series) is based on the assumption that inclusive education is far more than an effort to change the location in which special education services are provided. In fact, the IDEA itself defined *special education* as "specially designed instruction to meet the unique needs of a child with a disability" (20 U.S.C. § 1400; IDEA § 1602[29]), a definition that makes no mention of the place where this instruction is to occur. Instead, inclusive education is part of a comprehensive effort to transform schools by making them more flexible, prevention oriented, and responsive to children and their families (Schnorr, 1997). The seven critical characteristics of inclusive education are listed in Table 1.1. Because it is also helpful to know which parameters guide inclusion, Table 1.2 displays what York, Doyle, and Kronberg called "what inclusion is and what inclusion is not" (1992, p. 1). Although inclusive education

Table 1.1. Seven critical characteristics of inclusive education

1. All students are welcome to attend the schools they would attend if they did not have a disability, where they and their families are valued members of the school community.

2. The school culture reflects shared values of equality, democracy, high expectations, diversity, collaboration, and the belief that all students are capable of learning and contributing.

3. Students are full members of age-appropriate classes where the number of students with and without disabilities is proportional to the local population (natural proportions). Students with disabilities are not clustered into particular schools or classes.

4. School teams use flexible decision making to determine students' individualized education programs (including their special services and supports, accommodations, and modifications) that are not based on disability categories.

5. A coherent service delivery model allows general education and special education teachers and other personnel to collaboratively incorporate any special services and supports into age-appropriate school contexts and to coordinate special services with ongoing instruction.

6. Students with varied needs and abilities take part in shared learning experiences while working toward individualized learning priorities with necessary supports and adaptations.

7. Administrators motivate and support school staff toward the achievement of a shared mission and foster shared leadership in a professional community.

From Janney, R., & Snell, M.E. (2013). *Teachers' guides to inclusive practices: Modifying schoolwork* (3rd ed., p. 5). Baltimore, MD: Paul H. Brookes Publishing Co; reprinted by permission.

Table 1.2.   What inclusion is and is not

Inclusion *is*	Inclusion *is not*
Students with disabilities attending the same schools as siblings and neighbors	Requiring all students with any disability to spend every minute of the school day in general education classrooms
Students with disabilities being in general education classes with chronological age-appropriate classmates	Students with disabilities never receiving small-group or individualized instruction
Students with disabilities having individualized and relevant learning objectives	Students with disabilities being in general education to learn the core curriculum only
Students with disabilities being provided with the necessary supports to participate in learning activities and school routines with their classmates	Students with disabilities being left to "sink or swim" when outside of special education environments

Source: York, Doyle, and Kronberg (1992).

is a systemwide and schoolwide approach to schooling, each student with a disability still has an IEP team that defines the special education supports and services needed by that student. Defining those services and supports, and ensuring that they follow the student throughout the school day as needed, requires the collaboration of teachers, specialists, administrators, students, and family members. It is virtually impossible to imagine a school community that could be legitimately described as inclusive for all students yet did not value and practice collaboration.

Collaboration Is Essential to Schoolwide Systems for Student Support

Calls for improved collaboration in schools today do not come only from educators, parents, and others who seek more effective inclusion for students with disabilities. Many current school improvement initiatives focus on integrating available human and capital resources to address a single schoolwide goal—building school capacity to address student needs (Capper & Frattura, 2009; Causton-Theoharis, Theoharis, Bull, Cosier, & Dempt-Aldrich, 2011; Sailor & Roger, 2005; Waldron & McLeskey, 2010). Although reforms such as inclusive education, schoolwide positive behavior interventions and supports (SW-PBIS), and response to intervention (RTI)

originated in special education, they have an effect on all students and teachers in a school. Furthermore, many general education reforms (e.g., differentiated instruction, UDL, Common Core State Standards) are essentially tools for assisting educators to achieve excellence and equity for all students. The No Child Left Behind (NCLB) Act of 2001 (PL 107-110) also has contributed to the need for collaboration with its requirements that school accountability measures take all students' academic progress into account and that all students be taught by teachers who are highly qualified to teach the subject matter on which students are tested. Collaborative teaming among educators, other relevant professionals, and family members is essential to each of these initiatives.

Figure 1.1 depicts a framework for thinking about and organizing supports and interventions in schools that are committed to the success of all students. This three-tiered model for schoolwide prevention of academic and behavior problems builds on the logic behind the RTI model. It also is consistent with the framework used to organize the three tiers of interventions used in SW-PBIS (Copeland & Cosbey, 2008/2009; Sailor et al., 2006). This model, however, applies more broadly to sustained use of all supports and interventions available in a school and not only to the RTI process or the application of positive behavior supports. The

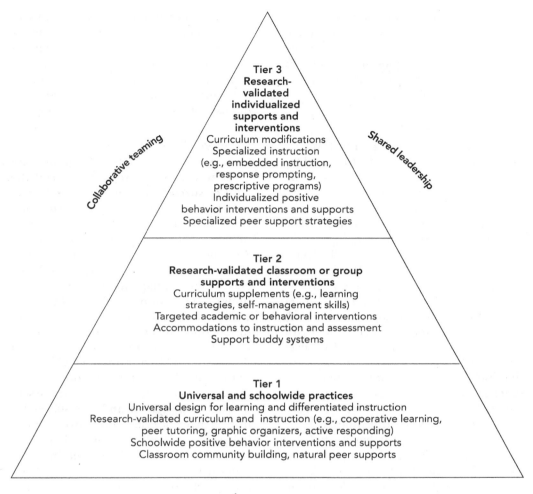

Figure 1.1. Three tiers surrounded by collaborative teaming, shared leadership, and an inclusive culture. (From Janney, R., & Snell, M.E. [2013]. *Teachers' guides to inclusive practices: Modifying schoolwork* [3rd ed., p. 9]. Baltimore, MD: Paul H. Brookes Publishing Co.; adapted by permission.)

triangle in Figure 1.1 is divided into three tiers of educational practices, with 1) universal practices at the base or first tier, 2) supports targeted toward specific groups of students in the middle or second tier, and 3) more individualized supports in the upper or third tier.

Collaboration in Tier 1

Universal or whole-school practices focus on prevention of learning and behavior problems and include UDL (Center for Applied Special Technology [CAST], 2010), research-validated instructional practices (also called *evidence-based practices*), and schoolwide discipline programs. Collaboration comes into play as school teams make decisions about and participate together in professional development to ensure that all students receive high-quality instruction and effective behavior support. Teams jointly determine when students need additional supports. Keep in mind that some students with IEPs have accommodations, which are adjustments to the school program that do not substantially change the curriculum level or performance criteria, such as needing visuals to accompany auditory information, using digital textbooks, or providing guided note-taking forms. These accommodating materials and techniques fit conceptually into Tier 1's universal practices when they are available to all students.

Collaboration in Tier 2

Tier 2's supports target the needs of students who exhibit risk factors and/or school performance that reflect less-than-expected gains. Students receive short-term, intensive instruction beyond the general curriculum based on performance data and team decision making. These interventions often target small groups of students with similar difficulties and include tutoring programs, prescriptive literacy interventions, and self-management support. General educators may team with specialists (e.g., reading, mathematics, or strategic instruction specialists) to deliver, and coordinate Tier 2 supports. Teams that include administrators, general and special educators, specialists, and family members make decisions about students' intervention goals and time lines.

IEP accommodations that fit into Tier 2 supports enable a student to gain access to curriculum content, demonstrate learning, and lessen the effect of a disability on the student's school performance. Examples of these accommodations include self-management instruction to increase on-task behavior and accurate work completion during mathematics, booster sessions for learning vocabulary for content area units, and learning strategy instruction for skills to write essays for English. Note that these accommodations may involve supplementary learning goals for the student (e.g., attaining fluency in the use of a self-management technique, essay-writing strategy). Such accommodations might require a special educator's expertise to match them with student needs, but other team members also can deliver them. Classroom teachers sometimes find that many of their students without IEPs

also benefit from these learning and self-management skills; teachers may decide to provide general instruction in their use to the entire class. Some students may still concurrently receive additional support and time to acquire proficiency, so more intensive explicit instruction is necessary.

Collaboration in Tier 3

Students who obtain Tier 3 supports are those who have not yet experienced the level of success targeted at Tiers 1 or 2. The team decides what other supports need to be used, based on the student's unique needs. Consider the Classroom Snapshot for Brad at the beginning of this chapter. The co-teachers had strong Tier 1 classroom management and instructional interventions in place. The teachers decided to provide self-management instruction during several study periods when Brad's disruptive behavior was not responsive to those research-based techniques. A Tier 3 intervention was not considered because Brad learned the self-management system and was successful using it in science class, but if his disruptive behavior persisted or was more dangerous to himself or others, then involvement by other team members such as administrators, psychologists, counselors, and other teachers would be appropriate. Tier 3 interventions go beyond adding intensive, short-term supports and/or providing reasonable accommodations. Specialized teaching methods with a confirmed track record (e.g., visual strategies, task analysis and chaining, systematic prompting and reinforcement) and individualized behavior interventions and supports fall into this category, as do curriculum modifications, which alter curriculum goals and performance criteria. Special educators may be the team members who are most familiar with these more unique interventions, but other team members may be instrumental in delivering them when the collaborative teaming practices described in this book are consistently applied.

Best Practices for Schoolwide Systems of Support

Integrated, responsive schoolwide systems for student support are associated with achievement gains, reduced rates of special education referral and placement, and higher passing rates on state tests (Burns, Appleton, & Stehouwer, 2005). The framework for schoolwide student support is consistent with the philosophy and practice of inclusive education and emphasizes 1) a unified system of supports to enhance achievement, rather than separate systems for special and general education; 2) use of least intrusive supports so that teachers turn to more specialized practices only when generally effective practices are inadequate to meet a student's needs; 3) use of student performance data—not disability classifications—to judge learning and the need for more specialized methods; and 4) services and supports that are viewed as portable and not available in only one special education location (Snell & Brown, 2011). It also is important to understand that a tier is not a place or placement, and students may be provided supports and interventions from various tiers at different points in time and for different aspects of their educational programming. For example, a student might need Tier 3 supports for behavioral issues and Tier 2 supports for literacy, yet participate in mathematics with the benefit of whole-class Tier 1 practices. Furthermore, the Tier 2 literacy intervention may be reduced or faded over time as the student progresses toward a more typical range of literacy skills.

Teachers and other school staff must have the skills and dispositions to implement evidence-based practices at each tier of the central triangle or pyramid of support in Figure 1.1 in order for schoolwide systems for student support and inclusive education to work. (These practices are the subject of companion books in this series: *Behavior Support* [Bambara, Janney, & Snell, 2015], *Modifying Schoolwork* [Janney & Snell, 2013], *Social Relationships and Peer Support* [Janney & Snell, 2006].) Surrounding the central pyramid of support are three additional features of a school's culture and structure that affect successful implementation of the integrated system of student support: 1) an inclusive culture, 2) shared leadership, and 3) collaborative teaming. An essential piece of the foundation for inclusive education and schoolwide systems of support is missing without effective collaboration among the various teams of educators, administrators, and family members. Administrators must provide strong leadership and support to facilitate these collaborative efforts and foster a school culture that values all students and their families (Ratcliffe & Harts, 2011; Thousand & Villa, 2005).

It is not difficult to make a convincing case for the need for improved collaboration in schools. Piercey summed it up well: "Teacher collaboration is a prime determinant of school improvement" (2010, p. 54). Research on efforts to make schools more inclusive and collaborative repeatedly has found that major barriers include 1) finding time to collaborate, 2) negative teacher attitudes about variations in ability and the feasibility of addressing them in general education contexts (as well as the influence of those attitudes on school climate), and 3) lack of a shared philosophy and understanding of inclusive education (Carter, Prater, Jackson, & Marchant, 2009; Causton-Theoharis et al., 2011; Frattura & Capper, 2007). Overcoming these obstacles requires focused, systematic planning along with reconfiguring the school's existing resources and supports. Appendix B provides helpful resources on the topic of successful adoption and sustained implementation of school improvement efforts.

COLLABORATION AND COLLABORATIVE TEAMING

Collaboration is often misunderstood. It is time consuming and requires different skills from working alone, so experts advise that we carefully select what needs collaborative work versus what can be tackled by individuals (Friend, 2000). Friend (2000), who is a recognized authority on collaboration, set forth and clarified several misunderstandings educators hold about collaboration (see Table 1.3). We will keep these in mind as we examine the components of collaborative teamwork in inclusive schools.

What Is a Team?

A *team* in education is "two or more interdependent individuals with unique skills and perspectives who interact directly to achieve their mutual goal of providing students with effective educational programs and services" (Friend & Cook, 2007, p. 113). General and special education teachers, related services providers, administrators, other school staff, and family members work together to implement collaboration in a variety of teams. These teams include teacher assistance teams, IEP teams, grade-level or subject-area teams, classroom or co-teaching teams, and student support teams. The collaborative teams addressed in this book are primarily those that focus on students who use special education

Table 1.3.   Myths and misunderstandings about collaboration in schools

Myth or misunderstanding	Reality of professional collaboration
Everyone is doing it.	Saying that every activity involving more than one person is collaborative diminishes the effort required. Collaboration requires ongoing commitment from every team member to sharing goals, communicating with care, and maintaining parity in communication.
More is better.	Collaboration is time intensive and must be kept at a doable level. Special educators and related services staff can have so many classroom teachers to collaborate with, students to support and follow, and planning meetings to attend that they have no time for direct service. Schools must set priorities on collaboration that put students and families first. Collaboration effort (time and number of staff) and outcomes (documented results) should be monitored to set priorities about what requires collaboration.
It is about feeling good and liking others.	"Collaboration is the conduit through which professionals can ensure that students receive the most effective educational services to which they are entitled" (Friend, 2000, p. 131). Feeling good at the end of a teaming session gives no guarantee of reaching this goal. The success of collaboration is measured by what it yields for students. If one teacher can achieve this goal as well alone, then collaboration is not worth its cost in time, despite the fact that team members may have been satisfied with the experience. Collaboration is about respect more than about liking one another. Having respect for each other makes team members more willing to take on the risks involved in teaming.
It comes naturally.	The skills needed to collaborate are often viewed in contradictory ways. Some complain that collaboration is difficult and they did not have coursework on it, whereas many claim they know all about communication skills and problem solving. It seems that some professionals equate collaboration with conversation, whereas others think that skills for interacting well with others come along with caring for children. Professionals are often lazy with co-workers they know well and use poor interaction skills, which contributes to being unprepared and out-of-practice for adversarial interactions that require extensive skills. Staff who gossip about others' noncooperative style, operate by under-the-table agendas, and adopt a blaming attitude to parents are exhibiting symptoms that cry out for professional development. Collaboration without the skills threatens the outcomes for students.

From Friend, M. (2000). Myths and misunderstandings about professional collaboration. *Remedial and Special Education, 21,* 130–132; adapted by permission of SAGE Publications.

services and supports; however, many of the principles of collaborative teaming that apply to these student-centered teams also apply to other types of teams that are formed within schools, such as teams to select textbooks, implement a new literacy program, or promote improvements in school–community relationships. Effective communication, mutual respect, and problem-solving strategies are relevant whether a team is addressing a student with disabilities or designing a mathematics curriculum.

What Is Collaboration?

According to Friend and Cook, *collaboration* is "a style for direct interaction between at least two co-equal parties voluntarily engaged in shared decision making as they work toward a common goal" (2007, p. 7). It is critical to understand that this definition views collaboration as a style for interacting, not as an activity. A team will not be effective if some members dominate and others have opinions and attempts to contribute that are ignored or discounted.

Collaboration is not simply another word for *cooperation*. Nor is it simply another word for *working together*. When teams work together in a collaborative style, positive interdependence exists among members who agree both to pool and partition their resources and responsibilities and to operate from a foundation of shared values. Team-generated goals determine the purpose of working together, and team-generated ground rules guide the way the team operates. The work can entail a wide range of activities, including assessing students' needs and skills, determining goals, exchanging information, reaching consensual decisions, making teaching and support plans, and implementing and evaluating those plans. Friend and Cook's (2007) definition directly or indirectly suggested these six core characteristics of collaboration:

1. *Collaboration is a voluntary relationship.* This is not to suggest that teachers

should not be assigned the students they will teach or that teaming with other professionals should be optional. It does mean that whereas proximity can be mandated, the use of a collaborative style of interaction cannot be mandated—it can only be voluntarily chosen. Participants who at first do not feel at ease with collaboration can be encouraged through example and discussion to develop a more collaborative style. Experiencing the rewards and benefits of collaborative efforts helps participants increase their appreciation of this interpersonal style (Hunt, Soto, Maier, & Doering, 2003; Malone & Gallagher, 2010).

2. *Collaboration is based on parity (or equality) among participants.* All participants and their contributions are equally valued and add to the team's outcomes. The disparity in the authority and status in relationships between professionals and parents can derail the development of productive partnerships. Professionals can help establish equality by actively encouraging family members to express their opinions and by acknowledging the validity of their points of view (Blue-Banning, Summers, Frankland, Nelson, & Beegle, 2004).

3. *Collaboration is based on mutual goals.* Team members must be clear about the short- and long-term goals that have been set for students. When engaged in problem solving and action planning, they must seek solutions to shared notions of what "the problem" is. For example, a classroom teacher concerned about a student with a disability who becomes upset and disruptive during large-group lessons may want the team to figure out how to get the student out of the room during those times. The special educator on the team might view the solution to the problem as making

large-group lessons more engaging and enabling the student to play a more active role. Having shared goals, such as the value of being included with peers, builds commitment to consensual solutions and shared responsibility for results.

4. *Collaboration requires shared responsibility for key decisions.* Although team members may take individual responsibility for completing particular tasks, the team shares responsibility for the decisions on which action plans are based.

5. *Collaboration requires participants to share resources.* Each participant is responsible for sharing his or her particular resources, including information, skills, equipment, and materials, with the rest of the team.

6. *Collaboration requires shared accountability for outcomes.* The team's success and its failure are shared by all team members. Individual members do not take credit for team success or blame others for team failures. When teams take time to celebrate their successes, they also are celebrating their cohesion.

In addition to these six key characteristics, collaboration has been described as having several *emergent* characteristics, or characteristics that develop over the course of time when a collaborative relationship grows (e.g., trust, respect, a sense of community) (Friend & Cook, 2007; Knackendoffel, 2007). The participants in a collaborative relationship begin their work together with a general attitude of respect and openness to learning. They are not likely to experience a true sense of community, however, until they have had the chance to get to know one another and share ongoing responsibility for achieving common goals. Participants earn the trust and respect of team members when they show that they are committed and dependable.

SERVICE DELIVERY MODELS AND METHODS

Schools traditionally have provided special education apart from the general education classroom by either pulling students out of a general classroom into tutoring sessions or resource rooms or by teaching students in self-contained classrooms that serve only students with disabilities. These approaches generally have not been coupled with ongoing, systematic joint planning or sharing of information between general education and special education teachers. The collaborative teaming that occurred primarily focused on the IEP process—determining eligibility, developing annual goals, deciding on the services to be provided, and so forth.

These traditional service delivery approaches contrast with approaches that are better suited to achieving the goals of collaborative teams in inclusive schools, which center on facilitating student learning and membership within general education classes, school activities, and peer groups. States and localities differ with respect to the specific terminology used to identify service delivery methods and the personnel who deliver them (e.g., some states and/or localities distinguish between special education teachers who provide direct services and consulting teachers who provide indirect services). In general, however, inclusive service delivery models utilize some version of the following three types of services.

1. Special education instruction is a direct service that may be delivered 1) through co-teaching in the general class or 2) through direct teaching to individuals or small groups in the general class (a push-in approach) or another area of the school (a pull-out approach). If direct teaching occurs in the context of an alternative lesson or activity, then it is scheduled and located in accordance with recommendations for making individualized

adaptations that are nonstigmatizing and respectful of the student's class membership (see Table 1.4).

2. Special education support is a direct service that is typically delivered by paraprofessionals who are acting under the guidance and supervision of the teachers on the team. (We use the term *paraprofessional* throughout this text, but schools and school systems may use other terms, such as *para-educator, instructional aide,* or *instructional assistant.*)

3. Special education consultation is an indirect service delivered by a special educator that may involve activities such as adapting materials, training and supervising paraprofessionals, gathering and analyzing student performance data, and providing information to other team members.

Students also may receive related services that may be delivered through 1) direct service (either pushed in to the general class context or, in certain cases, such as for a service that is most appropriately

Table 1.4. Collaborative service delivery approaches used by team members with three students

| Student | Special education and related services | | | |
	Special education instruction (with co-planning)	Special education consultation	Special education paraprofessional support	Related services
Abby (age 6), first grade (intellectual disability and cerebral palsy)	60 minutes daily for reading and language arts (co-teaching and push-in direct instruction) 30 minutes daily for mathematics (co-teaching)	20 minutes × 2 days per week for progress monitoring, record keeping, developing adaptations, paraprofessional training and supervision, and teacher consultation	2 hours daily for morning activities, school and class routines, lunch, self-care, and physical education	*Speech-language therapy:* 20 minutes × 3 days per week (direct service; 2 days pull-out, 1 day push-in within small-group activities) *Physical therapy:* 20 minutes × 1 day per week (pull-out direct service)
Devin (age 9), fourth grade (Asperger syndrome)	30 minutes daily for reading and language arts (co-teaching 2 days, pull-out direct instruction 3 days) 30 minutes daily for social-behavior skills (co-teaching)	15 minutes daily for progress monitoring, record keeping, developing adaptations, paraprofessional training and supervision, and teacher consultation	4.25 hours daily for mathematics, content areas, specialties, recess, school and class routines, and self-help	*Speech-language therapy:* 20 minutes per week (push-in direct service, within small-group activities) *Occupational therapy:* consult once per marking period
Stephen (age 16), 11th grade (learning disability)	60 minutes every other day (block scheduling) for English 11 (co-teaching and push-in direct instruction for writing strategy instruction) and academic lab as needed	30 minutes every other day (block scheduling) for progress monitoring, record keeping, and developing accommodations in all content classes	None	None

Source: Janney and Snell (2013).

delivered in private, in a pull-out location) or 2) consultation.

Teams plan ways to deliver these special education services that maximize learning and membership. Thus the most frequently used delivery approaches involve pushing in supports and teaching collaboratively and less often involve pulling the student away from class activities. This varies, however, depending on individual student needs. Table 1.4 lists the special education and related services required for three students of varying ages and support needs. All of the students' services and supports are determined by their IEP teams and delivered through collaborative planning that guides the students' special education instruction and support, as well as through differing proportions of co-teaching and collaborative consultation. Consider Figure 1.2 as you read the following scenario about Abby's delivery of services.

Student Snapshot

Abby is a first-grade student with multiple disabilities, including cerebral palsy and an intellectual disability. Abby's team created an individually designed plan that suits her IEP goals and meshes both with Abby's first-grade schedule and with the staff schedule. Abby's schedule is different from her classmates' only when she leaves the classroom for an assessment check by the physical therapist once each marking period and when receiving special education support for her personal needs. In-class special education support is provided daily by a paraprofessional during morning activities (arrival, lunch sign-up, morning meeting), classroom transitions and routines (e.g., moving from desk to table or learning center, gathering supplies and materials), and during physical education. Co-teaching occurs during language arts when her classroom teacher and special education teacher use a team teaching model during the first half of the lesson, and then the special education teacher instructs Abby along with a small group of classmates while the general education teacher instructs the rest of the class (a co-teaching model called *alternative teaching*). The special education teacher also co-teaches during math using various co-teaching arrangements, depending on the particular skills being taught.

⟳ ACTIVITY: *How do you envision Abby's relationships with her first-grade peers without disabilities, given that she is receiving most of her services alongside them in the first-grade classroom? Contrast that with her peer relationships if she were in a self-contained special education setting all day. What would be the difference for Abby? For her peers?*

Transdisciplinary Approach

Many collaborative teams include members other than those from the teaching profession or students' families. In addition to general education and special education teachers, other professional members might include physical therapists, occupational therapists, speech-language pathologists, counselors, school psychologists, vision specialists, orientation and mobility specialists, interpreters for students with hearing impairment, nurses, community agency representatives, and program administrators. Besides family members, other nonprofessional and paraprofessional members may include a family advocate, the student, friends of the student, and any paraprofessionals that support the student or the classroom.

Although discipline-specific skills and knowledge are necessary to meet students' educational needs, team members must conduct their activities—whether conducting assessments, providing academic instruction, facilitating social interactions, designing and implementing behavior supports, promoting physical health and safety, or providing service coordination—in coordinated and collaborative ways. Professionals who use a multidisciplinary approach conduct their activities independently, utilizing their disciplinary skills and knowledge

In *Modifying Schoolwork,* a companion book in the Teachers' Guides to Inclusive Practices series, Janney and Snell (2013) suggested two broad guidelines for teams to follow when creating individualized adaptations for students with individualized education programs (IEPs). Adaptations should 1) achieve both social and instructional participation for the student and 2) be only as special as necessary.

Providing a student with alternative instruction is one of the most specialized (and intrusive) adaptations. At times, teams may decide that a student's individualized learning target can only be achieved through instruction that uses student-specific methods, materials, and activities. Such a decision should be based on data, a sound rationale, and careful consideration of the costs and benefits to the student's social, academic, and other needs. In addition, alternative instruction should be scheduled with respect for the student's classroom membership (Ford, Davern, & Schnorr, 2001). If alternative instruction is delivered outside the general classroom (e.g., study center, computer lab, multipurpose room, media center), then the student's overall schedule should decisively maintain his or her class membership. In schools where differentiation and a variety of groupings are the rule for all students, and where special educators are viewed as teachers for the entire class, well-coordinated alternative instruction seems less atypical than in schools where these conditions do not exist. It is important for team members to ask the following questions when alternative adaptations are used:

1. Do we have reliable data showing that this approach is succeeding where less intrusive approaches have failed?
2. Is the lesson or activity timed to match natural transitions in the class schedule?
3. Are peers included as possible and appropriate?
4. Is the lesson or activity coordinated with classroom content and themes?
5. Does the alternative lesson or activity provide intensive, individualized instruction or other specialized services?
6. If the student leaves the classroom, is the alternative lesson or activity offered in a nonstigmatizing location and grouping?
7. Is the alternative lesson or activity monitored and adjusted to be less intrusive as the student makes gains and the team increases its skills? (Janney & Snell, 2013, p. 87)

Figure 1.2.   Questions to ask about alternative instruction. *(Source:* Janney & Snell, 2013.)

to address student needs that fall within the context of their specific disciplines. A common pitfall of multidisciplinary teaming is that a student's programs and services can be fragmented, incompatible, and even unnecessarily duplicated (Falk-Ross et al., 2009; Giangreco, Prelock, Reid, Dennis, & Edelman, 2000). A multidisciplinary team approach also fails to afford parity to nonprofessional team members, such as family members, who are placed in the role of being primarily consumers of information (Carpenter, King-Sears, & Keys, 1998).

In contrast with a multidisciplinary approach, a team using an interdisciplinary approach tends to act in a more coordinated and cooperative fashion during assessment and planning activities, but team members independently implement team decisions and then share the results

at team meetings (Carpenter et al., 1998). Therefore, services—and, as a result, students' learning—still may be fragmented and duplicated. Students may learn particular skills outside of the typical classroom and then not be taught to generalize and transfer those skills to natural contexts.

 ## Student Snapshot

Devin, a fourth grader with Asperger syndrome, participates in almost all of his class's lessons and routines with an array of adaptations and supports. His reading fluency and word recognition skills are well below the norm for his age, however. Participation in the regular classroom program during his second-grade year and the addition of a supplementary Tier 2 intervention in his third-grade year did not close the gap. Therefore, Devin's IEP team decided to provide him with a more specialized reading approach through direct instruction by a special educator. Devin and three other fourth graders with similar reading needs go to the resource room daily for a 30-minute reading group during the first part of the fourth-grade reading and language arts block.

A few weeks into the semester, Devin's fourth-grade teacher noticed several signs that she and the special education teacher needed to better coordinate Devin's reading instruction with the instruction that was provided to his classmates. She saw that Devin seemed lost and embarrassed when other students would refer to a book that the class had been reading when he was in his pull-out reading group. She also had been surprised when the special education teacher provided Devin with an individualized spelling packet that was different from the class packet. Whereas the class was given a menu of homework assignments from which they could choose how to practice their spelling words, Devin's spelling packet prescribed his practice activities. Devin's fourth-grade teacher also was concerned about the lack of information she was receiving about Devin's progress in his alternative reading group. As the semester progressed, Devin's team gained skills in planning as a team so that his reading materials and spelling assignments were better coordinated with ongoing class activities. The team also devised ways to better communicate about progress that occurred during alternative instruction. Team members gained trust in one another as they revealed their concerns about Devin's literacy program and resolved those concerns in a professional way.

⏱ ACTIVITY: *How are students like Devin affected when adults do not collaborate or share critical instructional information?*

Teams that include members of multiple disciplines and are collaborative (and not only coordinated and cooperative) throughout all phases of their work, from assessment to planning to implementation and evaluation, are called *transdisciplinary* teams; their approach involves agreement that the multiple needs of students are interrelated (Bruder, 1994; Rainforth & York-Barr, 1997) and that team members'

interdependence is essential to meeting those needs in inclusive contexts.

 ## Student Snapshot

Abby shares her morning news with her first-grade classmates with several individualized adaptations that enable her to communicate using skills that have been shaped by the efforts of her team members. For example, Abby first needs to be sitting upright with a lot of support from a special legless chair to communicate in class circle. She then touches the symbols on a Cheaptalk communication device (Enabling Devices) to activate a message corresponding to each symbol. Six of Abby's team members—her classroom and special education teachers; her mother; and her occupational, physical, and speech-language therapists—worked together to design and refine this arrangement.

⏱ ACTIVITY: *What reactions would you anticipate from peers in Abby's classroom?*

Role Release

Team members who use a transdisciplinary approach must fill their old roles in new ways and also fill new roles. Their roles become less defined along traditional disciplinary lines (although in reality there probably is much overlap in members' skill sets) as they share roles and integrate their skills and knowledge. Team members may extend or expand their previous roles, such as by participating in professional development activities about collaborative teaching or staying current with the latest research in their own and related disciplines. Team members also must release certain aspects of their old roles to other team members in order for students with disabilities—particularly those with the most complex support needs who receive full-time special education and multiple related services—to be effectively served in inclusive classes.

Role release at the simplest level means that team members step out of their usual roles to become either teachers of other team members or learners taught by other team members. Role release results not only in mutual learning but also in professional roles being combined so that one or several team members learn to deliver a variety of interventions to a student (Friend & Cook, 2007). Role release is accomplished through explicit collaborative consultation between the two team members so that the learner becomes an ongoing implementer of the new techniques, yet the teacher is still accountable for delivery of the support or intervention in question until the learner team member is up to speed.

To be a teacher of another team member requires sharing the knowledge and expertise of one's position as a teacher, parent, therapist, and so forth 1) at times when this information is relevant to the team's goals and 2) in ways that will yield learning from team members. To be a learner and benefit from other team members' experiences requires 1) the belief that each team member's knowledge and perspectives are valuable to other team members and will assist the team in reaching its goals and 2) the opportunity to receive instruction and feedback from the teaching team member. Two instruction and feedback strategies that have been found to be effective when team members teach other team members are praise and simple prompts given to the learning team member during his or her use of the new skill and brief (3–5 minutes) discussions of how the learning team member or the student actually performed during an observation (Noell et al., 2000). Teachers in one research study increased their use of specific academic praise (an evidence-based practice) when they were shown visual feedback on graphs (Reinke, Lewis-Palmer, & Martin, 2007). Technical assistance and support are critical when teachers (or any team members) are learning to use new approaches.

Student Snapshot

Jonah is an eighth-grade student with Asperger syndrome. His classroom teachers are eager to learn how to prevent his disruptive behavior. When he becomes anxious, Jonah can change quickly from being a talented student to being highly disruptive. During team meetings, Jonah's classroom teachers learn new methods of behavior management from the special education teacher and the school counselor, including redirection, behavior rehearsal, peer support, organizational support, and Social Stories. Because the methods were new to them, the classroom teachers then shared their expertise to help shape these new methods into strategies that would work in their classrooms. They role-played the methods with each other while getting feedback from the special education teacher and then discussed their performance as a group.

Role release enables Jonah's classroom teachers to implement team-developed behavior plans with Jonah even when special education staff are not present. Mr. Smythe, Jonah's U.S. history teacher, has learned to redirect Jonah when the bell rings for class change and rehearse his routine for staying calm. Mr. Smythe puts a checkmark next to the date on a data sheet and quickly notes Jonah's response. He and other team members will share notes at the next team meeting and make sure that the data sheet goes to Jonah's IEP manager, who retains responsibility for ensuring that the agreed-on strategies are used as planned and that Jonah's behavior changes are recorded.

↻ ACTIVITY: *If the co-teachers did not have a strong positive and proactive classroom management system in place, then what effect might this have on Jonah's behavior?*

Role release is most likely to occur when teams are operating in a cooperative atmosphere of trust and support and are working toward achieving a common goal (Thomas, Correa, & Morsink, 1995). Role release allows team members to move together with a uniform understanding of the rationale for their decisions and the techniques for implementing them.

COMPONENTS OF COLLABORATIVE TEAMING

Collaborative teamwork involves a set of different, yet overlapping, components. The first three components occur somewhat sequentially as a team forms and develops (see Figure 1.3); however, each component maintains its importance even after its initial implementation. For example, in addition to an initiative from administrators to get the team underway (Component 1), most lasting collaborative efforts rely on some administrative support to sustain themselves over time. Team members will learn communication skills and develop processes that enable them to work efficiently once a team is organized and operating (Component 2). Members also will repeatedly problem-solve and make numerous decisions during the school year about their students, their classroom, their instruction, and so forth and will repeatedly take team action (Component 3). The dynamics often change when teams add new members, such as at the beginning of a new school year; a reconfigured team should take some time to review teamwork skills (Component 2) while getting used to its internal changes.

Team members will use the activities of these three components as they participate in the three primary structures in which collaboration to deliver special education occurs: 1) student-level collaborative teams, 2) collaborative consultation, and 3) collaborative teaching (co-teaching). Participants in all three structures use a transdisciplinary approach and a collaborative interaction style to make inclusion work. They apply effective teamwork skills (e.g., defining roles and responsibilities, communicating unambiguously, resolving conflicts constructively, making decisions by consensus, using agreed-on problem-solving and action planning processes) to do the work involved in meeting students' educational goals. It is important to understand that teachers in inclusive schools typically will be involved in all three of these formal collaborative structures to some degree, as well as frequent informal collaborative exchanges with team members. For example, an elementary classroom teacher and a special education teacher might participate in student-level collaborative teams for several students in the class for whom the special educator is the IEP manager. The pair also might co-teach for a portion of the day and engage in weekly collaborative consultation with one another or with specialists as they work together to serve a classroom group of students. The special educator will likely participate in an assortment of collaborative activities with additional classroom teachers, family members, and specialists. If the special education teacher is a member of an elementary school grade-level team, a middle school family or core-subject team, or a high school departmental team, then collaborative teaming also occurs when the entire team conducts its planning and evaluation of instruction.

BENEFITS AND CHALLENGES OF COLLABORATIVE TEAMING

Research has verified what common sense easily suggests about implementing collaboration in schools: It is not always easy work (Friend & Cook, 2010). Teachers and other participants need to embrace (or at least be open to) this style for interacting, have the time and structures for engaging in face-to-face interactions, and have the skills to productively and harmoniously interact. This is a tall order. Many of today's educators have not received effective training to work collaboratively and therefore are learning teamwork at the same time they must operate as teams and without the needed infrastructure.

Evidence for Benefits of Collaborative Teaming

Inclusive education has gradually increased since the late 1990s, and

Component 1: Building team organization and supports	Set school policy on collaboration. Create administrative supports for teams and teamwork. Articulate personal belief system consistent with collective responsibility. Define team purpose and focus (e.g., shared values, common goals). Establish team membership. Define team roles and responsibilities. Create and protect time and space. Establish team meeting norms (ground rules), processes, and schedule. Establish the importance of trust and parity.
Component 2: Learning team-work skills	Listen and interact well. Communicate accurately and unambiguously. Give and receive information (including use of effective questioning strategies). Make decisions by consensus. Be sensitive to diverse cultures and languages. Foster positive staff–family interaction. Resolve conflicts constructively. Collaborate effectively on the go. Reflect on the team process.
Component 3: Problem solving, action planning, and coordinating team action	Identify collaborative team structures that use problem solving and action planning: teacher assistance teams, positive behavior interventions and supports teams, response to intervention teams, and other student support teams (i.e., core team focused on ongoing individualized support plans). Follow problem-solving steps: 1) identify priority student needs and concerns; 2) gather information from multiple sources; 3) generate possible solutions; 4) evaluate possible solutions and choose a solution(s); 5) develop an action plan (who, what, how, when, where); 6) implement the plan; 7) evaluate and improve plan. Use strategies to involve student team members. Identify and resolve common issues for student(s) and for the team. Organize documents. Coordinate with different team members, including teachers, paraprofessionals, related services staff, administrators, and family members.

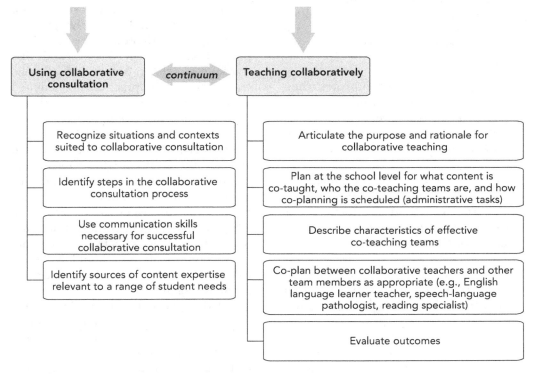

Figure 1.3. Components of collaborative teaming.

researchers reported a number of advantages of planning and creating solutions within collaborative teams and supportive administrative climates (e.g., Alquraini & Gut, 2012; Appl, Troha, & Rowell, 2001; Foley & Lewis, 1999; Johnson, Zorn, Tam, Lamontagne, & Johnson, 2003; Salisbury & McGregor, 2002; Santoli, Sachs, Romey, & McClurg, 2008; Snell & Janney, 2000). The benefits reported by participants in collaborative efforts include the following:

- Both teachers and administrators appear to be motivated by the advantages of shared decision making.

- Collaborative teaming is reported to enhance teachers' satisfaction with their jobs; they enjoy the regular exchange of resources and expertise, the sense of belonging, the freedom from isolation, and the intellectual stimulation.

- Team members report that they are more committed to the plan's implementation and success when they have been instrumental in forming the plan.

- Student achievement improves when teachers have opportunities to collaborate on issues related to curriculum, instruction, and professional development.

With the increased emphasis public education policy places on the use of practices based on scientific evidence, it is understandable that some educators and researchers will ask not whether members of collaborative teams perceive benefits for themselves and their students, but whether rigorous, quantitative research demonstrates that collaboration improves student achievement. It is more difficult, however, to verify the benefits of collaboration for students than it is to identify the challenges and benefits of collaboration for the adults for several reasons.

The first difficulty is that collaborative teaming is a complex process; it is not a single method, strategy, or intervention that can easily be defined so that comparisons can be made across various schools, teams, and classrooms. Collaborative teaming involves varying numbers of participants who are likely to have a wide range of perspectives, skills, and experience; they do their work using a variety of collaborative structures and with varying kinds and amounts of support. So, research on the effectiveness of collaboration must examine a specific collaborative structure (e.g., collaborative teaming to support an individual student or group of students, co-teaching using a particular co-teaching model) and/or processes used by teams (e.g., problem solving, action planning, coaching). Second, the collaborative structure and/or process under investigation must be operationalized and implemented with enough consistency for consumers of the research to believe the results and trust they can implement the practice themselves. As Friend and her colleagues pointed out with regard to research that studies co-teaching, "researchers must be confident that the practice implemented is defensible as co-teaching, and that it is consistently practiced" (Friend, Cook, Hurley-Chamberlain, & Shamberger, 2010, p. 21). A third complication is that collaborating teams use different curricular and instructional practices for actually accomplishing their work with students. Simply knowing whether teachers consulted, co-planned, or co-taught does not tell whether they selected appropriate instructional goals, used sound pedagogical methods, and practiced effective classroom management.

Although there are more reliable ways to measure student achievement than through team members' perceptions, understanding how teachers respond to their collaborative experiences is not without merit. For example, participation in certain collaborative teaming efforts accrues personal and professional support for special education teachers, which in turn bears a positive relationship with their job satisfaction and retention in the teaching field (Pugach, Blanton, Correa, McLeskey, & Langley, 2009). This finding is important because there is a critical shortage of special educators. Difficult working conditions and high attrition rates pose a great challenge to school systems as they seek ways to hire and retain qualified special educators (Billingsley, 2004; Boe & Cook, 2006). "Retaining a stable special education teaching force is critical to the quality of student learning. [H]ow schools create climates that encourage professional growth and teacher collaboration is critical to the retention of beginning teachers" (Pugach et al., 2009, p. 2).

Evidence for How to Collaborate Well

This chapter emphasized the critical role of collaboration in implementing inclusive education, schoolwide systems for student support, and other school improvement initiatives. A useful approach to learning more about collaboration is to locate schools where students are achieving and then ask, "What are the teachers, administrators, other personnel, and parents doing in these schools, and how are they doing it?" In numerous cases, the answer to a question such as this is clear: They are using a variety of collaborative structures and strategies to act on their collective high expectations for all students. The collaborative work in such schools is implemented in multiple ways, including co-planning, co-teaching, and collaborative consultation, and it occurs during both scheduled and unscheduled interactions. Schools that have demonstrated their success with students often are described as "cultures of sharing, collaboration, and inclusion" (Wallace, Anderson, & Bartholomay, 2002, p. 349). They are schools characterized by norms of continuous improvement.

Another distinctive characteristic of exemplary schools is that general education teachers and special education teachers alike accept increased responsibility for improving the performance of all students in their school, including those who have disabilities (Caron & McLaughlin, 2002).

Goddard and her colleagues (Goddard, Goddard, & Tschannen-Moran, 2007) took another approach to the study of collaboration in schools by assessing and comparing 1) the types and amounts of collaborative activity in several schools and 2) students' achievement on standardized tests. These researchers found that fourth-grade students had higher achievement in math and reading in schools characterized by higher levels of teacher collaboration in planning school improvement, making decisions about curriculum and instruction, and planning professional development.

Research on collaborative teams that have helped a particular focus student or students to meet important social and academic goals also can provide valuable guidance to the field. Hunt and her colleagues (2003) studied a specific collaborative teaming process that was applied to the development and implementation of support plans for individual students. These researchers documented the process by which collaborating teams of general and special educators and parents determined the academic adaptations and supports for classroom participation and social interaction for students with severe disabilities and also academically at-risk students in the same classrooms. The researchers conducted behavioral observations and team interviews to evaluate the students' academic skills, levels of engagement, and interaction patterns before and after the support plans were implemented. They also measured team members' ratings of the fidelity with which each element of the students' support plans were implemented. "Consistent implementation of the plans of support by team members was associated with increases in academic skills, engagement in classroom activities, peer interactions, and student-initiated interactions" (Hunt et al., 2003, p. 315).

Challenges and Overcoming Them

The challenges presented by collaboration are the time, skill, and risk it takes for educators to work collaboratively and reach good outcomes (Brownell, Yeager, Rennels, & Riley, 1997; Friend, 2000). Team members in inclusive schools work together to provide instruction and supports using a variety of approaches—collaborative team planning and problem solving, collaborative teaching, in-class support, collaborative consultation, and, when necessary and appropriate, pull-out instruction with teaming. Each approach entails overcoming vexing logistical issues, learning new skills, and taking risks. The outcomes reflect cooperative exchange and decision making among team members, however, and increase the likelihood that students with disabilities can be successful learners in general education classrooms alongside their peers. This book addresses many of the skills teams need to address this challenge.

2

Building Team Structure

FOCUSING QUESTIONS

- In what ways can administrators facilitate and support collaborative teaming?
- What team structures (e.g., norms and ways of operating) promote teams' effective and efficient operation?
- Who are members of collaborative teams, and what are their roles?
- In what ways can professionals facilitate and support collaborative teaming with family members?

 ## Team Snapshot

The middle schools in one school system were well aware that during the upcoming school year, fifth-grade students who had been served in inclusive elementary classes would be moving up to middle school and would continue receiving many of their services in general education settings. The principal at one middle school began arranging for departmental teams to visit their feeder elementary schools to meet with teachers and observe inclusive classrooms. Some middle school teachers could not even tell which students had disabilities. They were impressed with the way special educators and paraprofessionals serving students with more significant needs seemed a part of the class; seamless collaboration was evident. The principal scheduled summer professional development on collaboration and differentiated instruction and made sure that the middle school teachers were involved in the students' IEP meetings at the end of the school year. The middle school teachers felt far more confident about beginning the school year as collaborative teams, with students' needs as their focus.

The principal at another middle school in the same school system did nothing to prepare the staff. He thought inclusion was a fad that would pass. When he taught, he taught alone. He did not see why it needed to be different today.

⟳ ACTIVITY: *Compare the differences in the principals' approaches and how the school staff and the students (with and without IEPs) in the two schools will experience the upcoming school year.*

This chapter focuses on building support for collaborative teaming and organizing teams for effective and efficient operation (e.g., establishing membership, handling logistics, creating team meeting processes, delineating roles and responsibilities). Chapter 3 focuses on the development of a team's interpersonal attributes, such as building teamwork skills, establishing productive relationships, and effectively handling conflicts.

LEADERSHIP AND SUPPORT FROM ADMINISTRATORS

Principals are pivotal in setting the tone for movement toward an inclusive school model (Villa, Thousand, Meyers, & Nevin, 1996). In bringing about changes for collaborative teaming, Klar and Brewer found that principals were taking an important initial step for teachers in high-need schools when they created teams of individuals who had strong collaborative skills. Teachers at one school indicated that collaborative teams were supported by their principal's redesign of schedules so teachers could meet and learn from each other; they appreciated

> [The principal's] creation of teacher teams and provision of time to meet during the regular school day. An eighth-grade teacher noted, "We meet every Tuesday during our planning time, and more during the week if we need to." The opportunity to observe their peers teaching is another way that teachers formed collaborative relationships. (2013, p. 786)

Thus, there seems to be a relationship among principals' beliefs about inclusion, their previous teaching experiences, and the practices that are implemented in schools. School system administrators who were clearly successful with inclusive practices in five school districts were interviewed (Toson, Burrello, & Knollman, 2013). Some had almost doubled the percentage of students in inclusive classes since beginning their position; one had achieved the inclusion of 96% of students with disabilities. When asked why they promoted inclusion, all indicated they "did not see disabilities as deficits, but societal and educational designs and practices as the deficit" (p. 496). Their philosophical stances were deeply informed by an awareness of the strengths and competencies of each individual, and they believed instruction and curriculum needed to be

responsive to strengths and build competencies. Although school leaders may sometimes perceive mandates for inclusive education originating from their school system, superintendent, or state department of education, successful inclusive school leaders honor their personal philosophies and are guided more by their sense of what is right and fair for all students. Coelli and Green (2012) found that high school principals' effect on student outcomes positively increased over a period of years, supporting the often-heard claim that change does not happen overnight. The researchers noted the value of retaining strong principals who could, in turn, support building-based changes that accrue over years. Similarly, collaborative teams who enjoy strong support from principals can also become more effective over time (Raforth & Foriska, 2006).

Collaborative Teaming as Changed Practice

Building administrators need to do more than simply state their support of the change initiatives in order for the changes to be meaningful and sustained. Administrators, including the principal, assistant principal(s), and those in other administrative-level positions, who are the most effective at implementing change are directly and wholeheartedly involved with the change process (Fullan, 2007). They are willing to collaborate with staff and able to delegate responsibilities. Building administrators whose leadership styles promote collaborative change (Fullan, 2007; Theoharis & O'Toole, 2011)

- Clarify and support the innovation (e.g., collaborative teaming, inclusion) by talking with teachers and reinforcing their efforts

- Work in collaborative ways with others involved in the change (e.g., send support notes to staff, hold regular problem-solving sessions with staff)

- Have their finger on the pulse of the school (e.g., are frequently seen in the hallways and classrooms, even teaching a class; are knowledgeable about significant innovations in the school)

- Are actively involved in the school's work without being controlling of staff (e.g., monitor student progress by implementing a systematic policy of record keeping and review data but have teachers keep the records, are involved in curriculum decisions and in influencing content but do not take control)

- Implement strategies to transform the school's culture (e.g., take action to improve the culture and reinforce change, share power and responsibility)

- Involve stakeholders who will be affected by the change (e.g., community personnel, families)

Both the principal's background work and visible modeling make a difference in whether collaborative teaming continues in schools as a healthy, functional process or dies an early death.

Recognizing the integral role of collaboration in successful school reform is perhaps the central role of administrators in supporting collaborative teaming (Fullan, 2007). The extent to which a school can create conditions needed for successful collaboration will determine how meaningful inclusion becomes within the school community. Principals play a major role in creating and maintaining these conditions, one of which is a shared vision of the desired change. For example, one teacher in a school reform effort studied by Klar and Brewer noted that

> [The principal's] vision was not an immediate focus on scores, but instead a focus on relationships with students, teachers, and community members. She articulated his vision as follows: "We're going to jump in here and start trying to build some relationships with our students, with our community" and

> that these relationships would lead to communal sense of "the more we know, the more we grow, and the better we do things." (2013, p. 790)

Phases of Policy Development and Administrative Support for Teams

The process involved in implementing collaborative teams in a school can be broken down into three phases.

1. *Preparation phase:* Schools organize for collaborative teaming.

2. *Implementation phase:* Students are included, and teams become adept at planning, problem solving, and implementing student supports.

3. *Maintenance phase:* Teams are in use and relied on by staff and building administrators; self-evaluation and improvement are ongoing.

Building administrators play a critical role in each phase. Figure 2.1 provides a checklist of some actions administrators may take to develop these three phases of inclusion.

Preparation

Principals and assistant principals in many schools initiate discussions with staff members regarding potential school improvements and inclusion, which often lead to recommendations by the staff, particularly special educators, for collaborative teaming. District policy changes sometimes help initiate inclusion and make teaming a recommended districtwide practice; however, schools (and districts) need to examine their reasons for inclusively serving students and develop a mission statement or a shared purpose before there can be schoolwide adoption of a structure and a procedure for team development. Schools should not start forming collaborative teams without first taking some time to examine their values. Shared values provide a firm foundation for creating collaborative teams.

Phase			Actions taken by building administrators with school staff
P	**I**	**M**	
✓			Plan times for open dialogue at the district level and the school level about inclusive education and its benefits and challenges. Involve parents and students.
✓	✓		Arrange for staff to view and learn more about inclusive school models (e.g., visits, videos, panels from schools). Participate in these workshop sessions with staff.
✓			Engage staff in creating a common definition of their school community—one that addresses what it is (or is becoming) and why. Expand this definition into a philosophical position on inclusion and a mission statement to guide school improvement.
✓	✓		Explore and adopt a staffing arrangement that supports teaming between general and special education faculty. • Grade-level teams or families (elementary) • Interdepartmental teams, pods, or families (middle schools) • Departmental teams (high schools)
✓	✓		Determine the ways to deliver special education services. • Consultation • Instruction or co-teaching • Push-in instructional support • Limited pull-out (only with collaborative planning)
✓	✓		Consider reductions in the caseload for special educators and/or a staffing arrangement that limits the number of classrooms special educators serve.
✓	✓	✓	Identify relevant competency-based professional development on inclusion and related topics; attend, process, and implement professional development content as teams.
✓	✓		Recognize that staff have varying levels of comfort and understanding about inclusion; provide time and resources for staff to learn and experience the new philosophy and gain comfort with the changes inclusion brings.
✓	✓		With teachers, plan for a schoolwide program on disability awareness or climate for learning to emphasize themes of appreciation of diversity and understanding of disability.
✓	✓		Be alert to staff morale and use team-building activities during the school year to promote collegiality.
✓	✓	✓	Involve all stakeholders in reaching mutual decisions.
✓	✓	✓	Identify school- and grade-level inclusion goals, and support taking small steps toward those goals.
✓	✓	✓	Make use of round-robin discussions at meetings to hear all voices and reach creative solutions.
✓	✓	✓	Recognize that listening and being empathic may be more useful than solving a problem.
	✓	✓	Recognize and celebrate successes (incremental progress is good).
	✓	✓	Be alert and responsive to staff needs as they change over time.
	✓	✓	Make consultative services available to general educators and collaborative teams.
	✓	✓	Know that support takes different forms and functions for different classroom teachers; develop a school or district menu of support options.
✓	✓		Encourage staff/teams to share their ideas and resources with others.
	✓	✓	Orient new staff to school philosophy and progress; link them with strong teams who can mentor their development.
	✓	✓	Find ways to record, share, and publicize student success stories.

P = *Preparation:* As schools are preparing for inclusion
I = *Implementation:* As teams are being planned and implemented
M = *Maintenance:* Once teams are in use

Figure 2.1. A building administrator's checklist for building collaborative teaming during preparation, implementation, and maintenance phases. (*Sources:* Elliott & McKenney, 1998; Idol, 1997; National Dissemination Center for Children with Disabilities, 1995; Roach, 1995; Russ, Chiang, Rylance, & Bongers, 2001.)

Building administrators often schedule a professional development day to define a common mission or shared school values and explore questions such as, "What are our beliefs regarding learning and the students we serve?" and "What is our purpose?" Forums sometimes are held during which parents and other members of the school community who are interested in inclusion can voice their concerns and obtain answers to their questions. Information on inclusion is usually supplied in response to any concerns or questions that are raised and, as a consequence, a vision for a school begins to develop. School personnel, along with representative parents and students, then work toward consensus on the school's vision for inclusion. Mission statements can guide the design of a school's major goals and its instructional program and activities and often clarify the need for collaborative teams (Idol, 1997; Janney, Snell, Beers, & Raynes, 1995; Roach, 1995).

Having experience with educating heterogeneous groups of students seems to strengthen administrators' and educators' beliefs in inclusion over pull-out programs and self-contained classrooms (Toson et al., 2013; Villa et al., 1996). During the preparation phase, therefore, administrators are advised to provide positive, personal experiences, some of which may challenge existing beliefs and attitudes (Giangreco, Dennis, Cloninger, Edelman, & Schattman, 1993). When the focus for collaborative teaming is inclusive practices, school personnel may find it helpful to listen to teams from other schools who have been successful with inclusion and collaboration, view illustrative videos on these topics, and visit schools that practice inclusion and then evaluate these experiences as a group. Direct experiences with adults and students with disabilities are perhaps even more powerful than learning about methods of inclusion and collaboration.

The professional development planned for schools during this phase needs to be tailored to match the school personnel's concerns in addition to their skills; therefore, administrators should closely work with teachers to plan professional development topics. For example, general and special educators who were to collaborate for incorporating assistive technology with inclusive efforts desired professional development together (McLaren, Bausch, & Ault, 2007). The professional development can sometimes occur as colleagues learn from each other, when they have sufficient time to watch one another teach. In particular, general education teachers with little knowledge of students with disabilities want to see, not just read about, how it is done. In the words of one classroom teacher, "I could benefit from watching [the special education teacher] teach a lesson to the class and see how he would modify, to see what he would do during that class time to meet the needs of those kids" (Leatherman, 2009, p. 198).

Giangreco and his colleagues (1993) similarly found that traditional professional development for teachers that addressed the inclusion of students with extensive support needs in general education classrooms was not as beneficial as nontraditional ongoing professional development about inclusion and teaming (*nontraditional* meaning that both the content of training and the timing of its delivery were atypical). The most influential of these nontraditional professional development practices identified by teachers included the following:

- Hearing about the feelings and experiences of other teachers in inclusive classrooms

- Learning about the elements of inclusion that were critical to starting the school year: teamwork, ways to interact with and what to expect from the included students, roles and schedules of the special education staff, and methods for involving class members in creative problem solving

- Learning about successful approaches from experienced teachers: cooperative groups and activity-based teaching, group strategies, ways to use and adapt typical materials, and class activities for students with disabilities

These valuable nontraditional training methods were implemented during the preparation phase once class placement decisions were made and before the school year started.

Professional development activities also should be responsive to the specific type of concern held by teachers and others who will be implementing collaborative teaming or other inclusive practices. Hall and Hord (2011) developed a stage theory to describe the predictable evolution of educators' personal concerns as they adopt and apply an innovation. The Concerns-Based Adoption Model

(CBAM) is based on the idea that change is a learning process. Teachers and other professionals who are learning to teach all students through collaboration begin the process at the *awareness* stage ("I've heard about inclusion, but I don't know much about it"). They then progress through a sequence of stages of concern as they gain information, motivation, and skills to implement the innovation, and then have the opportunity to see its effect on themselves and students.

Hall and Hord (2011) noted that responsive actions for individual staff members depend on the stage of concern they are experiencing (see Table 2.1). For example, teachers may be at the *personal* stage when they complain about learning to collaborate; they are trying to figure out how the change will affect them. Validation of their concerns may be the responsive action ("I understand that you

Table 2.1. Applying the Concerns-Based Adoption Model (Hall & Hord, 2011) stages of change to collaborative teaming

Stage	Focus of concern	What people say	How to respond
0: Awareness	Unrelated	I have heard of people collaborating, but I am fine teaching alone.	Involve in discussions. Provide a brief handout or video.
1: Information	Self	I did not realize there were so many teaming models and skills involved in collaboration.	Give information in several ways and grouping formats. Compare with current practice.
2: Personal	Self	How can they expect me to collaborate? I do not have time.	Validate. Encourage.
3: Implementation	Task	When can we meet? We need to figure out our co-teaching roles for the new unit.	Offer enough information and resources on how to use. Figure out logistics.
4: Consequence	Impact	I think what we did really benefited the students. Students I have been concerned about scored higher than they have all of this grading period.	Arrange visits to other settings. Reinforce and support.
5: Collaboration	Impact	Let's talk with the other teachers to see what techniques they are using.	Mentor other teachers. Schedule opportunities to work with others.
6: Refocusing	Impact	If we use the three activities one after the other, then the students will be more actively engaged and we will have a chance to observe their social skills.	Encourage interest. Find out if other resources are needed.

Source: Hall and Hord (2011).

are feeling nervous about what is being expected of you"), along with encouragement and offers of support as they move into implementation. Members of a collaborative team need to hear what teammates or other colleagues are saying and determine the underlying concern.

Student Snapshot

Before Abby's transition to first grade, her kindergarten teacher met with the first-grade teacher to share her positive experiences of working with Abby, despite her initial fears. The kindergarten teacher explained, "I remember last fall, when we were trying to figure out how to include Abby, we were just learning to be a team. We did not know each other, and I did not know Abby very well, so I was nervous about it. But the team figured that if we could just get her communicating with the other children, it would help her so much. So we focused on that. There was no magical thing that would make her communicate overnight. We knew we had to figure it out."

Student Snapshot

Keith's IEP team eventually agreed that he would be half-day in the regular kindergarten class and half-day in the self-contained special education class. Although his mother had wanted more time with typically developing peers, she felt this was as much as she was going to get, at least for the beginning of the school year. It was difficult to understand why. Keith's kindergarten teacher, who was terrific with Keith, seemed so resistant to including him for more than half of the day. Keith's mother mentioned this to a friend of hers who was a professor of special education at the local university. Her friend said, "She may be at the personal stage of changing to more inclusive practices. Experienced and effective teachers may be resistant to trying new things because they have a reputation for a certain level of expertise, and they are comfortable with what they know how to do. Change is uncomfortable for people." Keith's mother noticed as Thanksgiving approached that Keith's kindergarten teacher was using more cooperative groups and Social Stories (recommended by the special education teacher). It did seem like she was changing. She mentioned this to her university friend, who said, "Sounds like she is more comfortable now that she has a better understanding of what is expected of her; she has moved beyond the personal stage of the change process to the next stage, where she can really focus on implementation of new strategies. That means she is noticing the positive results of these strategies." Keith's mother was relieved. Taking this perspective on Keith's school year helped her to see that progress was being made, even if it was not happening as fast as she would like.

↻ ACTIVITY: *Reflect on what you have heard school personnel say about inclusion and collaborative teaming. Try to match what they have said to a stage of concern, as described by Hall and Hord (2011).*

Implementation

Teachers experience a noticeable shift when they no longer focus on preparation and personal concerns and begin focusing on implementation efforts. Kaniuka documented how elementary teachers who taught in high-need low-performing schools experienced change as they implemented evidence-based techniques:

> During the startup phase, the teachers' logs evidenced doubts regarding their ability to teach the program and their students' ability to perform, followed by anxiety, and then optimism as the students began to perform successfully. During the implementation period teachers showed increased comfort with the program, surprise (as the students surpassed their prior expectations), subsequently higher expectations for their students, and increased levels of optimism. (2012, p. 335)

Kaniuka (2012) indicated that as teachers move beyond a teacher-centered focus (i.e., their startup phase), they move into *program-centered* ("How do I do this?") then *student-centered* ("Which students need more practice in what areas?") implementation phases.

Administrators play an important role during the team implementation phase because they exercise ultimate control over school schedules and space. Basic questions need to be addressed such as, "Why will we form teams (team purpose)?" "When will teams meet?" and "Where will we meet?" During the implementation phase, building administrators need to continue listening and responding to obstacles teams face as they form and develop. Using the teachers' input to arrange professional development and consultation on teaming topics that refine teachers' emerging skills (e.g., problem solving, reaching consensus, practicing teamwork skills) and address implementation issues (e.g., ideas for teaching and assessing collaboratively, modifying schoolwork, improving family participation) is one part of responding to obstacles teams face. Professional development should not be limited to a single day or the beginning of the school year; ongoing communication and sharing of information, along with technical assistance and support, are necessary.

It is often valuable for building administrators to hold regular discussions with staff regarding their successes and concerns about collaborative teaming or other aspects of inclusive programming during the implementation and maintenance phases. The meetings provide another collaborative forum for problem solving that involves the principal and extends to all staff.

Maintenance

Some actions that administrators have taken during preparation or initiation (e.g., problem solving at the school level, initial professional development sessions) will continue in the maintenance phase, whereas other actions will be added or discontinued. The emphasis during this phase is on the refinement and evolution of the collaborative team's function and process. Team functions and outcomes need to be visibly integrated into the standard school procedure so staff members see the significance of their work. Improving team function will continue to be a priority during this phase, though professional development might shift to more focused topics, such as improving communication, handling team conflict, and making the transition between grades and schools.

PURPOSE OF TEAMS

Promoting student learning and success in school is the overall purpose of collaborative teams. Teams may choose a narrow or wide focus in addressing these student-centered purposes. The team's focus for students with numerous support needs is often on that particular student; other times, teams may work to address the needs of all students from a single classroom who require specific support for success or attend to the entire classroom or grade level. Consider these two arrangements for collaborative teams:

1. *Individual student teams:* These teams are organized to address the needs of a single student. When a student is eligible for special education, this team also is involved in planning and reviewing the IEP. Although teams for students with IEPs are ongoing, an individual student team can be convened to assist any students for whom there is a concern. Individual students also may have a positive behavior support (PBS) team. *Behavior Support* (Bambara, Janney, & Snell, 2015), another book in this series, describes the work of PBS teams in detail.

2. *Classroom/grade-level teams:* These teams are organized to address support issues pertaining to small groups of students in a classroom, the entire classroom, or the entire grade level. The support may be for academic, social, or behavioral areas.

Student Snapshot

Devin, a fourth grader with Asperger syndrome, is a member of Ms. Greer's class. In addition to his classroom teacher, Devin's core team includes his special education teacher (Ms. Conti), his parents, and his speech-language pathologist. The core team meets once a month with frequent verbal exchange between meetings. Devin's teachers meet weekly but interact daily as they work together to implement and adapt classroom instruction and school activities for Devin. Also, Ms. Greer meets monthly with the other fourth-grade teachers and Ms. Conti to address grade-level issues. When Devin's parents are involved, his mother usually attends in person, but his father generally participates via Skype because his career requires frequent travel.

⟲ ACTIVITY: *Discuss the continuum of the frequency for team meetings in place for Devin.*

Although these two arrangements for collaborative teams (teams formed around a single student and those formed for small groups of students, entire classrooms, or grade levels) are the primary focus of this book, teams can organize other ways to fulfill their purpose and focus on students.

- *Middle school grade-level teams:* Middle schools often organize teams at single grade levels to share planning and instruction, problem solving, and evaluating student performance. Advantages of this approach include focusing on the different concerns regarding students just entering or preparing to leave middle school, students having specific problems in a subject, or students having general problems across that grade level.

- *Department teams:* Secondary school teachers, and sometimes middle school teachers, often organize themselves into teams by academic department. When special education staff are active members (or regular drop-ins) on these teams, the learning and success of students with special needs who are enrolled in general education classes in that department can be promoted.

- *Teacher assistance teams, RTI teams, intervention assistance teams, and ad-hoc problem-solving and round-table teams:* These teams vary in their membership, from having only teachers to consisting of teachers plus professional support staff, the principal, and sometimes parents. RTI teams, like the former prereferral teams, regularly meet to discuss specific students who are exhibiting difficulties and have been referred to them by a teacher. The teams provide assistance to the referring teacher in order to prevent a student's problems from worsening. Both approaches—teachers only and teachers plus specialists—have been effective over the years (Friend & Cook, 2003; Pugach & Johnson, 2002).

- *Related services teams:* These teams include teachers and therapists whose focus is on the students who receive the team's related services and the issues surrounding those services (e.g., scheduling, types of therapy support).

- *Building-level or system-level teams:* Teams also can form to address short- or long-term system-level and building-level goals. Schoolwide positive behavior interventions and supports (SW-PBIS) is an example of a building-level team, although all school personnel participate in developing the positive and proactive rules and procedures that everyone reinforces (Bradshaw, Koth, Bevans, Ialongo, & Leaf, 2008). System-level goals may also include writing a curriculum, discussing textbook changes, or resolving a problem that affects some or all students in the school (e.g., drugs, bullying). Building-level teams address school-specific issues and make recommendations, such as designing plans to involve families, making site-based decisions, and determining professional development needs.

- *Professional learning communities:* A professional learning community is another type of building-level team and is created by professional staff using collaboration and participation in decision making, enabling them to share power and authority, which helps them grow in professionalism and efficacy (Hall & Hord, 2011; Williams, 2006).

The general principles for building teams, learning teamwork skills, problem solving, taking team action, improving communication, and evaluating outcomes apply across all types of team arrangements, whether in schools or in other types of organizations. The configuration of collaborative teams chosen by a particular school should relate to classroom, school, and system needs in addition to the phase of team development that the school system or individual school is in (e.g., teams initially beginning, more experienced teams).

Student Snapshot

Ricardo, a fourth grader with Asperger syndrome, is a member of Ms. Lee's class. In addition to his classroom teacher, Ricardo's core team includes his special education teacher (Mrs. Bohr), his mother, and his speech-language pathologist. The core team meets once a month with frequent verbal exchanges between meetings. Ricardo's teachers meet weekly but interact daily as they work together to implement and adapt classroom instruction and school activities for Ricardo. Also, Ms. Lee meets monthly with the other fourth-grade teachers and Mrs. Bohr to address student-focused, grade-level issues.

⏱ ACTIVITY: *How do the purpose and focus of Ricardo's core team and the fourth-grade teaching team differ?*

ESTABLISHING TEAM MEMBERSHIP FOR INDIVIDUAL STUDENT TEAMS

Teams that focus on an individual student should consist of those people who closely work with the student and know him or her well. For students who have IEPs, team members should be those service providers listed on the IEP who work with the student. Family members (and sometimes the student) may also be on the team, depending on the types of decisions being made. Members of the student's core team are those who play major roles in planning, implementing, and overseeing a student's daily education schedule, including general educators, special educators, and family members. A student's whole team is often larger and typically consists of those who meet annually to review a student's IEP. The IEP team, in addition to the core team members, includes other people who are needed in the educational process but whose involvement is required less frequently (e.g., school psychologist, counselor). Three questions can be used to identify who should be on a single student's core and whole or extended (IEP) teams (Thousand & Villa, 2000).

1. Who has the talent and expertise that the team must have to make the best decisions for that student?

2. Who is affected by the team's decisions?

3. Who has an interest in participating?

How Many Members Should Be on a Team?

Every student who receives special education has an IEP team that operates in a collaborative style using a transdisciplinary approach. Although IEP teams do their formal, legally required work in a few annual meetings, implementing and evaluating the IEP requires ongoing collaboration among a subset of members of the IEP team as well as other staff who assist to implement the IEP. Although many people may convene for the IEP meeting, a smaller group from that team generally collaborates more frequently throughout the year to accomplish tasks. Examples of tasks that require ongoing collaborative teaming include

- Developing a student's schedule and program to fulfill the IEP

- Designing individualized adaptations and supports for particular students

- Finding ways to ensure consistency and quality among school staff implementing a student's support plan

- Problem solving about specific issues that arise: Why isn't Aaron passing his math tests? How can we prepare Abby for the upcoming field trip to the arboretum? Why has Chase stopped doing his homework?

- Planning for successful transitions within and between schools, as well as making successful transitions out of school

Core teams work together most frequently to achieve the team goals, whereas a student's whole team includes other team members who participate less frequently in the team meetings and have less frequent regularly scheduled contacts with core team members and the focus student (see Figure 2.2) (Giangreco, Cloninger, & Iverson, 2011). The core team includes those members most directly responsible for the student and who interact daily or almost daily to plan, implement, and evaluate a student's educational program. The members of core teams usually consist of teachers (the classroom teacher[s] and special educator[s] who serve the student with disabilities) and family members. Although the general education and special education teachers share the primary responsibility for teaching the focus student or students, other professional or paraprofessional team members sometimes contribute by teaching or by monitoring students' performance during certain learning activities or routines. Although it is unusual for family members to be physically present daily with other core members, their input can be regularly heard through mutually determined ways (e.g., telephone calls, traveling notebook, e-mail).

The whole team includes core members plus team members who participate with the student or team less often, yet are important to the achievement of team goals. Their participation at team meetings may be on an ad-hoc basis, when their expertise or authority is needed in order to solve a particular problem that has arisen or engage in planning for the future.

The contributions that family members make to the whole IEP team and the core team are equally important. The family's perspective on the student may differ from that of school personnel and, therefore, may provide a more complete picture of the student's abilities and needs. Also, the family's perspective on the child's educational priorities is often rich with implications for instruction and should influence team decisions about goals and programs.

Family members are part of the core team because they are the historians of what has occurred and the observers of what is current in their child's life beyond school (Hagner et al., 2012; Salisbury & Dunst, 1997). Limiting family members' involvement to attending formal meetings (e.g., eligibility and IEP meetings) or giving consent for decisions means that their input either is too little or comes too late. In addition to being listened to, understood, and respected by the other team members, family members should influence the child's program development (Park, 2008; Turnbull, Turnbull, Erwin, & Soodak, 2006). Professionals should recognize family members as experts on their child, draw on their knowledge, encourage their input, and seriously consider their ideas.

Family members—particularly those who are culturally and linguistically diverse or have a low income—often feel intimidated and unsupported by school personnel (Harry, 2008; Olivos, 2009). In addition, immigrant families may be even more reluctant to speak up, even to alert the team that they do not understand the acronyms and test scores when their child is being assessed to determine

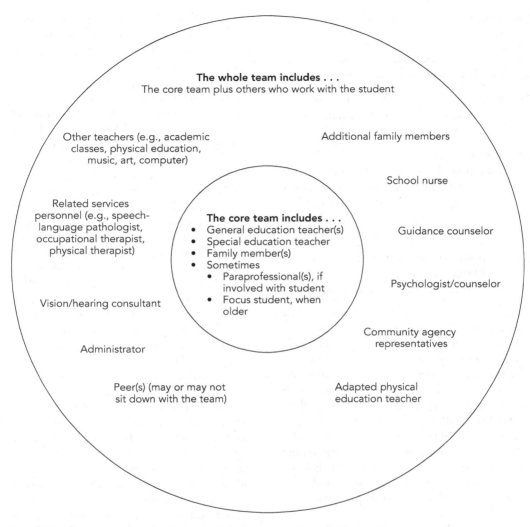

Figure 2.2. The core team and the whole team for students with individualized education programs.

eligibility for special education services (Schoorman, Zainuddin, & Sena, 2011). Establishing true equality with parents requires "active effort from professionals to empower families [such as] by actively encouraging them to express opinions and helping families gain skills to enable them to participate fully in decision making" (Blue-Banning et al., 2004, p. 177). Supporting family involvement in authentic decision making may require educators to inform parents of all options available for their child. Educators also should make sure that family members know how

and when to express concerns with the teaming process or the implementation of team decisions. Educators and other professional participants on the team may need to critically examine personal and/or institutional biases that can create barriers to collaboration with family members from different cultural, racial, or socioeconomic backgrounds (Olivos, Gallagher, & Aguilar, 2010).

Some students do not have family members who are able to represent them legally, typically because parental or familial rights have been terminated based on an inability to adequately care for the child (e.g., family members with significant drug abuse issues). In such a case, a state-appointed guardian may be designated to serve as the students' legal representative in regard to IEP-focused issues. In other similar situations, a Court Appointed Special Advocate (CASA) may be designated to participate on a student's educational team, albeit not in the role of the parent (Lawson & Berrick, 2013; Litzelfelner, 2008). The state-appointed personnel or CASAs fill valuable roles as representatives of the best interest of the child in either of these situations.

Families need to be involved in decision making, and they also should receive regular updates on how the team is implementing any decisions regarding their child. Teachers need to identify with family members how communication will occur and how much and what types of involvement the family wants to maintain. See Figure 2.3 for an example of how to elicit information from parents about communication preferences. (A blank, photocopiable version is available in Appendix A and the forms download.) Participation with family members is individually determined and allowed to change over time.

Students who have reached adolescence should participate as members of their own team so they can directly offer their perspectives. Students may learn to be more self-determined and feel more in control of their lives if they directly participate in planning their educational programs (Carter, Lane, Pierson, & Stang, 2008). Students typically should participate in meetings during which key decisions are made, but not necessarily in all team meetings. A few students will readily participate, whereas others will require encouragement and participate less. Many students benefit from being taught how to participate in team meetings, whereas some students will need family and/or school personnel support in order to have their say.

Smaller teams generally require less energy to gather together and fewer schedules to coordinate; as a consequence, they make communication easier. Members of smaller teams are more familiar with one another, which leads to more task involvement and a greater sense of responsibility (Johnson & Johnson, 2000). By contrast, larger teams often translate into more resources and greater expertise; however, coordination, accountability, and contribution by individual members may actually be reduced. Some team members, such as specialists and related-services providers who serve students in multiple schools, encounter logistical challenges when trying to attend team meetings. Careful planning around people's schedules is needed to either have all team members present or to find creative ways to give their input during meetings (see Figure 2.4). Sometimes participation via speakerphone, Skype, or FaceTime allows specialists to use their time more efficiently.

General education teachers are often overwhelmed by too many team members serving the same student (Snell & Janney, 2000). General education teachers conversely may find themselves as core members on many students' teams, depending on how many students with disabilities they teach. A study of team membership for students with multiple disabilities found that team size ranged from 5 to 11 members (Giangreco, Dennis, Edelman, & Cloninger, 1994). Very large teams can be difficult to coordinate (see Figure 2.5), but if the student's needs require multiple areas of expertise, then team members' contributions can be invaluable. Students with fewer complex needs, however, tend to have fewer core and whole team members.

Student Snapshot

Jonah is served by seven general education teachers (one from each of his subject areas), a number of paraprofessionals who alternate across his day, and a special

How Can We Stay in Touch?

Family member : _Mr. Warren (Devin's dad)_   Teacher: _Ms. Greer_   Date: _9/5_

_____ I would like to come to the school to meet with you. Days and times that work best are:
_____ Monday   _____ Tuesday   _____ Wednesday   _____ Thursday   _____ Friday
Times: _____

_____ I would like you to come visit at our house.

_____ I would like to write in and read a notebook that travels in my child's backpack.

_____ I would like to write notes back and forth.

_____ I would like telephone calls at home between the hours of _____ and _____
(phone number: _____).

_____ I would like telephone calls at work between the hours of _____ and _____
(phone number: _____).

__X__ I would like to use e-mail; my address is: __devinsdad@mymail.com__ .

_____ I would like to talk when I drop off or pick up my child on M T W R F (circle one) at _____.

_____ I would like to meet before _____ after _____ PTA meetings.

_____ I would like to have a school/class open house and meet there.

_____ I would like to observe in the classroom and talk afterward.

_____ I would like to receive school and classroom newsletters.

_____ I would like to participate in my child's individualized education program (IEP) meeting.

_____ I would like to bring a friend or other family members to meetings with me.

_____ I would like to talk and plan before the IEP meeting.

__X__ I would like to talk and plan via Skype.

_____ I would like to talk and plan with multiple people via speakerphone.

_____ Another way: _____

Figure 2.3.   Format to seek parent participation. (_Note:_ A blank, photocopiable version is available in Appendix A, and blank and filled-in versions are available in the forms download.)

education teacher (who also is his IEP manager). The guidance counselor and school psychologist are extended team members, and Jonah's parents both work closely with the team as core members. Because 14 people are involved in supporting Jonah, about the only time everyone is in the room together for a meeting is when they are discussing Jonah's IEP. A lot of communication is done in writing so that team members can provide input even if they cannot be at the more frequent planning meetings. Jonah's special education teacher requests input from team members prior to planning meetings, and then each team member—both those who were present at the meeting and those who were not—is sent information about the meeting's outcome.

Voices from the Classroom

My role as a behavior management teacher is to serve as an agent of collaboration among school teams, administrators, and families for students with autism spectrum disorder (ASD). As an itinerant, my position takes me across several school sites, ranging from elementary to secondary and spanning the full continuum of services, including general education, self-contained classrooms, and special education labs. I orchestrate my time between providing specialized staff development, conducting student or classwide observations, and participating as an individualized education program (IEP) team member. My method of organization and planning has become more refined over time. I prefer to utilize electronic calendar invites because it provides a color-coded visual layout of how my time is spent. In addition, the calendar invites are directly linked to those I work with, and they receive alerts about upcoming meetings and observations.

My specialized role on the IEP team is to collaborate with school teams, parents, and students in developing and implementing functional behavior assessments and behavioral intervention plans (BIPs), informal behavior plans, and classwide reinforcement systems. Communication among all team members is critical, and there are several regularly scheduled meetings that are held for the purposes of planning and supporting while implementing. These meetings are generally geared toward systematic implementation of BIPs; however, all behavior management plans require clear management and preparation. It is at these meetings where the development and use of graphic organizers that convey the plan for implementation are created, designating individuals' roles and responsibilities. I use a coaching model to provide direct support to teachers. I assess how much initial contact will be required (e.g., daily, weekly, intermittent), depending on the level of need (e.g., one student, entire class, BIP), and set up a plan that includes e-mail check-ins, data reviews, and regular revisions to the plan. Knowing firsthand that time is the most valuable resource to a teacher, it is not uncommon that I check in and meet with teachers via speakerphone or Skype. I have learned that becoming a clear communicator and effective collaborator requires practice and reflection.

Figure 2.4.   Time management for a behavior support specialist. (Contributed by Colleen Barry.)

ACTIVITY: *Describe the pros and cons of large teams.*

Many of the advantages of both smaller (core) teams and larger (whole) teams can be realized when core team members meet frequently and there is good communication with whole team members (Giangreco, 1996). Although the number of members is one way to limit the size of a team, an individual's time for involvement and his or her knowledge and skills are better selection criteria.

What Skills and Knowledge Do Potential Team Members Have?

Balancing the following factors is the guiding principle for selecting team members: teaming efficiency, team members' time available to work with students and other team members, and the match between members' abilities and students' needs. Teams that are selected to avoid role overlap are likely to be smaller, more efficient, and have less chance for territorial conflict. Successful teams in inclusive schools seem to change over time as the roles and duties of members progress from rigidly distinct to being blurred, with more cooperation between members (Wood, 1998). These changes appear to be related to several things: 1) communication and trust, 2) the amount of role release teams engage in as members teach each other about their specialties, and 3) the success experienced by members as they broaden their role and duties with the student with disabilities.

The degree to which a team member is involved on a student's team depends on the access he or she has to the student and the school, the distance that the member

IN AN EFFORT TO MAINTAIN A
WORKABLE TEAM SIZE, MR. MOODY
SUGGESTS LIMITING MEMBERSHIP TO
THE NUMBER OF PEOPLE THAT
CAN FIT IN A PHONE BOOTH.

Figure 2.5. Limiting team size can be challenging. (From Giangreco, M.F. [2007]. *Absurdities and realities of special education: The complete digital set [CD]*. Thousand Oaks, CA: Corwin Press; reprinted with permission of the copyright holder, Michael F. Giangreco.)

must travel to serve the student, and the caseload of students whom the member already serves. Sometimes, potential team members who do not have adequate access to the student or the environment will serve as consultants to the core team and visit on demand, focusing on a specific issue. Some specialists may feel there are not enough hours across the school day to attend to all tasks, so they figure out ways to be as efficient as possible (see Figure 2.6 for how one educator calculates time for a large caseload).

ESTABLISHING TEAM TRUST

A team can falter if there is a lack of trust among team members. Establishing trust requires both trusting others and being trustworthy (Johnson & Johnson, 2000). A sense of trust is manifested by each individual when a collaborative team is functioning well and also is reflected in team dynamics. DeBoer (1995) identified

three basic strategies for facilitating trust among co-workers and team members.

1. Empathy toward other team members occurs when one team member is able to take the perspective of others.

"You know I feel the same way sometimes. I see Jonah a lot every day, and he is not the first challenging student I have had; however, I remember that same fearful feeling when I first met Jonah!" says his special education teacher to a new member of Jonah's team.

2. Acceptance of the other team members for what they are means showing genuine positive regard for another person's capacity, experiences, talents, and unique viewpoints.

"I can understand how scary it can be—you have seen one of his worst explosions," says a counselor, who remembers Jonah's anger in English during the first week of classes. "He exploded the day he forgot to bring his lunch

Figure 2.6. Balancing special educators' caseloads. (From Giangreco, M.F. [2007]. *Absurdities and realities of special education: The complete digital set [CD].* Thousand Oaks, CA: Corwin Press; reprinted with permission of the copyright holder, Michael F. Giangreco.)

to school; school had just started, high school was brand new for him, and he was confused about his schedule. He has not fallen apart like that in a long time, thank goodness—and I think it is because of all of our supports, including his parents' help with Jonah's daily planner!" the counselor adds.

3. Credibility means that team members perceive each other as compatible or similar and competent (i.e., having talents to bring to the team that others value) and as someone who openly speaks his or her mind and takes the group's interest to heart.

The members of Jonah's team have many years of high school teaching experience among them. They have strong respect for each other's talents. Each team member interacts with Jonah regularly, and, for the most part, their team-generated action plan for supporting him has been highly successful.

Trust is built when an individual takes a risk in initiating an interaction with

another person and is affirmed, which leads to team members' open sharing (disclosure). Although trust is essential to team effectiveness, there are limits to trust. Trust in another team member is appropriate only when the potential for benefit is greater than the potential for harm. This requires sizing up the situation and initiating or reacting accordingly. Chapter 3 provides more detail on developing interpersonal and teamwork skills.

DEFINING TEAM MEMBERS' ROLES AND RESPONSIBILITIES

Staff roles frequently change in inclusive schools where collaboration is practiced (West & Idol, 1990; Wood, 1998). Collaborative teachers are more likely to seek help from other teachers and support staff than teachers who work alone. They are also apt to plan instruction together, draw on related services professionals, and solicit help from family members. General education teachers usually have command of the content and primary responsibility for the class. Special educators bring their complementary skills of designing teaching programs suited to students with special needs. Also consider that special educators who are highly qualified in a content area have expertise in both content and pedagogy. General educators, particularly those who have experience as co-teachers or in inclusive settings, likely have expertise in a range of pedagogical areas. As the term *transdisciplinary* indicates, the skills begin to cross over disciplines, whether from general to special educator, speech-language therapist to general educator, or within and among all team members.

Collaborative teaming requires that team members learn how to jointly communicate, plan, and deliver coordinated services. Teachers, related services providers, and other staff members report that their roles changed as a result of inclusion (e.g., Leatherman, 2009; Mackenzie, 2011; Snell et al., 1995). Team members should be actively involved in defining the changes because role changes and turf protection can cause considerable concern among staff. Conceptual barriers can also hinder special educators lending support to classroom teachers. For example, general and special educators may not know or agree with each other's teaching strategies, they might be divided by a feeling of hierarchy if special educators take on consultant or expert roles, and classroom teachers may view the increase in support staff traffic for students with IEPs as intrusive (Matzen, Ryndak, & Nakao, 2010; Wood, 1998). The hierarchy for co-teachers is usually reversed, with the general education teacher assuming the lead or expert role and special education teachers often in a more subordinate role (Scruggs, Mastropieri, & McDuffie, 2007). In addition, overreliance on paraprofessionals assigned to individual students with significant needs raises concerns about role definitions in inclusive classrooms

(Conroy, 2007; Giangreco, Broer, & Suter, 2011; Suter & Giangreco, 2009). Therefore, an early step in building teamwork is to think about, discuss, define, and clarify team members' roles and responsibilities concerning the student with disabilities and other students in a classroom or activity. Once these roles and responsibilities are defined and agreed to, teams can identify and problem-solve issues that arise and make revisions as needed.

Self-Perception of Strengths and Weaknesses

Personal style, professional training, and perception of strengths and weaknesses influence how team members envision their jobs and professional duties. The duties that teachers elect to fulfill will change 1) when they gain experience with a broader diversity of students in inclusive programs, 2) as the team to which they belong works to support various students, and 3) as the team's composition changes. In studies of collaborative teams seeking to include students in elementary schools (Wood, 1998) and middle schools (Matzen et al., 2010), researchers found that the role boundaries between general and special educators were initially rigid, with a clear division of duties. Special educators initially developed all of the academic and behavior programs for the included students and supervised the paraprofessionals in an effort to "ease the general educators' fears about workload and expected student outcomes" (Matzen et al., 2010, p. 293). This initial division of labor meant that classroom teachers 1) were less involved in the core team, 2) had less influence on how services were pulled into the classroom, 3) focused mainly on the child's social goals, and 4) were unable to express their dislike of disruptive push-in schedules and special teaching. Middle school general educators expressed concern when there was no clarification of their roles: "Even when students attended their general education classes, they usually arrived late and left early, thus missing both the naturally occurring opportunities to interact with their general education classmates and the organizational activities that occurred at these times" (Matzen et al., 2010 p. 295). Role clarification can be facilitated in several ways (Damore & Murray, 2009; DeBoer & Fister, 1995–1996; Gurgur & Uzuner, 2010):

- Professional development is provided for grade-level teams or for entire schools on topics such as effective teaming, collaborative problem solving, and methods of pushing in special education services and co-teaching. Professional development helps teachers and other team members define the skills needed to include students and presents teachers with different models for planning and delivering coordinated special education supports.

- Special education and general education teachers meet individually to determine who does what, including preferences for teaming roles and responsibilities.

- Team members identify and share their responses to questions about their strengths/resources and needs/fears regarding inclusion and teaming: What skills, talents, knowledge, and experiences do I bring to the team? What are my emerging skills? What supports and resources do I need? What supports can I provide? What situations do I find stressful? What fears do I have about inclusion and teamwork?

 ## Student Snapshot

Abby, a 6-year-old first grader, has a diagnosis of multiple disabilities, including an intellectual disability and cerebral palsy. She actively participates in many classroom activities with a variety of supports and adaptations. Abby uses a walker but is a bit unsteady and needs assistance to sit and stand. She mainly communicates through nonsymbolic communication but is learning to use picture symbols, simple voice-output communication devices (e.g., a Cheaptalk), and a few words to express her needs, make choices and requests, and greet people. Abby's curricular adaptations involve a combination of simplified literacy and numeracy goals as well as functional goals in school routines, self-help, and communication. (See Figure 2.7 for a brief listing of Abby's IEP goals and other key information about her special education services. A blank, photocopiable version of this form is available in Appendix A and the forms download.)

Abby's core team includes her mom; Ms. Becker, her first-grade teacher; Ms. Montague, her special education teacher; and two paraprofessionals who support Abby at various times during the day. A speech-language pathologist, physical therapist, and the school district's consulting specialist on including students with significant disabilities attend team meetings on an intermittent basis, when their particular expertise is needed by the team. The two teachers and Abby's mom met before the school year started to get to know one another better and talk about some of the work the team would need to do to ensure a good school year for Abby. First, the team reviewed Abby's Program-at-a-Glance. Ms. Montague stressed the importance of addressing Abby's IEP goals in the context of ongoing academic lessons and classroom routines throughout the day, and she emphasized the need for all adults working with Abby to be familiar with those goals and the other key provisions of the IEP.

Next, they discussed their preferences for teaming roles and responsibilities. Abby's IEP team already had determined that Abby would receive her literacy and numeracy instruction through a combination of co-teaching and push-in direct instruction by a special education teacher. Ms. Becker thought she would feel comfortable carrying out team ideas when Abby was in the classroom for most other whole-group instruction and for any small-group instruction in which the teaching focus for Abby was a simplified version of the curriculum objective for most students. The two teachers discussed how they would handle adapting materials for Abby when

Program-at-a-Glance

Student: _Abby_   Date: _September 2014_

IEP goals (in a few words)	IEP accommodations and modifications
Communication, socialization, and self-management	• *Receive special education instruction for academics; support for daily routines, transitions, communication techniques, peer interactions*
• *Use gestures and words, augmented by pictures or picture symbols or simple devices, for expressive communication (e.g., greetings and farewells, expressing needs, making choices).*	• *Modified curriculum emphasizing basic academics, functional skills, social-communication skills, and school and classroom participation*
• *Follow directions (e.g., get materials, sit at desk or floor, line up) from teacher cues and peer models.*	• *Home–school communication log*
Functional skills and school participation	• *Educational team familiar with and supports use of all augmentative communication methods and adaptive seating and materials*
• *Use picture schedule to begin and end activities.*	• *Variety of manipulatives for math activities*
• *Participate in large and small groups (e.g., take turns; volunteer; follow directions; color, cut, and paste).*	• *Anecdotal records and skill acquisition data for IEP progress*
• *Increase participation in school routines: arrival, departure, lunch, and classroom jobs.*	
Math	
• *Recognize numbers 0–10.*	
• *Count and compare objects to 10.*	**Academic, social, and physical supports**
• *Use mouse or keyboard to navigate computer.*	• *Peer planning and problem solving at beginning of year and as needed*
• *Build A–B patterns with manipulatives.*	• *Assistance and support for arrival, lunch, departure, and restroom routines*
Reading and language arts	• *Position close to classmates in variety of suitable positions per physical therapist's or occupational therapist's plans*
• *Hold print materials in correct position, identify front and back cover and title page, and turn pages.*	• *Core team meetings weekly; whole team meetings monthly*
• *Answer basic comprehension ("wh") questions.*	
• *Read high-frequency words (match, point to).*	
• *Sort or match pictures with words or initial consonants.*	
Science and social studies	
• *Participate in science activities: focus on animals and plants, living and nonliving, weather, and senses.*	
• *Identify classmates, school personnel, school, town, and state.*	

Figure 2.7. Program-at-a-Glance for Abby, a first-grade student. (*Key:* IEP, individualized education program.) (*Note:* A blank, photocopiable version is available in Appendix A, and blank and filled-in versions are available in the forms download.)

necessary; Ms. Becker felt that she would be able to adapt science and social studies materials after some initial guidance and input from Ms. Montague and Abby's mom. She wanted Ms. Montague to take responsibility for finding and/or adapting reading, language arts, and math materials for Abby, but the team would decide together on an overall plan for the general ways that Abby's schoolwork would be individualized. Ms. Becker raised concerns about the training and supervision of the two paraprofessionals who would be assisting Abby with her physical and personal needs; the team agreed that Ms. Montague would use part of the time allotted on Abby's IEP for special education consultation to train, observe, and confer with the paraprofessionals every other Friday. Another decision about roles and responsibilities made at this meeting was that Ms. Montague would handle any IEP-specific communication with Abby's parents and other team members, but Ms. Becker would be the point person for daily communication with parents—just as she did for all other students in the class.

⟳ ACTIVITY: *Describe the potential undesirable outcomes if Ms. Becker and Ms. Montague had not directly and explicitly discussed how they would share and divide responsibilities for Abby's educational program.*

The Program-at-a-Glance should be shared with all team members as a way to help establish shared expectations about a student's educational programming and also to prompt the discussion about the roles and responsibilities team members will have to fill in order to implement the IEP and ensure that the student is a full member of the class.

Team Roles and Responsibilities Worksheet

Discussions about roles and responsibilities, such as the one described in the preceding vignette about Abby's team, can be further facilitated by using a matrix that lists team members across the top and typical responsibilities for delivering coordinated programs on the left-hand side. Figure 2.8 is an example of such a checklist that Devin's team used in planning their roles to support him. (A blank, photocopiable version is available in Appendix A and the forms download.) Notice that the responsibilities are truly shared among Devin's team members, but the people with the primary responsibility for a task are identified.

The worksheet will need to be expanded for teams for secondary students to include other general education teachers who are team members and who share responsibilities. Focus should be redirected to assigning roles and responsibilities whenever a new member joins the team or the team re-forms at the beginning of a new school year. A student's team may need to be completely re-formed when he or she moves from one school to another. Teams can smooth these major transitions by meeting with new team members well before the change.

Teams share ownership of the students on whom they focus, although special education teachers ultimately are responsible for knowing and implementing special education procedures consistent with school policy and state law. Accommodations and other content on the IEP, however, may specifically note involvement of general education teachers. In classrooms that are truly inclusive, however, the special education teacher does not have primary responsibility for every item on the Team Roles and Responsibilities Checklist, and the general education teacher is not left to figure things out alone.

TIME TO MEET, PLAN, AND IMPLEMENT

Several guidelines determine the amount of time teams need both for sit-down meetings and for on-the-fly communications.

- Students with more complex disabilities, less supportive families, and/or atypical or disruptive social behavior usually need more support and require more involvement and time. The core

Team Roles and Responsibilities Checklist

Student: _Devin_   Date: _September 2014_

Teaching and support team members

Teachers: _Greer (4th grade)_   Paraprofessional(s): _Johannsen, Barnes_
Conti (special education)   Others: _Mr. and Mrs. Warren (parents)_

Key:
P = Primary responsibility
I = Input into implementation and/or decision making

Roles and responsibilities	Who is responsible?			
	Classroom teacher	Special educator	Paraprofessionals	Others
1. Developing lesson and unit plans	*P*	*I*		
2. Developing individualized adaptations and support plans	*I*	*P*	*I*	*Parent input*
3. Providing instruction (with accommodations and modifications; list subjects or other targeted goal areas):				
a. Communication, social, and behavior	*I*	*P*	*I*	*SLP*
b. Functional skills and school participation	*I*	*P*	*I*	
c. Academics: Reading, language arts, and math	*I*	*P*	*I*	
d. Academics: Science and social studies	*P*	*I*	*I*	
4. Adapting instructional materials	*P (content areas)*	*P (basic skills)*	*I*	
5. Assigning grades/report card	*P*	*I*	*I*	
6. Monitoring progress on individualized education program (IEP) goals	*I*	*P (reports, IEP)*	*I (data log)*	
7. Assigning duties to and supervising paraprofessionals	*P (daily)*	*P (long term)*		
8. Training paraprofessionals	*I*	*P*		
9. Scheduling and facilitating team meetings	*P (core team)*	*P (IEP)*		
10. Daily communication with parents	*P*	*I*	*I*	
11. Communication and coordination with related services	*I*	*P (service coordinator)*	*I (logs)*	
12. Facilitating peer relationships and supports (modeling and prompting appropriate ways to interact, organizing formal peer supports)	*P*	*P (peer support network)*	*I*	
13. Assigning student to partners or cooperative groups	*P*	*I*		

Figure 2.8. Team Roles and Responsibilities Checklist. (*Key:* SLP, speech-language pathologist.) (From Ford, A., Messenheimer-Young, T., Toshner, J., Fitzgerald, M.A., Dyer, C., Glodoski, J., & Laveck, J. [1995, July]. *A team planning packet for inclusive education.* Milwaukee: Wisconsin School Inclusion Project; adapted by permission.) (*Note:* A blank, photocopiable version is available in Appendix A, and blank and filled-in versions are available in the forms download.)

team members of students with high support needs often meet weekly and communicate daily.

- The core team members of students with fewer support needs may meet every 1–3 weeks but communicate at least weekly.

- Paraprofessionals who are involved in the support should communicate daily with the special and general educators.

- Related services personnel who are involved in the support should communicate with the classroom staff whenever they are scheduled with the student and should give verbal or written comments to the special educator on a preplanned basis.

- Schools and teams decide on written approaches to preserve the decisions made in meetings (e.g., notes on issues, actions, or people responsible; meeting minutes) and share the decisions with team members.

- Family members and teachers decide how they will communicate (e.g., in person before or after school, traveling notebook, telephone, voice mail, e-mail) and how often, as well as what meetings families want to attend.

Communication among team members between meetings must also be planned and valued. The preceding guidelines for meeting frequency are only general rules, and most teams will adopt the general principle, "Meet when there is a reason to meet, and let the agenda drive the meeting."

Finding the Time to Plan

Finding the time to meet is probably the biggest challenge for most teams (e.g., Carter et al., 2009; Santoli et al., 2008). General and special education teachers may not have common planning times. Special education teachers in elementary schools often have no planning time. Paraprofessionals sometimes have contracts that do not pay after-school hours, or paraprofessionals have after-school duties or other jobs. Related services personnel frequently rotate across schools. Although public school teachers and school staff will always find scheduling difficult, there are some solutions.

First, building administrators and teachers need to confront schedule conflicts and the shortage of available time. Meeting times for teams will always be influenced by building-wide scheduling decisions (e.g., start and end of school, assemblies) as well as by the staffing assignment approach a school adopts for its special education teachers. Three common staffing approaches that facilitate collaboration include assigning special education teachers with the training to serve a broader range of students with disabilities to 1) grade-level or multigrade teams in elementary schools; 2) interdepartmental, grade-level teams or families in middle schools; and 3) departmental teams in high schools. Teachers or therapists who are highly specialized (e.g., severe disabilities, mobility specialists) might rotate across all grades in a larger school or across several schools. Most special education teachers will have a defined caseload that matches the way general education teachers are organized, making common meeting times more likely and reducing the number of special educators a group of teachers must call on to collaborate. Furthermore, principals who understand the value of team meetings and have a logical staffing plan in place can work with teachers to explore ways to make time available and coordinate staff schedules (Idol, 1997; Raforth & Foriska, 2006; Walther-Thomas, 1997).

Second, creative approaches make use of in-school planning time before tapping after-school or before-school time. Several common options are used for creating shared planning time (Carter et al.,

2009; Friend & Cook, 2003; Rainforth & England, 1997).

- *Early school release or late arrival:* Adjust school schedules so that dismissing school early or starting late creates time for weekly or monthly planning with no reduction in student learning time. Get community support first and preserve the time for teaming.

- *Substitutes:* Hire a permanent substitute who is scheduled to teach across schools (e.g., one day on alternate weeks) or hire substitutes to rotate across classes, freeing up teachers to meet with special educators. Select substitutes who are able to rotate from class to class, save planning time by having substitutes review material rather than teach new material, and keep teachers accountable for their teaming interactions.

- *On-the-spot teaming strategies for co-teaching:* At the scheduled time for co-teaching, the classroom teacher tells students (and the co-teacher) what they will be working on and may stop instruction to let students review in an effort to check their understanding and to orient the special educator.

Third, therapists or specialized teachers who regularly serve students with low-incidence disabilities (e.g., severe disabilities, deafblindness, autism) can be scheduled for longer, blocked time periods in schools to increase the likelihood that they will be available to meet with core teams. Scheduling therapy becomes difficult for included students because they are not clustered in self-contained classrooms. *Block scheduling of therapy* (e.g., occupational, physical) refers to

> Allocating longer periods of time than usual (e.g., a half or full day instead of 30–45 minutes) to provide the time and flexibility needed to work in and move between the learning environments in which students with disabilities are

> integrated. (Rainforth & York-Barr, 1997, p. 267)

Therapists who go to a particular school less often but stay longer reduce travel time between and within buildings and create teaming possibilities by being available before and/or after school or during planning periods:

Finally, efficiency is often the best antidote to a shortage of time. Several practices will increase the efficiency of even short periods of available time:

- Teams should use and mutually enforce a regular schedule and process for meetings.

- Team members show respect for each other's time by adhering to time limits—start on time, stay on task, and end on time.

- Teams use an agenda, take notes, share notes with all members, and use notes from earlier meetings to review progress.

When these three practices are applied, a great deal can be accomplished in a 20- to 30-minute period. The following section offers guidance to help teams do their work more efficiently and effectively.

ESTABLISHING A TEAM MEETING PROCESS AND SCHEDULE

A team's initial meetings make important impressions on members; therefore, the initial team leaders, organizers, and supporting administrators should strive to make the team's first meeting successful (Katzenbach & Smith, 1993). Initial meetings should focus on team-building activities such as redefining the school's mission into goals that are specific to the team, defining shared values, identifying ground rules, determining members' roles and responsibilities, and clarifying the teaming process members will use. Once teams have established these fundamentals, they are ready to tackle specific issues concerning students. Initial meetings and group interactions often determine team members' impressions of the team's future success. Whether all members attend (particularly anyone seen as being in charge or an organizer), show up on time, play by the established rules of conduct, participate, and stay the entire session are good indicators of whether team members will view initial sessions as successes. Team members tend to focus on the person perceived as being in charge, observing his or her behavior more closely than his or her words and making predictions about the future of the team based on these impressions (Johnson & Johnson, 2000). It is helpful for team members to answer several questions to establish the team process they will use.

• How will we develop the team's agenda?

• How will we conduct our meetings?

• When and how often or long will we meet?

• Where will we meet?

• How can we use collaborative technology?

• How will our process be suited to the student's family members?

How Will Team Members Develop the Team's Agenda?

Team goals can be either 1) broad, overall goals (reflected in shared values and roles and responsibilities) or 2) immediate goals (reflected in ongoing action plans and current meeting agendas). Awareness of and attention to both levels of team goals is evident in almost every step of conducting a team meeting. Researchers found that reaching and implementing responsive actions was far more difficult when team members were unprepared for meetings or were unaware that their philosophies differed (Carter et al., 2009). Teams need to be aware of their purpose

and their reasons for gathering. Several indicators of potential trouble will arise when overall and immediate goals are vague or undefined (Senge, Roberts, Ross, Smith, & Kleiner, 1994):

• Repeated changes in direction during a meeting

• Recurrent disagreement about team action

• Concerns about the size or appropriateness of the goals or team's focus

• Inaction and frustration

• Extreme lack of confidence regarding team decisions and actions

Forging ahead with the agenda when problems arise often simply results in more frustration. Instead, it helps to refocus on the team goals, such as by saying, "Let's identify what is reasonable to accomplish for our first steps." Responsive actions can include clarifying the parameters of the team's most immediate purpose, reaching agreement on the priority for the student and the team, or simplifying or combining goals to workable sizes and complexity.

What occurs during meetings is closely related to team roles and responsibilities and students' status as class or school members and their progress as learners. For example, if and when teams have concerns about students' academic progress or social acceptance, these concerns can be aired during team meetings, and teams can determine whether to take action to address them. In general, most student-centered teams direct their energies toward facilitating student learning and membership within classes, school activities, and peer groups. For example, they develop lessons; adapt curricula, teaching methods, and materials; assess student progress; assign grades; and address interaction issues. Teams use agendas to guide them when defining the primary (i.e., priority) and secondary (i.e., could be discussed and acted on this week or next meeting but needs to be on everyone's mind) tasks that they need to accomplish.

- An agenda, even if just verbal, is established prior to a team meeting (or in the minutes of the prior meeting) and provides the reasons for meeting.

- The agenda is reviewed at the beginning of the meeting; revisions are made until the team agrees on the content, number and order of items, and time needed for each item.

- The agenda is used to guide the meeting once it is reviewed and agreed on by all members.

- Agendas include student-focused items and team-focused items (e.g., action items, who does what by when, "kudos to . . .").

- At the end of the meeting, any agenda items that still need to be addressed in addition to other items that have cropped up during the meeting are placed on the agenda for the next meeting.

How Will Team Members Conduct Team Meetings?

Although meetings are conducted according to the process team members have designed, this design will be fairly similar for all collaborative teams that focus on students.

- Team members take a few minutes to socialize with each other.

- Someone (perhaps a predesignated facilitator) opens the meeting.

- Team members volunteer to fill roles that will help the group accomplish their tasks and allow leadership to be distributed among team members (see Table 2.2). These roles should rotate each meeting.

- The facilitator leads a discussion about agenda items (e.g., clarity, priority, team time required to address each item).

- The facilitator leads a review of action plan progress; the team celebrates successes.

Table 2.2.   Roles team members take to accomplish team tasks and distribute leadership

Team role	Leadership role description
Facilitator	Leads the meeting, keeps members focused on the agenda, encourages all members to participate, and suggests other options for reaching agreement. Takes responsibility for preparation before the meeting.
Timekeeper	Watches the time and warns others when the designated time for each agenda item is almost over and is finished.
Recorder	Writes down team meeting details (e.g., people present, agenda items, roles) and takes brief notes on relevant information and team decisions. Quickly captures the essence of group ideas without evaluation. May read notes back to group for clarification. May use two recorders: one to take notes that are visible to team members on wall-hanging paper and another to put the notes on a meeting minutes form or in a laptop file for distribution later.
Jargon buster	Is alert to terms used by members that may not be understood by others present. Signals the speaker to explain or define the term in simpler or more complete ways.
Processor or observer	Pays attention to the teaming process and whether members work together collaboratively. Reminds team to process. Praises good team communication. Alerts team when group tension requires discussion or problem solving.

Note: All team members participate in the meeting while also filling one of the following roles.

- Using the team process and assigned roles, the facilitator provides structure and helps members focus on each agenda item as time allows, the time-keeper reminds the team of the meeting's schedule, and members filling other roles play their part (e.g., jargon buster, notetaker, process observer, encourager).

- For each agenda item that requires action, team members discuss and identify the issue or concern, share information, generate ideas, problem-solve and select potential solutions, and create an action plan. (Chapter 4 details the problem-solving and action-planning processes teams use during this step.)

- Members work to process the functioning of the team.

- The facilitator brings the meeting to a close and summarizes outcomes.

- Notes taken by the recorder are disseminated to team members.

Teams develop or adapt a meeting form that reflects their procedures and facilitates notetaking. Meeting forms may be fairly simple, providing a place for noting who is present and recording agenda items and expected times, team decisions and action plans, and information about the next meeting (see Figure 2.9; a blank, photocopiable version is available in Appendix A and the forms download). If the next meeting is not set at this time, then someone on the team may be designated to send out an e-mail with a Doodle poll (http://doodle.com) requesting responses for the next meeting. Practiced teams, however, typically use a set meeting schedule.

Most members leave with a defined part in one or several action plans at the conclusion of the meeting. Team members should prepare to update others at the next meeting on whatever part they were assigned.

 ## Student Snapshot

Each member of Abby's team was handed a printed copy of the meeting minutes that listed new issues and responsibilities when they left the previous meeting. All had a part in implementing or assisting with Abby's use of her communication switch, adjusting the wheelchair footrests, using the slant board, or getting Abby to participate in the "coat off and hung" routine. Each member came to the next meeting prepared to report the status of these old issues. Likewise, members had signed on for new responsibilities to carry out before the next meeting.

⟲ ACTIVITY: *Contrast Abby's team's experience with that of Joe (see Figure 2.10).*

Team morale is low and team effectiveness suffers when team members come to a meeting unprepared. A consistent lack of preparation by one or more team members is a clear indication of team trouble and requires team processing. Some questions to explore when determining the reasons why team members are unprepared include

- Are team members overloaded with too many competing commitments?

- Are team responsibilities distributed unevenly in their action plans?

- Do action plans set forth workable and defined responsibilities?

- Are those responsible for action plans in agreement with the plans (was consensus reached)?

- Are team members in agreement on their team's general goals and purpose?

- Do team members share and operate by a common set of values?

When and How Often or Long Will Team Members Meet?

Teams need to determine a meeting frequency and duration that suits team members and allows enough time to address

Generic Meeting Form

Meeting purpose: *Monthly meeting for Abby*

Date: *10/1*　　　Start time: *8:00 a.m.*　　　Next meeting date: *11/2*　　　Next start time: *8:00 a.m.*
　　　　　　　End time: *8:20 a.m.*　　　　　　　　　　　　　　　　　　End time: *8:30 a.m.*

Members present:

Name: *Ms. Becker*   Position: *First-grade teacher*

Name: *Ms. Montague*   Position: *Special education teacher*

Name: *Mrs. Park*   Position: *Speech-language therapist*

Name: *Mr. Meeks*   Position: *Physical therapist*

Agenda topics:	Decisions:
1. *Use of communication switch*	1. *Need to assess several options during class activities.*
2. *Adjusting wheelchair footrests*	2. *Need tools to make adjustments.*
3. *Using the slant board*	3. *Need to assess different implements (crayons, pencils, markers).*

Action Plan

Who	Does what	By when
1. *Mrs. Park*	1. *Bring switches from technical assistance center to test with Abby and peers during morning meeting, snack, and reading.*	1. *10/15/14*
2. *Mr. Meeks*	2. *Find tools and make adjustments during pull-out therapy session with Abby.*	2. *10/8/14*
3. *Ms. Becker and Ms. Montague*	3. *Conduct brief assessments of writing tools during language arts activities.*	3. *10/10/14*

Figure 2.9. Generic Meeting Form. (*Note:* A blank, photocopiable version is available in Appendix A, and blank and filled-in versions are available in the forms download.)

team goals. Teams should identify a regular time to meet once frequency and duration have been established. Whole team meetings should be scheduled less often and be less flexible; core team meetings should be scheduled more often, and their times may need to be more flexible. The following guidelines may assist teams in planning this part of their process:

- Meet only when there is a clear purpose.

- Promptly address current and serious student or staff issues.

- Meet when necessary material and information is available and key members can attend.

- When a team meeting is held to provide new information, consider distributing printed information before the meeting or instead of holding the meeting.

- Regularly held meetings (e.g., 4 p.m. on Tuesdays) are predictable and easier to schedule.

- Schedule meeting times early in the year for the whole school year or at

Voices from the Classroom: A Mother's View

I had experienced two uneventful years of middle school for Joe. He had been in totally inclusive classes and was a member of the swim team. Academically and socially, he was doing the best he had ever done in school. During Joe's IEP meeting for ninth grade (high school), Joe was placed in special education classes for all of his academics. I was not sure why he was placed in such classes, and I asked that he be placed in regular classes because he was doing fine in them while in middle school. I was instructed to wait until the school year started; any changes could be made then.

The issue was still not addressed in September of Joe's ninth-grade year. Joe was having behavioral issues, which was a new thing. There was a breakdown in communication from the middle school team to the high school team regarding Joe's placement once the new school year began. No one asked to reconvene the IEP meeting, so I requested an IEP meeting to discuss Joe's behavior and placement. During the IEP meeting, I was informed that none of Joe's classes in special education would count for credit toward a regular high school diploma. This meant he was not being prepared for college as an option. After several meetings and evaluations to determine Joe's ability to make the transition back to the general education environment, it was time for his IEP for the 10th grade. Joe ended up repeating the ninth grade in order to receive the academic courses he needed to graduate from high school with a regular diploma. After 5 years in high school, Joe was a high school graduate.

In spite of starting out high school with a weak collaborative team, Joe is working toward his goal of an undergraduate degree. Joe is currently a junior at a major university.

Figure 2.10. A mother's experiences with individualized education program (IEP) team meetings. (Contributed by Karen King Scanlan.)

least an entire semester (Rainforth & York-Barr, 1997); unnecessary meetings can simply be canceled.

- Meetings must be long enough for team members to address the essentials (e.g., build relationships, celebrate, organize, discuss, problem-solve, plan, process the discussion). Skilled core teams with an agreed-on agenda can accomplish these essentials in meetings as short as 20–30 minutes.

- Teaming procedures require high-energy thinking and interaction and can be exhausting, especially after a long school day. Twenty- or thirty-minute meetings often allow many issues to be adequately addressed (Thousand & Villa, 2000).

Teams initially may construct long agendas, thinking they can accomplish more than they actually can; over time, teams increase their productivity without increasing their meeting time as team members learn to use the process and procedures and work with each other (Thousand & Villa, 2000).

Where Will the Team Meet?

Choose a pleasant location that is quiet and has comfortable chairs, a seating arrangement that facilitates face-to-face communication, a table surface to ease notetaking and examination of materials, and refreshments to provide needed energy and create a collegial atmosphere. Classrooms that are free of students and nonparticipating staff sometimes are suitable, but other staff members or students should not be able to hear or observe the meeting. Staff members may need to post signs on meeting room doors to prevent unwelcome interruptions, turn off cell phones, and explore how to lower or eliminate the school intercom volume in the meeting room. Some teams prefer to use two team recorders: one to take notes on a worksheet or a laptop and another to take notes on a blackboard or on large newsprint that can be taped to the wall for all members to see. It is particularly advantageous to display the meeting notes on the wall or blackboard when the team is large; remarks are easily referred to, memory needs be relied on less, and progress made on action plans can be easily reviewed. A blackboard and chalk; easel, markers, tape, and newsprint; or laptop computer should be available in the meeting location.

How Can Team Members Use Collaborative Technology?

With the increased likelihood of team members participating in meetings using videoconferencing technology (refer to Appendix B for examples of videoconferencing technology), it is important to be attentive to how team dynamics and processes are affected when one or more members is not physically in the same room as the other team members. In addition, any of the note-sharing strategies previously mentioned may need to be adapted to ensure everyone is able to view the changing information. Certain web sites can help address this concern by enabling team members to view and work on materials in real time during their meeting. (Refer to real-time whiteboard options in Appendix B.)

All systems, devices, or programs to be used in meetings should be tested in the specific locations in advance. If there are potential issues with firewalls, connections, software licenses, or other matters, then solutions can be found without slowing down the team.

How Will the Team Process Be Suited to the Student's Family Members?

Teams that include family members need to ensure that their team meeting process works not only for staff but also for students' families. Teachers may need to

individualize their approach to suit family members' level of sophistication, comfort, and preferences. For example, parents may or may not want to fill a role during the meeting, and other family members will initially participate by listening and only later by talking. Many barriers can hinder parents from being active participants in their child's education, such as economic constraints on their time, cultural discomfort, and negative school experiences as a child or as a parent. Parents can gain new confidence about their interactions with teams when team members communicate respect to parents for knowledge about their child. Some school systems provide advocacy training or parent support groups to ensure family members are aware of the ways they are team members (Burke, 2013).

Family members are not available for face-to-face interactions as often as teachers. However, as a part of the core team, their input needs to be ongoing, and their attendance at some team meetings is essential. Educators on the team should be sensitive to family logistical needs (e.g., convenient scheduling, child care, transportation) and seek ways to work around those needs whenever possible, including using technology to maintain participation (e.g., speakerphones) and face-to-face interactions (e.g., webcams and applications such as Skype that allow instant messaging over the Internet).

If parents (or their designees) are able to meet regularly with the core team, then communication prior to each meeting allows a check on the time and place and a review of the agenda. Conroy (2012) found that families in rural areas who are culturally and linguistically diverse may feel more sensitive about language differences, geographic isolation, and lack of transportation. It can be difficult to travel or take time off work during the school day, even for families in urban and suburban areas. Premeeting communication is still valuable when family members cannot meet regularly because it allows current family input to be considered; communicating with family members following the meeting helps keep the student's family linked to the team process. Effective collaborative teams are immediately responsive to family needs and requests. Team members will find that the following practices communicate sensitivity to the concerns and perspectives of family members:

- Treat team minutes as confidential, and do not list specific details about students in the team minutes.

- Teach and prompt teaming procedures by using simple guidelines for problem-solving methods (see Chapter 3). Hand out a printed list of team roles and their definitions.

- Strive to generate an action plan for implementing solutions.

- Attend to interpersonal aspects. List people's names (including the parents) and roles on a whiteboard or wall poster. Be aware of how your outward behavior in meetings communicates interest and disinterest. Avoid professional jargon, be a good listener, and monitor dominance by staff members. Seek the input of family members by posing open-ended questions one at a time and listening to their comments.

- End meetings on time, but also be sure to review major outcomes and plans, thank team members, and establish a time for a follow-up meeting or contact.

- When parents cannot attend meetings, include their input and then share the meeting decisions with them. Also consider how parents can be present via technology (e.g., speakerphones,

videoconferencing). If there are cultural and/or language differences between the team's staff members and family members, then staff should take steps to prevent those differences from becoming barriers.

- The composition of the student's team could be reconfigured to include a staff member of the same culture, one who speaks the family's native language, or one who is well informed and can heighten the awareness of other staff members.

- Staff members could ask a family member to regularly share information on the student's home and culture to enlighten staff and assist them in relating to the family and student more meaningfully.

- Staff could seek professional development on multicultural sensitivity, family-centered programs, and ways to provide services that are culturally responsive. (Appendix B includes a listing of some helpful resources on these topics.)

CONCLUSION

Inclusive schools cannot succeed without the work of collaborative teams. Effective teamwork rests on a foundation of mutual trust and equity, with team members coordinating their efforts through face-to-face interactions involving problem solving to achieve a common goal. Although team-based decision making is clearly a part of all special education procedures, there is no guarantee that teams will operate in this manner. Educators may have to learn these strategies, and administrators may need to support them in this process (Alquraini & Gut, 2012). Chapter 3 describes the skills team members need to use as members of collaborative teams.

3

Learning Teamwork Skills

FOCUSING QUESTIONS

- In what ways can teams make the most of formal and informal meetings, given limited time?
- What are the basic communication skills and outward behaviors that team members exhibit to promote team effectiveness?
- In what ways can individuals facilitate and support collaborative teaming?
- How do teams create consensus?
- How do teams deal with conflict and disagreement?
- How might team dynamics change when videoconferencing?

Student Snapshot

Mr. Li, the fifth-grade teacher, explained to Ms. Southard, the special educator, why he thought Jose, who had learning disabilities and read at a second-grade level, needed more time during the school day for intensive reading instruction. Ms. Southard perceived his explanation as a way of saying he (Mr. Li) did not want Jose in his class for language arts. Mr. Li perceived he was voicing a valid concern based on several reasons. Most important, he felt Jose needed to increase his decoding and comprehension skills this year so that he would be able to learn better from textbooks used in middle school content classes next year.

(↻) ACTIVITY: *Think about situations you have experienced in which the intended message was not the message received. When did you realize you were missing each other? What did you do to repair the miscommunication?*

Calling people a team is no guarantee that they will operate as a team (Lee, 2009; Sargeant, Loney, & Murphy, 2008; Villa & Thousand, 2000), which requires an array of collaborative skills and growth of positive relationships among team members (Appl et al., 2001; Chen & Reigeluth, 2010; Frankel, 2006). Some even suggest that a super anatomy is required (see Figure 3.1). This chapter addresses these teaming skills, from the most basic skills of active listening and setting up for positive and productive interactions, to the more complex skills of dealing with conflict and disagreement. Methods of setting ground rules, establishing team trust, promoting accurate and unambiguous communication, being sensitive to diversity and avoiding stereotyping, and fostering positive staff–family interactions are also described.

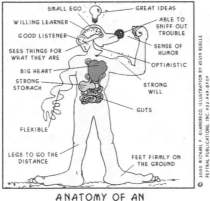

ANATOMY OF AN
EFFECTIVE TEAM MEMBER

Figure 3.1. Anatomy of an effective team member. (From Giangreco, M.F. [2007]. *Absurdities and realities of special education: The complete digital set [CD]*. Thousand Oaks, CA: Corwin Press; reprinted with permission of the copyright holder, Michael F. Giangreco.)

SETTING GROUND RULES FOR TEAM MEETINGS

Ground rules are informal directives set by the team that reflect each member's view of conditions that enable comfortable, honest, and productive communication. Ground rules provide team members with shared expectations about the team's norms and ways of operating. Team members may initially think "it goes without saying" for what are appropriate or inappropriate, desired or undesired, or supportive versus nonsupportive actions (whether verbal or nonverbal) and activities during team meetings. Seemingly trivial disagreements or misunderstandings can become problematic over time, particularly when teams realize they need ground rules or they need to add to the ground rules they already have. The following are examples of topics to discuss when setting ground rules:

- *When does the meeting start?* If members are expected to be on time, then that needs to be clear, enforced, and reinforced.

- *How are people introduced?* Remember that parents and community or other personnel find it difficult to remember who is who and who does what with the student.

- *How are the roles used during team meetings assigned?* Do people volunteer at the start of the meeting, or will it be more efficient to establish a system of rotating roles? For example, people can volunteer to fill certain roles during an initial team meeting; at each subsequent meeting, the role of facilitator is assigned to the previous meeting's recorder, the role of recorder is assigned to the previous meeting's timekeeper, and so forth.

- *How flexible is the content of the agenda?* If issues or areas for updates have arisen since the agenda was developed and disseminated, then teams may agree to add new issues or updates after quickly reviewing the agenda items. Be sure to disseminate the agenda to all team members, including family or community participants, prior to the meeting.

- *Should the topics on the agenda be discussed in order of priority?* Agendas often simply provide a list of topics, but the topics have not necessarily been prioritized or placed in a particular sequence. Teams may want to adopt a ground rule stipulating that the topics on the agenda be sequenced in priority order before discussion begins, along with an estimate of how much time will be spent on each item.

- *What are the parameters for using technology such as cell phones, laptop computers, and two-way radios?* Is it okay for the technology to be on and audible? Some administrative personnel may need to have a two-way radio on when in meetings in case of an emergency. Using other technology (e.g., receiving and responding to cell phone messages, using laptop computers for purposes other than the meeting's focus), however, can be distracting. The team needs to discuss these issues and determine guidelines on which all members can agree.

- *Are there guidelines for food and beverages at meetings; is it okay to eat meals?* Some

team members may need to eat specific foods throughout the day for medical reasons, and other individuals on the team might be distracted by sounds such as the crunching of potato chips or even sickened by the smell of certain foods. The team may decide to establish ground rules on eating and drinking that will make meetings more social, inviting, and inclusive (see Figure 3.2).

- *When does the meeting end?* Is there a designated time for adjournment, or does the meeting end when the issues are resolved or discussed? Experienced teams often decide beforehand how long their meetings will last and then move through the agenda at a pace that will ensure they address each topic by the meeting's end.

- *How are follow-up meetings scheduled?* Is the next meeting scheduled right then, does someone send out an electronic meeting scheduler such as Doodle, or is there another efficient

Voices from the Classroom

As one of several special educators at a large high school, one of my responsibilities was organizing and running some of our collaborative team meetings, whether for the individualized education program team or a student's core team. Team members for any given meeting could include general educators, special educators, related services personnel, and parents. I found over the years that being organized, modeling respect, having a sense of humor, and bringing food were the keys not only to productive collaboration meetings but also to everyday working relationships.

Food was always involved in our meetings. Different team members often volunteered to bring a snack, but I always kept an emergency package of cookies handy in case there were not any other options. The food factor, especially for meetings at the end of a long day, made the meeting something to look forward to and helped to keep the mood light. I learned this from the department chair at the middle school where I had taught for many years. She not only provided chocolate and other snacks at all the meetings but also hosted one department meeting a month at her home, which was close to the school, so that the meeting was more relaxed and the snacks more involved and varied. It worked.

Being organized, having a good sense of humor, bringing food, and modeling respect for each other was an important part of our everyday interactions with each other. Keeping all interactions professional and respectful gave our team the foundation for dealing with whatever issues we needed to deal with in a positive and productive manner.

Figure 3.2. Organizing and conducting collaborative meetings. (Contributed by Melissa Ainsworth.)

method to target the next date, time, and location? At the very least, teams may want to designate an approximate date for the next meeting and decide if others not at that team meeting should participate.

One way for a team to compile ground rules involves each team member writing down his or her answer to a stimulus question, such as "What does it take for our team to get its work done?" or "What would it take for me to feel safe communicating openly and honestly in this group?" Responses can be anonymously compiled into a single list. Some teams use a more informal approach, openly discussing their own suggested rules and rewording them until agreement is reached. The following are some examples of ground rules:

- Begin and end team meetings on time.

- Start every meeting with celebrations (i.e., recognition of recent accomplishments).

- Share responsibility for staying focused and following the agenda.

- Be kind and respectful; refrain from complaining and finger-pointing.

- Appreciate feedback, and provide feedback and recognition for others.

- End every meeting with an action plan.

- Nothing discussed leaves the room without team permission.

 Team Snapshot

Mrs. Anderson was the state's designated representative for DeShaun at his IEP meetings. DeShaun, who was labeled as having serious emotional disturbance, had legally been removed from parental care because the environment was extremely volatile. He currently lived in a group home. Mrs. Anderson arrived early to her first IEP meeting for DeShaun to ensure she would be on time. After signing in

at the school's office and getting directions to the meeting room, she found a place to sit at the long table. As people arrived and sat around the table, she wondered if she was in someone else's seat because it seemed that people had a designated seat. She asked if she should sit somewhere else, and it was only then that someone spoke to her: "Who are you?" She introduced herself and explained she was the state-appointed designee for DeShaun's IEP. She held out her hand to shake hands and continue introducing herself to the eight other people already seated. She was interrupted by the person who was apparently the team leader, however, who said: "We will do introductions when everyone's here. It is the first item on the agenda." Mrs. Anderson sat quietly until all team members had arrived, and the team leader announced the first agenda item: introductions.

⟳ ACTIVITY: *How would you have felt if you were Mrs. Anderson? How does your team handle introductions? How does your team ensure members new to the team feel welcome?*

ESTABLISHING TEAM TRUST

Establishing trust among team members is not a simple process; it requires both trusting others and being trustworthy (Johnson & Johnson, 2000; Williams & Baber, 2007). Lee (2009) noted that trust is built over time and that a team's interdependency can help or hinder trust. For example, if one team member does not usually follow through on action plan tasks assigned to him or her, then the trust—the interdependency—is hindered. Team members initially may be cautious in stating their opinions or seeming critical of another team member's idea. When members are more open to others' ideas, then any given member can feel less criticized when a different idea is suggested, but these feelings are shaped by how the team members interact. Building trust is dependent on several things:

- *Interdependence:* Team outcomes depend on individuals doing their part. Interdependence involves a willingness on the part of all team members to contribute to the achievement of team goals by 1) sharing their resources for group gain (e.g., talents, materials, ideas, time, energy), 2) giving help to others, 3) receiving help from each other, and 4) dividing the team's work.

- *Active participation:* Team members feel free to voice their ideas, even if the group seems to have decided about the group's plan for action. Better decisions may be lost if the group begins an action plan too soon. Good ways to discourage active participation are to never use other people's ideas, criticize others' ideas, and enumerate why others' ideas will not work.

- *Shared risk:* Team outcomes may not work as intended, but the team agrees that the solution is well developed and worth trying. The team members set time lines and benchmarks to monitor progress so that refinements can occur, but they are also open to the idea that when a solution does not work, they need to develop another one. They trust that no one blames each other or criticizes a team member for the idea that did not work.

- *Confidence:* The team believes in its potential to positively influence students' academic, social, and behavioral achievements.

LISTENING AND INTERACTING EFFECTIVELY

Spending time with experienced teams and watching them work together is one of the best ways to understand effective interaction among team members. Effective teams do not avoid conflict; instead, they minimize conflict by using productive teaming skills, recognize it when it occurs, and establish strategies to address it. Smoothly functioning teams spend most of their time cooperatively engaged in student-focused discussion and working

toward common goals. They typically use many strategies to effectively communicate, and they rely on one or several processes to identify and resolve problems. Verbal language and nonverbal behaviors are powerful communicative tools; yet, people in any profession may not have been prepared to use these tools to their advantage (Fortenberry, 2011).

Effective teams also regularly reflect on themselves as a team in order to build teaming skills, improve relationships among members, and resolve conflict. Observing teams who alternate their student focus with a team focus reveals the following predictable characteristics (Chen & Reigeluth, 2010; Dulaney, 2012; Johnson & Johnson, 2000; Lee, 2009; Thousand & Villa, 2000):

- Positive interdependence and mutual respect ("We are in this together, and we can all contribute.")

- Frequent, focused, face-to-face exchanges

- The use of processes to facilitate communication and shared decision making (e.g., problem identification, consensus on decisions)

- The use of methods for being responsible and accountable (e.g., setting an agenda, keeping written records of decisions, developing action plans, monitoring student progress via action plans)

- Team trust derived from trusting one another and being trustworthy

Basic Communication Skills and Outward Behavior

Several basic strategies of effective interpersonal communication strongly influence whether teamwork skills will be successful (Chen & Reigeluth, 2010; DeBoer & Fister, 1995–1996; Symeou, Roussounidou, & Michaelides, 2012). Positive interaction starts with the outward behavior of team members and polite consideration of others. Information in most interactions is communicated most powerfully through one's facial expressions and body language in nonverbal ways. "Facial emotions can be interpreted differently by every person. Each facial emotion has its own meaning and message and every receiver takes the message in a different way. Body language is the most important part of nonverbal communication" (Sethi & Seth, 2009, p. 34). Voice (i.e., pitch, tone, and timing) is the second most powerful means for communicating information; actual words can be the least effective means. Body language that can be received as inappropriate (e.g., facing away from speaker, looking down) can be part of the noise that goes along with messages sent and received (e.g., pointing, lack of eye contact, folded arms) (Sethi & Seth, 2009). What if it is just chilly in the room, so a person crosses his or her arms? The person may be communicating, "I am not open to receiving information." The following nine guidelines reflect the power that nonverbal communication and facilitative listening have on interactions:

1. *Attend to verbal and nonverbal behavior; look for teammates' responses to your behavior.* This includes body orientation, eye contact, facial expressions, gestures or touch, response time, interrupting others, and volume and tone of voice.

2. *Listen first; then, respond in ways that facilitate the exchange.* This includes encouraging ("Mm-hm," "What happened then?"); paraphrasing without judgment ("What I hear you saying is . . ."); clarifying without judgment ("Are you saying that . . . ?"); reflecting on the person's feelings ("What I hear you saying is . . ." "I get the feeling that . . ."); and perception checking ("You seem to be asking for more support. Is that accurate?").

3. *Avoid common barriers to effective communication.* Barriers include offering advice when none was requested

("Why don't you try . . . ?"), interrogating ("Why did you do that?"), lecturing ("Don't you realize . . . ?"), ridiculing ("And you're the adult?"), and diminishing others' feelings ("Cheer up!") (Briggs, 1993).

4. *Avoid interrupting others when they are speaking.* Instigate a way of indicating whose turn is next (usually a facilitator will do this by noticing raised hands, such as, "Mr. Jorge, Mrs. Tarry, then Ms. Farland").

5. *Contribute in ways that do not waste team time.* Make points succinctly, and state factual information, preferably with data.

6. *Speak clearly, and use a vocabulary that others can understand.* Be vigilant about whether acronyms or other terms are familiar to all team members.

7. *Use team members' names.* If members are not well acquainted, fold 8.5" × 11" cardstock paper in half, then write each person's name and position on the paper. Place in front of the corresponding person.

8. *Avoid storytelling.* Try not to tell lengthy anecdotes, especially if they are not directly relevant to the meeting's purpose. Even if stories are relevant, remember that the team's limited time needs to be spent productively.

9. *Limit conversation to the general topics of concern and some (versus all) details.* Prepare in advance with input on the topic and clear details or examples, but do not feel all instances of inappropriate behavior (for example) need to be voiced. Determine summary statements beforehand.

Although these nine basic communication guidelines are simple, team members may not automatically practice them. These skills need to be habitual enough to withstand the disagreement and discussions of challenging issues that teams face.

If training has not been a part of the professional preparation of team members, then in-service professional development may be necessary.

Strategies for Leading Communication

Leading strategies can be used to keep an interaction going and direct it in a particular way. Use leading strategies carefully because they do not work if you have not first thoroughly listened to the team member or if you do not fully trust the person (DeBoer, 1995; Frankel, 2006). Start by using an explaining strategy to clarify your understanding as you look at each person you name.

"Here is the picture I get, although I am not sure it is fully accurate. Mr. Folsom feels we should not teach Miranda to use the personal digital assistant (PDA), which has picture, auditory, and video prompts, at lunchtime. But Mrs. McLaughlin thinks this is a natural time for Miranda to use the PDA, and Mrs. McLaughlin wants Mr. Folsom's support. Mr. Pope, because you are the teacher with Miranda prior to lunch, you feel caught between them and want team agreement."

Next, encourage ("You certainly have been trying to incorporate more technology this semester, Mrs. McLaughlin") and assure ("I know that we can reach consensus as a team"). Present tentative ideas as one equal talking to another, such as, "Here is an idea I think may work with Miranda, but Mr. Folsom may be in a better position to know if it will work." Use agreement or disagreement statements to clarify a team member's perspective or to bring up criteria that should be considered in reaching a decision ("It does seem that lunch is a natural time to teach Miranda how to use the PDA, but will the instruction during lunch take her away from natural opportunities to interact with peers?"). Spontaneous humor can relieve tension and create a connection between you and your teammates ("Some teams do not even bring up different perspectives, but we need to do that so we can discuss your ideas. Certainly no one can say we do not have different ideas!").

Questioning Strategies to Facilitate Communication

Questions can be used to keep a discussion going by encouraging responses. Questioning methods include open- and closed-ended questions, as well as direct and indirect questions (Cheatham & Santos, 2011; DeBoer, 1995; Symeou et al., 2012). Both open-ended and indirect questions are inviting strategies used to 1) summon others to listen and 2) move through the difficult times of stalled interaction and disagreement. By contrast, closed-ended and direct questions do not invite others to freely respond, unless the speaker is simply seeking information.

- *Use open-ended questions to encourage people to describe their perspective.* The questions are broad and invite people to share their views, feelings, and ideas. Open-ended questions usually begin with *how* or *what* and allow team members to explain their ideas or explore further (e.g., "How does this math adaptation for Daniel seem to you?" "What kinds of things does Vanessa do when she does not understand the science material?").

- *Closed-ended questions need to be used carefully because they can leave colleagues with the feeling that they must agree or be rejected.* Closed-ended questions may intend to bring out factual details, but sometimes they impede generation of ideas (Selvalakshmi, 2012). Closed-ended questions tend to seek a *yes* or *no* response or specific information and usually begin with *are, do* or *don't, have, should, will, can, when,* and *where* (e.g., "How many students do you have in each of your reading groups?" "It seems clear that Vanessa is not really disruptive. Do you agree?")

- *Use indirect questions to create a cooperative climate.* They are statements that ask without appearing to ask; listeners understand that their response is being sought (e.g., "I guess this approach will be difficult to use." "I really do not understand what Asperger syndrome is, and I would like to know more.")

- *Be aware that direct questions may create a nonequitable climate.* The listener may feel put on the spot or spoken down to. Direct questions are clear questions with a rising intonation and a question mark at the end. They may be open (e.g., "How hard would it be to use this adaptation in your class?") or closed (e.g., "Yes, it is hard to plan for three reading groups, isn't it?").

Signs of Difficulty

Many signs indicate that teams are challenged by their shortcomings with communication (Briggs, 1993; Carter et al., 2009; Johnson et al., 2003; Leatherman, 2009; Senge et al., 1994).

- Nonverbal behaviors suggest that attending and listening skills are missing or trust is lacking (e.g., members have poor eye contact with each other; members appear tense, rushed, or preoccupied).

- Speaking skills are poor (e.g., rambling, speaking too quietly), and there is little evidence of effective verbal skills (e.g., using encouraging words or phrases, clarifying ideas through restatement, checking for agreement).

- Team members are overly cautious and make many conditional statements.

- Words are mismatched with speaking tone and mannerisms.

- Team members rarely acknowledge one another.

- Viewpoints are stated as facts or formed into questions.

- Differences in philosophies become apparent.

- Stressful behaviors (e.g., withdrawal, nonresponsiveness) are observed.

When these behaviors occur during team exchanges, team members must evaluate their communication. Recognizing, verbalizing, and agreeing that a difficulty exists are important first steps. An outside observer can give unbiased comments and honest feedback on team dynamics. Viewing videos of both model and problem teams at work can also be an excellent method of isolating, observing, discussing, and practicing collaborative communication skills.

Difficulties can also arise when one or more of the team members are tasked with implementing something with which they are unfamiliar and their initial reaction is resistance or frustration (Doll et al., 2005). Responsive actions may be to provide information, technical assistance and support, and encouragement to promote individuals' movement from awareness of the new technique to information about the new technique (Hall & Hord, 2011). Anticipating reactions reflecting personal concerns is natural. Expressions of personal concerns, however, may also be perceived as resistance or disagreement. Yet, personal concerns are valid, and it will be difficult to promote movement to implementation if personal concerns are not recognized. As is important for all interpersonal skills observed and heard, analyze whether the disagreement a person is voicing is the true reason for opposition or if there are underlying feelings or experiences that need to be uncovered and addressed.

Improving interpersonal skills does not happen quickly. Team members must pay attention to the ways in which they interact with each other in order to reach their goals for students without becoming sidetracked by unnecessary hurt feelings, incompatible communication styles, mis-understandings, or disputes.

PROMOTING ACCURATE AND UNAMBIGUOUS COMMUNICATION

For giving and receiving information, Sethi and Seth (2009) referred to *communication channels,* which can be direct or indirect. Direct channels are under the direct control of the speaker, and these channels consist of intentional verbal and nonverbal behaviors. Indirect channels include what the speaker unintentionally communicates. Team members receiving the message are the ones in control of how the message is interpreted by each of them. Indirect channels also include abstract concepts such as intuition or gut feeling. Team members who want their messages to be understood have to meet three rudimentary requirements (Johnson & Johnson, 2000):

1. *Phrase the message in a way that listeners can understand.* Avoid acronyms and technical terminology, use examples, and adjust language to the audience.

2. *Be a credible message sender and receiver.* Table 3.1 provides examples of effectively sending and receiving messages.

3. *Ask others for feedback* regarding their understanding of and reaction to what was communicated.

Communicators have credibility when they are viewed as being knowledgeable about the content under discussion, when their motives are not suspect, when their tone and style are friendly, when listeners regard them as trustworthy, and when they are appropriately assertive in communicating their messages.

The skill of listening to or receiving a message has two fundamental requirements (Johnson & Johnson, 2000; Symeou et al., 2012): 1) communicating, primarily through nonverbal behavior, that you want to understand the speaker's message and feelings and 2) actually understanding the speaker's message and feelings. Communicating intent is achieved mainly through the

Table 3.1. Being effective senders and receivers of messages

Sending messages effectively	Receiving messages effectively
Own your messages by using first person (i.e., *I, my*).	Check your understanding of the message by paraphrasing as accurately as possible, without any judgment of the sender's message or feelings. To do this,
Use complete and specific messages (as needed, communicate your frame of reference, assumptions, and intentions).	• Restate the message in your own words.
Be congruent in your verbal and your nonverbal messages.	• Do not communicate any approval or disapproval.
Repeat your message in more than one way and through another channel to be clear.	• Do not add to or take away from the message.
Seek feedback from teammates on your message.	• Step into the speaker's shoes to understand the meaning of his or her message.
Match the message to listeners' frame of reference (e.g., student, another teacher, parent, administrator).	• Communicate that you want to fully understand before you make an evaluation.
Be unambiguous by describing your feelings (e.g., name them, use figurative speech, state actions): "I feel happy," "I'm down in the dumps," or, "I want to run away from this."	Check your perceptions of the sender's feelings by describing them:
Describe the behavior of others but do not evaluate or interpret it (e.g., "You keep interrupting," not "You are a horrible listener").	• Describe tentatively; seek confirmation. • Do not communicate any approval or disapproval or try to interpret or explain your perceptions (e.g., "It seems like you are worried about Melanie being in middle school. Am I right?").
	Talk to the sender and negotiate the interpretation of his or her message until you both agree on the meaning.

Source: Johnson and Johnson (2000).

receiver's nonverbal behavior (e.g., facing the speaker, establishing eye contact, looking interested) as well as not interrupting.

> Listening with attentiveness begins by focusing on what is being said, not thinking about what you are going to say next, not assuming you know what the other person is going to say before they say it, and not interrupting. It is a common deception to think that listening happens simply through not talking. (Bumann & Younkin, 2012, p. 13)

In addition to listening well, effective communication requires checking for understanding of what someone else has said (Bumann & Younkin, 2012). When a receiver makes immediate judgments regarding a speaker's message without first confirming his or her understanding of the message, he or she often stops listening or leaps to conclusions based on a premature or erroneous evaluation of the message. Trust is consequently eroded. Premature evaluations by receivers also cause senders to be defensive, closed, and less able to explain or expand on their message.

Listening can be difficult when a speaker sends a message that takes a judgmental position (DeBoer, 1995). The message often conflicts directly with strongly held beliefs or values of the listener, but the listener should still listen to what the speaker is saying during these situations before responding or wait until later to make a reasoned response. Figure 3.3 provides examples of these situations, in addition to guidance on how to listen. If team members' comfort level is low when seeking clarification of a message through questioning each other, then they might want to 1) devise interesting exercises to practice the skill (e.g., give incomplete directions, tell a story or joke but leave out a key line), 2) modify their ground rules ("Listen and understand me before you judge my ideas"), and 3) recall examples of their own tough listening situations and discuss alternative ways they might have used effective listening strategies.

Giving and Receiving Feedback Effectively

Any improvement that results from constructive feedback given to a teammate depends equally on the skills of the giver and the recipient of the feedback. Givers must be sensitive to the receptivity of the receiver, only provide credible feedback, tailor their wording to suit the individual, and have positive motives. Receivers must be able to listen, seek clarification without being defensive, explore suggestions regarding change, take steps to self-improve, and seek feedback from teammates on their behavior (see Table 3.2). Members' openness to giving and receiving positive and constructive feedback may be the best way to prevent conflict among team members and improve effectiveness in collaboration.

MAKING DECISIONS BY CONSENSUS

Making decisions by consensus means that all team members agree on a solution; the group's collective opinion is determined after hearing each team member's viewpoints. Although it is best to reach consensus on important decisions, it is not always possible. Decisions can also be made in ways other than by consensus:

- The group takes a poll or majority vote.

- Team members average their opinions.

- A subset of the group makes the decision (e.g., the occupational and physical therapists decide on a therapy issue).

- A person who has authority over the group (e.g., building administrator) makes the decision.

- A person viewed as an expert in a discipline of central concern (who may or may not be a member of the team) makes the decision.

All of these nonconsensus options for reaching a decision have problems, especially lack

When team members are in tough situations, it is critical that they hear what others are saying. Only then do they have any hope of influencing the beliefs, feelings, or behaviors of their co-workers. The following are examples of tough listening situations:

- *A teammate who was absent from a meeting tears apart the team's carefully developed action plan, which you had a big part in developing; to make things worse, some of her strongest complaints seem to have some validity.* You listen.

- *A colleague openly cuts down your values on inclusion, hitting on many things you hold dear.* You listen, although only because you know that if you try to defend yourself now, she will not pay attention later.

- *In the presence of others in the teachers' lounge, a fellow teacher severely berates a student whom you know well and care for greatly. Several teachers who are listening agree with the complainer and sympathize with her miseries of having him as a student.* Your admiration for that student is great; however, given the negative and heated climate, you decide not to say anything now but to listen to her message and plan your response for a less emotional opportunity.

- *As the team focuses on several teaching challenges, you are brimming with ideas that you think are brilliant and could resolve all the challenges.* You resist jumping in and dominating the discussion and sending messages of your impatience with their contributions. Although you think you could outline the entire action plan, you know it would be your plan and not the team's plan. Instead, you take your turn, contributing the best of your ideas, listening to others' ideas, and looking for chances to integrate the team's ideas into a creative plan that is truly team generated.

All of these tough listening situations involve team members sending clear messages about their feelings and their needs. The nonverbal behaviors that speakers and listeners use—facial expressions, gestures, physical stance, voice volume and tone, and eye contact—are the primary ways such messages are sent. Although it is not easy to listen under these tough conditions, it is essential to do so; "until people feel certain you have heard their message, it is impossible for them to listen to you" (DeBoer & Fister, 1995–1996, p. 71).

To gain a complete understanding of other team members' messages, skilled listeners can use the following facilitative listening skills: 1) attending, 2) responding (e.g., by paraphrasing, clarifying, reflecting, checking perceptions), and 3) using leading strategies (e.g., interpreting, explaining, encouraging, assuring, suggesting, agreeing/disagreeing, challenging, humoring).

Figure 3.3. Good listening is tough listening. (From DeBoer, A., & Fister, S. [1995–1996]. *Working together: Tools for collaborative teaching.* Longmont, CO: Sopris West; adapted by permission.)

of commitment to implementation and the erosion of team values (e.g., all opinions are valued, team members have parity with each other). Some of the previous methods can lead to consensus if they are combined with open discussion. For example, listening to an expert and then batting around team reactions and viewpoints may lead to agreement on an issue. Most experts on teaming agree that making decisions through consensus has more benefits than other decision-making approaches because 1) team members share a commitment to resolve the issue and implement a solution and 2) decisions made by consensus usually reflect a broader set of perspectives and talents.

Deciding How Consensus Is Reached

Teams determine how they will make decisions, when they should reach a decision by consensus, and when they should rely on one of the other methods of decision making. For example, team members' positions on some issues can be explored by taking a vote verbally or in writing, whereas other issues should be decided by consensus (Baron, 2008; Meleady, Hopthrow, & Crisp, 2013; Wodak, Kwon, & Clarke, 2011). Of course, even this decision will be difficult to make if group members do not feel as if they are valued members of the team who have productive contributions to make.

Table 3.2.   Giving and receiving feedback from teammates

Providing positive feedback	Providing constructive feedback for improvement	Receiving constructive feedback for improvement
Goal: To help another realize the way that his or her behavior has had a positive influence on a person, group, or issue; to encourage the person to continue or to expand the behavior	*Goal: To help another receive information about improving or changing his or her behavior; reaching this goal depends on the receptivity of the recipient, the capability of the sender at giving feedback, and the credibility of the feedback*	*Goal: To hear what is being offered nondefensively and to consider feedback as an opportunity for self-improvement*
The person will understand more clearly when you mention specific behaviors, acts, or events.	Be perceptive to the recipient's readiness for feedback.	Keep your mind open, and listen; quell judgments, and focus on what is being said.
Tell why you think the behavior had a positive impact (e.g., your feelings, others reactions).	Word your feedback in ways that do not hurt or damage.	Do not interrupt. Make notes now to help clarify your understanding later.
Give only sincere praise; undeserved praise can have bad effects, and insincere praise can threaten relationships.	Identify specific behaviors and situations; be unambiguous, and do not generalize beyond the specific or exaggerate.	Hold your desire to react in check. Take a deep breath, be quiet, and think through your questions.
Sincere praise is easy to give and goes a long way.	Address behavior and actions, not personality traits.	Confirm your understanding of the message with the sender right away or later if you need time to gain self-control; sooner is better than later because you may misunderstand the feedback.
Positive feedback is easier to hear than constructive criticism and still effective in shaping improved behavior.	Tell how you feel, but omit any judgments or speculations on the recipient's motives.	
Find appropriate opportunities to give public credit that is due—orally or in written reports.	Give feedback promptly; time erodes our memory of events.	Seek clarification—ask about confusing aspects, request illustrations, and avoid being defensive in the process.
The team trait most often cited that enhances teamwork is positive communication conducted in flexible ways, characterized by honesty, positive tone, and tactfulness.	Make your feedback brief, and avoid unneeded repetition; this helps minimize defensiveness.	Size up the situation: what the sender is saying reflects how he or she feels—his or her reality.
	Confirm understanding by listening to the person's reaction or thoughts regarding self-improvement.	State your appreciation, even if you do not agree; try to regard feedback as a "gift of information" (Lundy, 1994, p. 164).
	Preface your suggestions with introductory questions: "Have you considered . . . ?" "Do you suppose . . . ?" "Would it help . . . ?"	Seek more information to clarify whether the viewpoint is shared by other teammates. If so, or if you agree with the criticism, continue the following steps.
	Suggest, but do not dictate.	Discuss ways to improve; those giving feedback may be good sources for ideas.
	Check back with the person on his or her comfort level with suggestions.	Focus on changing your behavior; seek the assistance of teammates.
	Make the person's needs the focus, not your needs as the helper.	Ask for feedback on progress.

In building consensus, a team leader or facilitator needs to first make sure team members have enough information to make an informed decision about the issue under consideration (Dulaney, 2012). The team should take sufficient time to clarify the issue, discuss major advantages and disadvantages of the possible solutions, and discuss how implementation might occur (Baron, 2008). When deciding if they concur with a decision, team members can ask themselves three questions:

1. Can I live with the decision?

2. Can I support my team members in implementing the decision?

3. Can I commit to doing nothing to undermine implementation of this decision?

Teams can test for consensus in several ways. First, they can use data as the basis for decisions. Second, the meeting facilitator can ask whether the entire team consents when several members appear to be in agreement. ("Mr. Bryant and Mrs. Jackson have made a case for involving Shaun in the Activity Club. What do the rest of you think? Do you feel you have enough information for us to make a decision?") It is important for the facilitator to ensure that input and potential solutions come from all members, not only those who are more vocal or more experienced with teaming. Third, the facilitator can let the meeting time determine whether discussion should be shifted to consensus building, although team members should also speak up if they feel hasty decisions are being made because the meeting is about to end. Discussion during team-building sessions should be directed to these options for collaborative decision making, and teams should identify their preference. If teams reflect on the pros and cons of using noncollaborative decision-making options, then they are more likely to decide in favor of using one or more of the collaborative approaches.

Signs of Difficulty

It is critical to recognize the verbal and nonverbal signals that indicate team members' ability to positively and productively contribute may be deteriorating. Each team member should be vigilant about signs of difficulty. There are several indicators of potential difficulty in reaching consensus and finalizing decisions (Meleady et al., 2013; Senge et al., 1994; Wodak et al., 2011):

- Team members cave in to others' opinions when no supporting data exist or are presented.

- Decisions are made by default. Members do not respond, and silence is interpreted as agreement.

- One or several team members either strong-arm or cajole the others into agreeing.

- One or several team members make the decision, despite a lack of team agreement.

- The person with the perceived power makes the decision, and others are extremely reluctant to disagree.

- Consensus is attained by team members in attendance at the meeting, but key stakeholders (e.g., the parents, the general educator) were excluded from the meeting and have not been part of the decision making.

- Hasty reversion to "the majority rules" occurs in order to avoid open disagreement.

A team discussion on decision making is necessary when any of these indicators are present. Some team facilitators might preface an open discussion with data about the team's behavior; an outsider could be asked to observe how the group makes decisions and give the team feedback.

BEING SENSITIVE TO DIVERSITY AND AVOIDING STEREOTYPING

Cultural and linguistic diversity, when combined with intercultural knowledge, communication, and positive experiences, is an asset; however, misunderstanding, stereotyping, prejudices, and even racism can result when knowledge, communication, and experiences are lacking (Harry, 1997; Olivos, 2009; Trainor, 2010). Team members' background experiences may not include interactions with or knowledge about the practices, beliefs, and characteristics of the members of a culture or group in a particular environment. Stereotypes reflect false beliefs about causal connections between two unrelated, and often negative, factors (e.g., being poor and being lazy). They are dangerous because they guide thinking about groups of people and are highly resistant to change. Sethi and Seth (2009) referred to cultural disparities, whether intended or not, as "noise" in team meetings that interferes with effective communication. Lee concurred about the dangers of stereotyping and the corresponding impact on trust.

> One of the most insidious challenges to trust is the situation in which individuals make assumptions about others. At best, such assumptions cause misunderstandings and perhaps some embarrassment that could be avoided by asking rather than assuming. At worst, such assumptions represent biases, prejudices, and intolerance that poison the possibility of trust. (2009, p. 48)

Cheatham and Santos (2011) identified two characteristics that vary widely by culture—how time is perceived and how communication is perceived. The variances substantiate that generalizations about people from any given culture should be avoided. For example, being on time in some cultures does not mean arriving at the predesignated time, whereas families in other cultures adhere to deadlines and schedules. Another time-related cultural orientation is the extent to which following the agenda is valued versus spending time building relationships, developing trust, and opening up lines of communication. An example of cross-cultural variation in communication styles is that people in some cultures believe it is disrespectful to voice any level of disagreement. As a consequence, they may verbally and nonverbally convey that they are pleased and agree with what people are saying, when in fact they disagree. In contrast, people from other cultures may be very direct with what they communicate. Although what is said and how it is said may seem confrontational to some, the speaker may not have intended that at all. Professional development to assist

teachers and other school staff to identify their own cultural orientation toward time and communication and to be aware of and sensitive to diversity in values and norms such as these can help avoid the stereotyping of family members based on cultural differences. Johnson and Johnson (2000) listed the ways that stereotypes are perpetuated:

- Stereotypes influence what people perceive and remember about the actions of nondominant group members.

- Stereotypes create an oversimplified picture of nondominant group members; the larger the nondominant group, the more likely oversimplifications are to occur.

- Individuals tend to overestimate the similarity of behavior among nondominant group members.

- People tend to have a bias toward false consensus: They believe that most people share their stereotypes.

- Stereotypes tend to be self-fulfilling.

- Stereotypes lead to scapegoating.

- People often develop a rationale and explanation to justify their stereotypes and prejudices.

Collaborative teams must be vigilant in identifying, discussing, confronting, and eradicating the conditions that breed or perpetuate stereotypes.

- When one or several team members' cultures are different from that of the rest of the team, the familiarization phase should involve time for the team member to share information about his or her culture. This might include learning vocabulary, recognizing a holiday, sharing ethnic food, or learning personal information about the individual.

- When the dominant culture of the professional staff differs from that of the paraprofessional staff and the students in a school, the effort to educate dominant and nondominant groups must be extensive and ongoing.

- Schools should prepare staff and students to understand the background of the nondominant group(s) in ways that do not overgeneralize the information. For example, consider the large range of linguistic and intracultural differences among people often identified as Hispanic, including Cubans, Puerto Ricans, Central and South Americans, Spaniards, and Mexicans (Conroy, 2012; Harry, 1992a; Mardinos, 1989; Olivos, 2009). Likewise, individuals who are recent immigrants often differ in their cultural practices and language from first- and second-generation immigrants (Schoorman et al., 2011).

- Professionals must recognize their own cultural values prior to developing sensitivity to the diversity in language, culture, customs, and attitudes of the students and families with whom they work (Harry, 1992b, 2008; Salisbury & Dunst, 1997).

Several steps should be taken to make team members' styles more congruent when family members are from a nondominant culture (Burke, 2013; Conroy; 2012; Sileo, Sileo, & Prater, 1996). First, differences in team members' regard for time might mean that the team needs to allow more time to think aloud together and not aim for a "quick fix." Second, when there are conflicts in beliefs concerning the target student's independence, professionals should encourage extended family members to join the team to design programs that reflect their home practices of shared child-rearing responsibility. Third, families can benefit from schools and school systems that set up family support systems, including cultural liaisons, parent-to-parent partnerships, and preparing parents to be advocates. Similarly, school

personnel's professional development should include characteristics of diverse cultures and how to be responsive and respectful. Finally, when the equity beliefs of team members differ from those of the student's family, professionals should regard the focus student's family's view of itself as an expert view in its own right.

FOSTERING POSITIVE STAFF–FAMILY INTERACTIONS

Some teachers, particularly at large schools, form smaller schools within schools so that students are less overwhelmed and a group of teachers get to know students better and can more readily address their social and academic needs. This model can also ease communication with families because a team-based approach prevails instead of each teacher knowing a "piece of" the child. These team-based approaches are not solely focused on students with disabilities; their focus is on all the students served by that team. The team proactively works to communicate with families on an ongoing basis rather than only when an issue arises. Ensuring that communication is not confined to times when there are problems is one way to foster positive staff–family interactions. The same mechanisms used to make contact with parents when a student has difficulties at school (e.g., e-mail, notes home, telephone calls) should occur when there is progress or success to report.

Bennett and her colleagues (2012) analyzed team members' communication patterns during collaborative team meetings and found that active participation from parents and administrators was at such low levels that the researchers had insufficient information to analyze their patterns. These findings should caution team members to promote active participation from all, with extra effort directed to parent and administrator contributions. Family involvement needs to be nurtured, and school personnel should be vigilant of team communication patterns that exclude parents, intentionally or not. Figure 3.3 and Tables 3.1 and 3.2, presented previously in this chapter, describe types of responses that can encourage or discourage parents and other team members from participating in team meetings.

For families who are involved with the special education process, the initial meetings that family members attend—evaluation and identification, IEP planning, and placement—are the most critical and often the most difficult for several reasons: 1) Parents and professionals usually do not know each other (especially when a child is first considered for special education); 2) team membership has not yet been established because eligibility, program planning, or placement have not yet been determined; and 3) family members are presented with information about their child that is often new, complex, confusing, unpleasant, and scary. Parents in one study indicated that their experiences in school-based team meetings were both positive and negative, with their responses clustered into five categories (Esquivel, Ryan, & Bonner, 2008):

1. *Meeting context and organization:* Some parents preferred smaller teams, such as core teams, because they got more accomplished and seemed less rushed. Other parents indicated they appreciated meeting notes, facilitation of the conversation, and clear conclusions and follow-up plans (see Figure 2.9).

2. *Relationships:* Parents indicated that tension influenced the meeting's dynamics when school personnel did not like each other or were in disagreement. Most parents, however, commented on the positive relationships between school personnel and their child.

3. *Communication:* Parents felt more positive about the meeting when their ideas were acknowledged and accepted. In addition, parents felt good when everyone on the team contributed and participated. On the contrary, parents did not like it when a teacher showed up to contribute his or her part and then left the meeting.

4. *Problem solving:* Parents reacted negatively when problem solving occurred without follow-through on team-developed action plans. The issue became more troublesome for parents when they thought plans were in place but found out later that nothing had been done. Yet, parents appreciated the dialogue and back-and-forth quality of productive problem solving.

5. *Emotions:* Some parents noted they experienced stress just because the team was meeting, which they acknowledged was sometimes unrelated to their relationships with school personnel. Other parents noted that the meeting's focus was on areas where progress had not occurred, even though their child had made progress. One parent indicated that the more complex the needs of her child became, the more challenging the meetings were for her.

As revealed by the mixture of feelings parents reported experiencing in team meetings, school personnel should be sensitive to the fact that what may be just another meeting for them can be a high-stakes and highly emotional experience for parents. School personnel should be attuned to the unique vantage point that parents bring to team meetings and recognize that parents have a significant investment in celebrating their children's successes as well as prioritizing other areas to work on.

School personnel may not be aware of challenges facing some families at any given time, so it is important to be alert and sensitive when parents share key information (sometimes with only one team member or the core team). For example, imagine the teacher who contacts the mother when her son has not consistently been turning in homework assignments. The teacher learns during the telephone conversation that the parents are separating. It is critical that the teacher's response be empathetic and understanding to the mother during the telephone conversation. Realizing the home issues, the teacher's approach might shift from assuming the mother will be able to address the homework issue single handedly to helping her to devise a plan that will support the mother's efforts.

School personnel on collaborative teams can foster family members' involvement in the teaming process through the attitudes they communicate and the teaming procedures they use (Conroy, 2012; Frankel, 2006; Losen & Losen, 1994; Symeou et al., 2012; Turnbull & Turnbull, 2000). Team members can

- Be cognizant of, sensitive to, and respectful of the family's culture, values, and viewpoints

- Spend a few minutes socializing with family members before the formal meeting begins

- Communicate in multiple ways that family members' knowledge, information, concerns, hopes, and opinions about their child are valuable

- Realize there may be family issues school personnel are unaware of and those issues may be influencing family members' reactions (e.g., negativity, concern, frustration, preoccupation), whereas team members may assume it is the meeting content evoking those reactions

- Be sensitive to communicating doubt or superiority; members should question for clarity, not accuracy

- Accept that there is no standard measurement for family involvement. Just getting the child dressed, fed, and to school on time is a major undertaking for some families

- Be vigilant about not feeding into any parental guilt over a child's disability or learning or behavioral challenges

- Communicate that they (the core team, the whole team) share the responsibility for designing and implementing programs to support the student's learning and behavior

- Examine any forms that will be used during a meeting (e.g., permission to test, IEP, transition plan) and review the procedural steps with the parents

- Understand that cultural perceptions of disability vary

- Recognize that cultural perceptions about school personnel vary (e.g., their cultural perspective may be to defer to the experts)

- Acknowledge that cultural perspectives on family priorities may differ from what the school would prioritize (e.g., absences for helping the family may be the cultural norm, while not necessarily the school norm)

Although family members typically are not present at every team meeting and rarely are present for on-the-fly interchanges (i.e., informal, quick exchanges; check-in opportunities) between staff members during the school day, their role as team members must not be forgotten. Teams should guarantee that family members will be able to contribute their input on every issue and every action plan. Members can seek the family's ideas beforehand, include them in the meeting process, and check team decisions with them before assuming team consensus.

Team members need to avoid limiting on-the-fly meetings with family members to a paraprofessional. For example, if a paraprofessional is assigned to ensure the child walks safely from or to a parent's car before or after school, then it can seem quite natural to have brief conversations about the child's progress or needs.

Because the special educators and other professional members of the team are ultimately responsible for what is communicated, paraprofessionals (and the teachers who supervise them) must be aware of the unintended consequences that can result if key information is communicated by the paraprofessional to the parent or from the parent to the paraprofessional. Educators should work to communicate this to paraprofessionals in ways that are positive and supportive (e.g., focusing on their rapport with a particular parent) rather than in ways that sound distrustful (i.e., the issue is not that the paraprofessional communicated with the parents; it is that the team needs to know the information). Teams should discuss guidelines for how and when ongoing, everyday information is to be shared with family members. Similarly, there needs to be some mechanism in place to ensure the relevant aspects of communication are shared with other team members when any members of the team confer through on-the-fly interactions.

Respect Advocates Who Accompany the Family for Meetings

Parents rarely bring legal counsel to team meetings, even though it is their right. It is more common for parents to bring advocates or parent advisors with them. Public law encourages parents to invite trusted friends, advisors, or family members to attend team meetings with them to lend support and assist in their understanding and their articulation of concerns. The presence of some individuals, such as lawyers, can be perceived as adversarial for professional staff. Lawyers rarely feel obligated to follow a team's procedure because their dedication is to their client; therefore, the presence of lawyers may be not only psychologically but also procedurally disruptive (Losen & Losen, 1994; Trainor, 2010).

Legal counsel is more often sought by parents because of a dispute with program administrators than a dispute with specific team members; the controversy, however, often seeps into the team as well and may be impossible to ignore. Recognizing the rightful presence of legal counsel and acknowledging the right of legal counsel to interrupt, the team facilitator can appeal to the group for cooperation and request team members' help in avoiding confrontation.

The team meeting facilitator needs to remind the team members that their focus must remain on the student. It is crucial not to forget the agenda, team procedures, or team processing steps (e.g., "How are we doing?" "Is each person having a chance to speak?" "If someone feels shutdown, can that be addressed within the meeting, or is it better to meet with people individually afterward?") when legal counsel is present, even though they may be difficult to carry out. Well-established teamwork routines can help overcome a difficult atmosphere and allow the important day-to-day decision making to get done. Although the team facilitators will not want to alienate parents by limiting the guest's participation in the team meeting, facilitators should interrupt when a guest's comments are out of place, premature, or not suited to the team's current task. Facilitators can remind the guest and the other team members to follow the agenda and to focus on their purpose— meeting the student's educational needs.

Team members need to realize that they are usually involved in a child's life for a year, or sometimes several years. Families, however, have that child for a lifetime. Sometimes school personnel do not understand what previous years' team meetings were like for the parents, but those previous experiences influence parents' feelings and perspectives about team meetings (Esquivel et al., 2008). For example, if parents are accustomed to being challenged by school personnel who maintain that the LRE for their child is the special education classroom, then those parents may anticipate that they will need to be prepared for another year of struggle for their child to be included. If parents have felt in past years that their signing the IEP was a perfunctory gesture, then they may expect to have little say in their child's educational program and services. It behooves school personnel to gain an understanding of the family's past experiences with and expectations of the collaborative teaming process and to seek ways they can work more productively with the family across the school year.

Other personnel such as state-appointed individuals who are legally authorized to be in the parental role throughout the IEP process also are child advocates, as are CASAs, who are appointed through the court system to provide independent appraisals of what is in the best interest of the student (see Chapter 2). The greater the extent to which all team members can agree on services and settings that promote students' academic, behavioral, and social achievements, the more cohesive the team can be.

BUILDING TEAM COHESION

Even the best collaborative teams run into communication blocks and get side-tracked by conflict. Routine self-evaluation or reflection of team processing is the best prevention for uncooperativeness and competition among team members. Fleming and Monda-Amaya (2001) examined the process variables related to team effectiveness and found team cohesion to be one of the most critical of the six categories of process variables identified. Team cohesion was demonstrated by members' respect for one another and also by behaviors such as taking time to celebrate, providing recognition for efforts, and using ongoing conflict-resolution procedures to resolve disagreements (which were openly expressed by team members).

Take Time to Process

Well-functioning teams often begin their meetings by celebrating their successes, an activity that contributes to team building. Teams may stop halfway through their agenda, and again at the end of the meeting, to process interpersonal dynamics and meeting progress. Processing often consists of posing questions such as the following.

- How are we doing?

- Are we making progress?

- Do we need to adjust our agenda to reflect what now seems to be the priority?

- Do we have interpersonal problems that are blocking our progress?

- If we do, what can we do differently?

When teams learn to schedule and then pose processing questions, they briefly shift their attention to themselves during the meeting, thereby increasing the probability that interpersonal channels will operate more smoothly (Johnson & Johnson, 2000).

Assess Group Functioning and Reflect on the Team Process

Regular self-assessment of team health is a good preventative measure for serious conflict (Bennett et al., 2012; Bumann & Younkin, 2012; Olson & Murphy, 1999). Procedures teams use to process group functioning include effective ways to give feedback to team members. One member is designated to be the group observer; this person not only contributes to work on agenda items but also watches interactions among members and helps team members self-examine in a number of ways.

- Team members each self-evaluate against a checklist of communication skills (see Figure 3.4) or their own ground rules and then reflect as a group.

- Team members regularly review responses that encourage or discourage participation (see Figure 3.5),

Checking Out My Communication Behavior

Directions: Complete all the questions by yourself. Review your answers in a round-robin fashion by having each member summarize his or her current communication performance. Discuss any implications for individual and team improvement.

1. If I were to explain something to teammates and they sat quietly with blank faces, I would:

    _____ Try to explain clearly and then move on

    _____ Encourage members to ask questions until I knew everyone understood

2. If our facilitator explained something to the team that I did not understand, I would:

    _____ Keep silent and find out from someone else later on

    _____ Ask the facilitator to repeat the explanation or to answer my questions

3. How often do I let other members know when I like or approve of something they say or do?

    Never   1 - 2 - 3 - 4 - 5 - 6 - 7 - 8 - 9 - 10   Always

4. How often do I let other teammates know when I am irritated or impatient, embarrassed by, or opposed to something they have said or done?

    Never   1 - 2 - 3 - 4 - 5 - 6 - 7 - 8 - 9 - 10   Always

5. How often do I check out teammates' feelings and not just assume that I know what they are?

    Never   1 - 2 - 3 - 4 - 5 - 6 - 7 - 8 - 9 - 10   Always

6. How often do I encourage others to let me know how they feel about what I say?

    Never   1 - 2 - 3 - 4 - 5 - 6 - 7 - 8 - 9 - 10   Always

7. How often do I check to be sure I understand what others are saying before I think judgmentally (e.g., "I don't agree" "She's right!")?

    Never   1 - 2 - 3 - 4 - 5 - 6 - 7 - 8 - 9 - 10   Always

8. How often do I check to be sure I understand what others are saying before I express my judgments nonverbally (e.g., head shake, frowning) or out loud (e.g., "I don't agree" "She's right!")?

    Never   1 - 2 - 3 - 4 - 5 - 6 - 7 - 8 - 9 - 10   Always

9. How often do I paraphrase or restate what others have said before I respond?

    Never   1 - 2 - 3 - 4 - 5 - 6 - 7 - 8 - 9 - 10   Always

10. How often do I keep my feelings, reactions, thoughts, and ideas to myself during meetings?

    Never   1 - 2 - 3 - 4 - 5 - 6 - 7 - 8 - 9 - 10   Always

11. How often do I make sure that all information I have regarding the topic under discussion is known to the rest of the group?

    Never   1 - 2 - 3 - 4 - 5 - 6 - 7 - 8 - 9 - 10   Always

Question Content

Questions address the following aspects of communication: 1 and 2—One-way and two-way communication; 3 and 4—Your willingness to give feedback to others on how you react to their messages; 5 and 6—Your willingness to ask for feedback on your messages; 7–9—Your receiving skills; 10 and 11—Your willingness to contribute (send) relevant messages about the team's work.

Figure 3.4. A quiz for team members to assess their communication behavior.

In *Teachers' Guides to Inclusive Practices: Collaborative Teaming, Third Edition* by
Margaret E. King-Sears, Rachel Janney, and Martha E. Snell (2015, Paul H. Brookes Publishing Co.)

Team Profile

Reflect on your team as a whole. For each item, circle the appropriate number that best corresponds with your view or opinion.

Our team as a whole	Almost never	Some-times	Often	Very often	Almost always
1. Team members are clear on their roles.	1	2	3	4	5
2. Team members listen to one another.	1	2	3	4	5
3. Team members check to understand what others are saying.	1	2	3	4	5
4. Team members understand and could identify group norms.	1	2	3	4	5
5. Goals and objectives are set by the whole team.	1	2	3	4	5
6. Time lines (due dates) are set for each team goal.	1	2	3	4	5
7. Goals are accomplished within set time lines.	1	2	3	4	5
8. All members are encouraged to participate.	1	2	3	4	5
9. Differences of opinion are expressed face to face.	1	2	3	4	5
10. The usual reaction to disagreement is a willingness to listen and problem-solve.	1	2	3	4	5

Our team meetings	Almost never	Some-times	Often	Very often	Almost always
11. Start on time.	1	2	3	4	5
12. Have an agenda.	1	2	3	4	5
13. Face a facilitator.	1	2	3	4	5
14. Have time limits for agenda items.	1	2	3	4	5
15. Include a plan for "who will do what by when."	1	2	3	4	5
16. Are summarized in writing at the end of the meeting.	1	2	3	4	5
17. Are evaluated by members for effectiveness.	1	2	3	4	5
18. Have a recorder who writes down outcomes.	1	2	3	4	5
19. Are productive and an efficient use of time.	1	2	3	4	5
20. End on time.	1	2	3	4	5

21. To what extent do I feel a real part of the team?

1	2	3	4	5
Not really a part of this team	Generally outside, except for one or two short periods	Sometimes in, sometimes out	A part of this team most of the time	Completely a part of the team

22. How safe is it in this team to be at ease, relaxed, and myself?

1	2	3	4	5
It would be foolish to be oneself on this team	I am fearful about being myself	Generally, I feel I have to be careful about what I say or do	Most people accept me if I am myself	I feel perfectly safe to be myself

Figure 3.5. Team profile. (From Olson, J., & Murphy, C.L. [1999]. Self-assessment: A key process of successful team development. *Young Exceptional Children, 2*[3], 4–5; adapted by permission of SAGE Publications.)

(continued)

Figure 3.5. *(continued)*

23. To what extent do I keep my opinions "under wraps;" that is, have ideas or feelings that I do not bring into the open?

1	2	3	4	5
Almost completely under wraps	I am fearful about being myself	Sometimes free and expressive	Quite free and expressive much of the time	Almost completely free and expressive

24. How effective is the team in including all members in making decisions?

1	2	3	4	5
We do not encourage everyone to share their ideas	Only ideas of a few members are used in making decisions	We hear the views of most members before making decisions	A few are hesitant about sharing opinions, but we generally have good participation	Everyone feels his or her ideas are given a fair hearing before decisions are made

25. How clear are the goals that the team is working toward?

1	2	3	4	5
I do not understand the goals of our team	Much of what we are doing is not clear	Sometimes I am clear on goals, other times I am not	I understand most of what we are doing	I am well aware of all the goals of our team

26. How well does the team progress toward its goals and related tasks?

1	2	3	4	5
Coasts, loafs, makes no progress	Makes a little progress, most members loaf	Progress is slow, spurts of effective work	Above average in progress and pace of work	Works well, achieves definite progress

27. The way the team operates is largely influenced by:

1	2	3	4	5
One team member	A clique or group	Shifts from one person or clique to another	Shared by most members	Shared by all members

28. Who accepts responsibility for most of the tasks of the team?

1	2	3	4	5
Nobody (except perhaps one) really assumes responsibility for work done	Only a few assume responsibility for work done	About half assume responsibility for work done	A majority of the members assume responsibility for work done	Each person assumes personal responsibility for work done

29. How are differences or conflicts handled by the team?

1	2	3	4	5
Differences or conflicts are denied, suppressed, or avoided at all costs	Differences or conflicts are recognized, but discussed outside of the team	Differences or conflicts are recognized and some members attempt to work through them	Differences and conflicts are recognized and most (but not all) members attempt to work through them	Differences and conflicts are recognized and the team works through them satisfactorily

30. What is the typical style of leadership on the team?

1	2	3	4	5
The leader dominates the team	The leader tends to control the team, although people generally agree	There is some give and take between the leader and team members	Team members relate easily to the leader and are able to give input	Team members respect the leader, everyone participates, and no one dominates

Please list the areas or items that you would like to see your team work on:

_____

_____

then self-assess by asking themselves the following questions: Are you an encourager or discourager? In what ways can you self-regulate to become more of an encourager and eliminate discouraging statements?

- Teams target one or several areas on which to focus in the next meeting.

- At the next meeting, the team observer reminds team members of the targeted areas, observes these areas, and then shares the observations with other members while giving feedback to each member.

- Team members comment on the observations.

- The observer shares incidents of positive teamwork and encourages others to contribute their observations.

- Team members discuss the observations and then identify or refine goals for improvement at individual and group levels.

Feedback can be better absorbed by team members if observers are positive and direct in their reports. Observers should establish eye contact with team members, present them with objective data, and be honest (Thousand & Villa, 2000).

Members should be involved in discussing and resolving agenda items and tuned into group process (teamwork) when teams are in full motion. Teams sometimes resist devoting a few minutes to team processing; many team members have found, however, that this time is critical to maintaining productive collaborative interactions (Chen & Reigeluth, 2010). Processing often consists of posing simple questions about team functioning and progress.

- Questions about prior team achievements and student progress should be asked at the beginning of meetings: *What have we accomplished since our last meeting? Let's celebrate the successes. Let's reconsider the areas of little progress.*

- Questions regarding individual team member accountability may be asked when team members give and receive information and report back to each other: *Is each team member held accountable for completing his or her work? Would more assistance or encouragement help?*

- Questions about ongoing interpersonal relationships and their impact on teamwork may be asked at any time during or near the end of a meeting: *How are the relationships among us as team members? What can we do to reduce the tension? Let's discuss our teamwork skills.*

- Questions regarding progress being made in the current meeting may be asked any time during or near the end of a meeting: *Are we making progress on our tasks for this meeting? Do we need to make agenda adjustments? Is each team member held accountable for his or her participation?*

- Questions about accomplishments made in the current meeting should be asked at the end of the meeting: *How well did we do as a team? As problem solvers? In pulling together an action plan?*

Hong and Reynolds-Keefer (2013) noted that sometimes it is the nature of different preparation programs completed by multidisciplinary team members that can lead to confusion and conflict. For example, speech and language pathologists are prepared with different pedagogies from special educators, who also differ from how physical therapists are prepared. In addition, general educator preparation programs differ from all of these. As such, the multidisciplinary team may have different pedagogies and repertoires of instruction and interventions. Team members on transdisciplinary teams expect to share roles and integrate (versus fragment) services. Hong and Reynolds-Keefer described the transdisciplinary process as progressive.

- Role exchange (giving and accepting feedback)

- Role expansion (acknowledging others' expertise)

- Role release (using other disciplines' perspectives)

- Role transformation (discussion across perspectives, incorporating multiple perspectives)

The researchers found that intentional reflection on team functioning was key to the success of transdisciplinary teaming.

> The intentional time together as a team created a reflective atmosphere that supported professional relationships, provided respectful interaction among professionals, and allowed team members to gain an understanding of each other's stance and practice including professional value system. One important aspect of this relationship was the development of the ability to listen across disciplines. (Hong & Reynolds-Keefer, 2013, p. 38)

An observer can help team members reflect on their interpersonal interactions and their actual work progress. When problems are identified in either area, the team should determine its course of action (e.g., set aside, discuss, collect observation data on group, problem-solve, develop an action plan).

RESOLVING CONFLICT CONSTRUCTIVELY

Healthy, cohesive teams do not refrain from expressing disagreement; they have a healthy regard for appropriately expressed disagreement and knowledge of conflict resolution techniques (Bumann & Younkin, 2012; Fleming & Monda-Amaya, 2001; Frankel, 2006). When disagreements or conflicts arise within a team, they must first be identified. Once disagreements are identified, teams need to decide whether they want to address them. Some conflicts are best handled by being ignored, especially if they are minor. Other conflicts are

best just acknowledged, particularly when their open recognition is adequate to sensitize members (e.g., "Gosh, you can tell by the way we are picking at each other that we are really ready for spring break!").

 ## Student Snapshot

Ms. Decker is late once again to Raul's team meeting—this time by 30 minutes—and the meeting is almost over. Ms. Regan reacts, "How do you expect us to work together if you are never here on time?" "You always blame me," Ms. Decker retorts and stomps out of the room in tears.

To make matters worse, Raul's mom refuses to sign his IEP, even after the lengthy process his teachers used to involve her. Team members are disappointed and angry. "What does she want anyway? We put everything in his program!" "She does not know how good that IEP is!"

⟳ ACTIVITY: *There are several issues described in this brief scenario about Raul's IEP team meeting. How would you handle the issues?*

Frankel (2006) urged team members to find ways to work toward solutions that are a win-win for all involved. Bumann and Younkin (2012) similarly noted that conflict is a sign that team members are in continued discussions and relating to each other, even if in disagreement. They cautioned that how individuals deal with conflict determines whether the teaming process is "productive or destructive" (p. 16). Bumann and Younkin suggested that team members directly and respectfully communicate about the conflict, and the conflict should be addressed immediately. The conflict can be immediately addressed, even if the solution is not immediately developed. Avoidance hinders the team's progress.

Communication skills described earlier in this chapter are even more critical to use effectively when conflicts arise—give and receive feedback in nonjudgmental ways, articulate feelings in a nonblaming manner, and identify behaviors that are perceived as blocking the team's progress.

Handling conflict well is likely the best indicator of an effective communicator, so it is a good idea to learn (and practice) different ways to neutrally and objectively communicate, particularly for uncomfortable situations that involve conflict.

Teacher Snapshot

During a core team meeting requested by Nathan's parents, they asked that he be reevaluated to determine whether continued resource room reading instruction by Ms. Kennedy, the special education teacher, was necessary. Ms. Kennedy had not been aware of the context for the meeting and had thought Nathan's parents were pleased with his reading progress. Nathan's fourth-grade teacher, Mrs. O'Rourke, enthusiastically supported having Nathan in the regular class for reading and had been discussing the possibility with the parents. Ms. Kennedy felt blind-sided. She felt like she had to talk about the issue with Mrs. O'Rourke, fearing that if she did not say something now, similarly uncomfortable situations would arise in the future.

Ms. Kennedy approached a colleague she trusted and who was also on Nathan's IEP team. Her colleague had observed Mrs. O'Rourke in other team meetings, and she felt some empathy for Ms. Kennedy. "How do I talk to her?" Ms. Kennedy asked. "I am very nervous and not sure what I should say." Ms. Kennedy's colleague coached her on using "I feel . . ." statements, followed by her description of what Mrs. O'Rourke had done and what that felt like to her. Ms. Kennedy was to end her encounter with Mrs. O'Rourke with a statement of what she would like Mrs. O'Rourke to agree to in the future.

⟳ ACTIVITY: *Recall a conflict situation you experienced or observed. Discuss ways conflict was addressed that were either productive or destructive.*

Identify the Conflict

Although some unaddressed conflicts will diminish over time, others have a way of festering. Many team conflicts involve school staff on one side and family members on the other side (Snell & Janney, 2000).

- *Disagreement about student goals and problem identification:* A lack of consensus on student goals sometimes leads to disagreement regarding what is or is not a problem.

- *Coordination problems:* Conflict sometimes arises while making or implementing plans that results from logistics (e.g., class schedules, available equipment, movement of students) and fragmentation of services and time.

- *Implementation and evaluation problems:* These problems often concern the skill of the person implementing the solution, lack of team consensus in developing a solution, inadequate solutions, or a failure to improve and refine solutions over time.

- *Communication problems:* These problems may be due to inadequate time to fully discuss supports, second-hand reporting, or lack of trust.

When problems seem to be primarily associated with one team member, a subset of the team (often the core teachers) may separately discuss the concern from the rest of the team. Although this method is usually the best way to explore the problem initially, any action will ultimately need to involve the target team member.

Use Nonconfrontational Solutions

At times, a simple, indirect intervention will diminish the problem enough for the team to once again function normally. If ground rules are being broken, then teams might review these rules and discuss potential changes (e.g., "Do we need to start the meeting at 3:15 p.m. if everyone cannot arrive by 3 p.m.?"). In other cases, team members might choose to work around the problem instead of confronting it.

Use Indirect or Gentle Confrontation

Team problems frequently stem from one person's failure to follow team procedures (always late, often absent, does not follow through on team solutions) or from the behavior of a team member during meetings (overly negative or critical, interruptive, dominating, frequently off task). Other problems stem from philosophical and methodological disagreement. Indirect or direct confrontation may be pursued when these problems cannot be ignored and do not respond to modeling and shaping and an exploration of their cause seems unhelpful.

Indirect confrontation involves calling attention to the troublesome behavior in a meeting but without identifying the person who engages in that behavior. Such confrontation is sometimes followed by team problem solving but often involves defusing rather than directly resolving the conflict. Team members can use humor to call attention to the difficulty ("How many strong personalities can we fit into one room?") or suggest an alternative to the problem behavior. They can turn the unfavorable behavior into a favorable behavior without confrontation. They can also make the difficult member an "expert" on certain team needs: A team member who is viewed as "always critical" may be the only one who has completed a series of specialized reading courses and learned new approaches for grouping and adaptations that the team could use. That person can offer some of his or her ideas during the next problem-solving session. Teams can also encourage self-assessment.

- "Why do we engage in (the problem behavior)?" "What function does it serve?"

- "How might our team procedures be changed to help reduce the problem behavior?"

- "When someone engages in this behavior, what do the rest of us do to encourage it?"

- "In what other ways can we behave toward this person to help change the problem behavior?"

Combine Direct Confrontation with Interpersonal Problem Solving

A more direct approach should be considered when indirect confrontation strategies do not work (Johnson & Johnson, 2000). Polito (2013) maintained that having difficult conversations is critical for open lines of communication; if people avoid discussing the hard topics, then they may be stepping around their capacity for progress instead of directly dealing with topics that may be impeding their progress. Direct confrontation involves several steps: describing the problem behavior to the person who engages in it, finding a solution, implementing the solution, and assessing satisfaction.

A face-to-face confrontation may mean that one team member decides or is elected to confront the problematic behavior of another team member, but only if the behavior regularly occurs and cannot be ignored. If there is more than one team member involved in what is perceived as problematic for other team members, then more than one person may be confronted face to face. This approach must be taken with care. Team members should plan who undertakes the task. Sometimes it helps to have the confronter be someone who knows the receiver (or receivers) well and can personally relate to him or her. Confrontation in private is often preferable to confrontation in front of the entire team, especially if it is likely that the person will be unhappy, embarrassed, or angered by the feedback. The approach one uses to confront another must be carefully thought through; address issues, not people; and avoid anger and blame. Polito (2013) noted that practicing or role-playing prior to confronting can be helpful for confronters.

It is often best to describe the troublesome behavior to the individual in objective terms in addition to describing its effect on the team and possible solutions. *I*-messages are an effective way to confront without attacking (DeBoer,

1995). *You*-messages should be avoided because they often sound condescending, abrasive, and judgmental (e.g., "You need to . . ." "You did not understand my question"). In addition, *never* and *always* should be avoided (e.g., "You are always late").

Although *I*-statements may be less offensive than *you*-statements (remember that the offense is perceived by the receiver, even if not necessarily the intent of the sender), *I*-statements are still difficult to deliver and somewhat unnatural to construct. Harms and Roebuck (2010) developed the BEAR acronym that can be used by team members to structure what to say (see Figure 3.6):

Behavior: Explicitly describe the behavior demonstrated by the person, including frequency (but avoid use of *always* or *never*).

Effect: Identify the effect that person's behavior has on you. Use *I feel, I believe,* or *I think* statements.

Alternative: Provide a replacement behavior the person could use that would not have the same uncomfortable or emotional effect on you.

Result: Describe the positive result that can occur if the person chooses to use the alternative behavior. Describe the consequences of continued use of the initial behavior.

A BEAR sequence might sound like this: "When the meetings start with solutions that are already developed [Behavior], I feel I do not have a chance to provide my input [Effect]. If meetings could start by following the agenda and involving others for suggestions in clarifying the problems, then discussing solutions [Alternative], we all have a chance to share and contribute [Result]. If the solution is determined in advance, then people feel their ideas are not valued."

Goldsmith (2008) suggested writing down what you want to say if you are having a difficult conversation. He acknowledged

---

I-messages are

- Messages that you own (*I* and *my*, not *you* and *your*)
- Straightforward, open, and honest statements
- Statements that communicate how something is affecting you and what you need

Use I-messages when

- You need to communicate to others that their behavior is unacceptable or is creating a problem for you.
- You need to be assertive so a solution can be found.

BEAR as the four elements of I-messages (Harms & Roebuck, 2010)

- *Behavior:* Explicitly describe the behavior demonstrated by the person, including frequency (but avoid use of *always* or *never*).
- *Effect:* Identify the effect that person's behavior has on you. Use *I feel, I think,* or *I believe* statements.
- *Alternative:* Provide a replacement behavior the person (or people) could use that would not have the same uncomfortable or emotional effect on you.
- *Result:* Describe the positive result that can occur if the person (or people) chooses to use the alternative behavior. Or, describe the consequences of continued use of the initial behavior.

"The meetings begin late when people arrive late, and we have started at least 15 minutes late for the last few meetings [Behavior]. I feel it is wasting valuable time when we begin late [Effect]. I would like everyone to be on time [Alternative]. We could use our time more productively if we started on time [Result]."

Figure 3.6.   Use *I*-messages to confront conflict that gentle approaches have not resolved.

the emotions involved, so advance preparation can help the message stay on target while still conveying feelings. The giver should practice confronting the problematic behavior exhibited by the team member (or members) ahead of time. In addition, Goldsmith noted the importance of having difficult conversations as valuable to relationships. Allowing one or more team members to regularly exhibit behaviors that interfere with the team's communication and collaboration is damaging to the team's capacity to work well together.

One of the biggest challenges of direct confrontation is getting the person to be part of the problem solving. That person may be feeling a variety of emotions: anger, embarrassment, defensiveness, guilt, or surprise. Once an *I*-statement has been used to confront a teammate, the giver should shift from the speaker role to the listener role. DeBoer suggested that active listening be conducted "with an attitude of empathy for the person's situation and an acceptance of them as an individual" (1995, p. 108), which does not mean that the person confronting the team member must agree with the troublesome behavior. The confronting team member could ask the person what his or her thoughts and feelings are and what might be done. The problem-solving discussion should occur at a second meeting when emotions are lower and should produce mutually generated suggestions for reducing the problem during future team sessions. It may be necessary for the confronting team member to restate the original *I*-message or rephrase the message after listening to the confronted team member's perspective in order to remind the person of his or her viewpoint and move toward a resolution.

The emotional stakes may feel greater for parents who are part of the team because their child's education is the focus. Harry (1997) and Kalyanpur and Harry (2012) described a five-step approach teams can use to bridge the differences between the cultures of diverse families and the culture of schools. The issues of disagreement between professionals and family members (e.g., amount of services, these services and not those services, location of schooling, this label not that one) often are only part of the picture. Both parties are trapped in conflict, however, when the issues of disagreement become the only focus. The researchers' message is that an individual's underlying beliefs and values provide the logic for the person's position. The researchers give examples of differing beliefs, stereotypes, or values we hold about 1) groups of people, 2) the meaning of disability, 3) parenting styles, and 4) goal setting. These differences may relate to one's culture, background, upbringing, heritage, language, religion, and education. The process for resolving conflict is to bridge that gap between the two viewpoints by first identifying the issues of disagreement and then understanding the underlying beliefs and values supporting each viewpoint. The five-step approach for resolving conflict (i.e., building the bridge) between parents and professionals follows.

- *Step 1:* Identify the issues.

Everyone left the last IEP meeting for Darrell feeling discouraged that the transition plan was not completed. Darrell's parents did not want him to learn how to travel the bus system to worksites, but the school personnel felt that was a valuable component of career readiness for him. The school personnel did not understand why the parents were so resistant to something that promoted Darrell's independence for getting to and from worksites.

- *Step 2:* Identify the professionals' underlying values.

The school personnel strongly felt that if Darrell could travel independently, then his reliance on family members or others for transportation would not be an issue that could prohibit career choices in the future.

- *Step 3:* Identify the parents' underlying values.

Although Darrell's parents understood the school personnel meant well for Darrell, his mother feared for his safety on the bus. The family also regularly relied on family members (including relatives) being able to drive Darrell to worksites. Having their own transportation was a source of pride for them; they did not need to ride on the bus.

- *Step 4:* Discuss both sets of beliefs.

Later that week, the special educator, who had worked with Darrell and his family for several years, walked with Darrell to his mother's car when she came to pick him up after school. The special educator asked his mother, "Please tell me why preparing Darrell to ride the bus is something you do not want. If we taught him how to get different places on the bus, then he could also get to the movie theatre, the mall, and other places for his free time on his own." Darrell's mother responded with stories she had read about teenagers getting into trouble on the bus. She shared her concerns for his safety. Then she looked at the car she was driving and told the special educator, "We worked very hard to get this car. My sister and her family also have a car. So does my brother-in-law, who lives near us. We help each other all the time for driving." She continued, "I want Darrell to find good jobs. I appreciate what you and others are doing to prepare him for careers after graduating from high school. But I do not want to worry about his safety on the bus."

The special educator now realized that why Darrell's mother was so resistant about the bus transportation. First, it was a safety concern. Second, it was a source of pride that the family had their own transportation.

- *Step 5:* Collaborate by focusing on values shared with the parent.

The special educator said, "I understand what you are saying. We both want Darrell prepared for a career with a good salary that also has benefits. We did not mention this at the last team meeting, but Darrell is not riding the bus alone. An adult from school would always be with him and some of his peers who are also learning how to use the bus. I have read about the safety on the bus, too. Those incidents happened in the evening and in other parts of town. But we would not be on the bus at that time or in those places. Would you be okay if an adult and some other students were on the bus with Darrell?"

Darrell's mother agreed for Darrell to learn to ride the bus under those conditions.

Effective collaborative teams are not about any one team member getting what he or she wants; effective collaborative teams are about each team member contributing in ways that enable students to get what they need.

ADJUSTING INTERPERSONAL SKILLS WHEN VIDEOCONFERENCING

Although using technology during and for meetings (videoconferencing using Skype or some other platform) sounds like more efficient use of people's time (e.g., reduces travel time), there is the potential for the nuances of what is communicated by verbal and nonverbal behaviors to be missed (not seen) or unrecognized (not perceived) by members at different locations. Of course, what is missed or unrecognized because everyone is not in the same room must also be balanced against the fact that people can misunderstand communicative behaviors (verbal and nonverbal) when they are in the same room.

Andres and Akan (2010) analyzed behaviors of newly formed teams when problem solving in face-to-face environments compared with videoconferencing. In addition to observations, members of each team completed a team interaction quality questionnaire after the meeting. Team members who were videoconferencing to collaborate were

- More likely to talk to members in the same location rather than to all team members

- Less attentive to verbal and nonverbal behaviors, which affected their capacity to share ideas, understand others' ideas, and come to consensus

- More likely to have misunderstandings and then to resolve those misunderstandings

The researchers cautioned that technology, albeit convenient for individual users, can lead to team dysfunction if not properly monitored. In addition to increased awareness of the potential for negative effects on teams' problem solving, they suggested using facilitators who were mindful of the potential for miscommunication and could steer individuals and the team to more productive meetings. School personnel who work together on a more consistent basis may have the capacity to avoid these pitfalls, but it may be that these school personnel typically are not the ones involved in the videoconferencing. Team members need to be extremely mindful that they appropriately include members who participate via technology and be particularly attentive to both the verbal and nonverbal communication they may inadvertently be sending; they should also ensure they are receiving the intended messages from team members who are virtually present.

Some videoconference meetings have one or more people participating from one or more sites. Vigilance is needed to ensure that team members from each site are actively participating as if everyone is in the same physical room. Andres (2011) maintained that the following are more easily achieved in face-to-face team meetings than in technology-facilitated meetings:

- More effective communication of the intended message (i.e., sending the message)

- Recognition of when repairs for communications need to occur when intended messages are not communicated

- Clarification of misunderstandings via feedback

- Deduction of team member meaning (i.e., receiving the intended message)

- Keeping pace with the team's discussion

Andres's (2011) research findings for newly formed teams indicated that it is not simply a matter of team members' communication and social interaction that were affected when comparing face-to-face meetings to videoconferencing. Teams meeting at different locations experienced more problems interpreting and evaluating ideas as well as having shared understanding of ideas. In addition, team members found it more difficult to reflect on the task, focus on the solution, and make decisions for the future related to their given task. It may be that as teams meet more frequently using videoconferencing their capacity to become more adept when not face-to-face increases. As teams become more familiar with each other and the problem-solving process, the familiarity may somewhat mitigate the mode of the meeting.

Team Snapshot

Mr. Miller, the school psychologist for quite a few schools in his region, was participating in today's team meeting using Skype. Although he realized he missed out on some nuances of the team's content and interactions when he was not physically present, he felt that this "cost" was balanced by the amount of time it would have taken him to drive to and from the meeting. During today's meeting, Mr. Miller would be sharing the results of the assessments he had conducted with a student. Additional school personnel and the student's parents were present at the other end of the meeting. He knew the parents might find some of the results upsetting because their child had several areas of low scores.

⟳ ACTIVITY: *Should Mr. Miller have made it a point to be physically present during this team meeting? What is your rationale for your response?*

TEAMING EFFECTIVELY ON THE FLY

Teaming interactions occur within two basic formats—planned, sit-down meetings (formal) and on-the-fly interactions (informal) between team members. Informal teaming can promote role exchanges between and among members (see Chapter 1). In addition, there is no need to have more frequent formal meetings than are necessary (Boerner, Schaffner, & Gebert, 2012). Boerner et al. suggested that both formal and informal team meetings are complementary to each other and can enhance team effectiveness. Figure 3.7 compares and contrasts the characteristics of each of these two formats. Person-to-person sensitivity must occur regardless of the format because productive communication is the desired outcome during both planned formal meetings and informal (often hurried) on-the-fly exchanges.

Team members who only have a few minutes to touch base or update others may need to improve their communication over time so they are not perceived as too abrupt, and they may need to carefully choose their words and tone so they provide specific information in an objective manner. Conveying the need for more information before the next team meeting, however, is also appropriate: "Although the new point system works well some days for Kwame, I am not sure I am using it right. I know we will need to discuss it at the next team meeting, but in the meantime, can you drop by during reading to observe for about 20 minutes?"

Planning Team Communication Between Meetings

Team members should plan or establish routines for how they will communicate with one another and with the student's family members between meetings. Strategies for communicating with family members often differ from those strategies used by team members, partly because family members are not walking the school hallways or dropping by offices or classrooms, which are

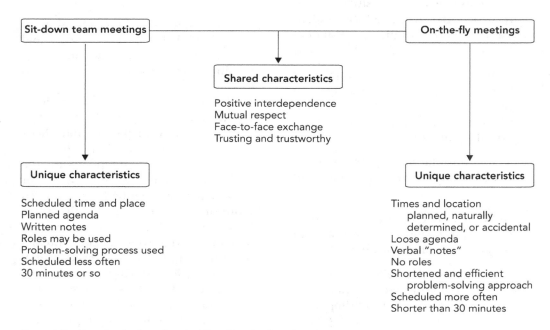

Figure 3.7.   Shared and unique characteristics of teaming formats.

typical ways informal quick conversations occur.

There are two methods of informal professional communication: 1) written (including e-mail), which is delayed, and 2) person-to-person (including telephone or technological face-to-face), which is live. Text messages are omitted from this list, unless the school personnel either have a cell phone provided by the school or the school personnel are not reluctant to share their private cell phone numbers with others. Students' initials instead of names could be used, particularly for written communication that may be inadvertently left in public areas of the school or in the classroom where others (including other students) can see the information. Types of written communication from which team members can select include the following:

- Informal notes in school mailboxes or sent home

- Rotating notebook (notebook between home and school), which is an excellent way to alert teachers if situations or events may affect the student's performance that day (e.g., the student was ill the previous night, the student had a restless evening with little sleep)

- Stationary notebook (notebook that remains in a secure predesignated place in a classroom so team members who come and go can write comments for others to see)

- Team consultation logs (related services staff record their presence and general activity)

- Individual student progress notebooks or specific forms to record student progress (see Janney & Snell, 2013)

- Specific forms that reflect or preserve team decisions or describe team plans for modifying schoolwork or supporting students' problem behavior (see Bambara et al., 2015; Janney & Snell, 2013)

- Blackboard or similar site (password accessible for confidentiality so team members, including parents, must sign in) where information can be exchanged

- Calendar back and forth between home and school, which may be daily to communicate performance each day, weekly to communicate performance at the end of the week, or monthly to indicate performance during the month (could be daily performance using monthly calendar, such as "homework turned in: yes or no")

- A graph of the student's performance that can be updated any time more data are gathered

Some families will desire to communicate between meetings, so school personnel could develop templates to individualize for students related to the communication topic and establish the frequency of touching base. Request input on what approaches would best suit that particular family. Parents should be given the opportunity to determine how they want to be involved with their son or daughter's program and to what degree (Salisbury & Dunst, 1997; Valle, 2011). The type and amount of involvement is likely to change over time in response to family and child circumstances.

Beyond formal scheduled sit-down meeting times, team members need to find time to talk in person and check on student progress or team efforts to implement team plans. Options for on-the-fly interactions include obvious or creative times that may be 1) prearranged before or after school, 2) highly probable because work schedules place team members in the same location during school (e.g., lunchroom, planning time), or 3) spontaneous during or after school (Doyle, York-Barr, & Kronberg, 1996). Team members obviously need to devise their own plans for keeping communication current in between meetings;

although these communication plans must be taken seriously, they also need to be kept flexible and revised if they are inadequate.

Implementing Team Recommendations and Meeting on the Fly

On-the-fly teaming among team members in inclusive schools frequently takes place throughout the school day; the focus of these interactions typically relates to implementing team decisions made for the action plans. These informal meetings are described by teachers as "checking back," "comparing notes," or "touching base" (Snell & Janney, 2000, p. 483). The meetings entail ongoing communication about students' progress with (or without) an adaptation or accommodation. In addition, on-the-fly meetings serve to construct an ongoing larger picture of what is going on for the student and teacher by ensuring the special educator (if not present in the general education setting) has an intermittent view about the larger picture. The intent for on-the-fly meetings is not to make core or whole team decisions but to refine solutions that the team's action plans set into motion.

Team members will communicate between sit-down meetings during the school day regarding the implementation of their plans, regardless of the intensity of a student's needs. Regular informal interchange between teachers is an essential supplement to weekly team meetings for students who need extensive support. These exchanges allow teachers to refine their plans by reducing, strengthening, or changing instructional and behavioral supports depending on the student, the day's conditions, and team goals. Meeting on the fly may become the primary collaboration strategy for students whose instructional support program is easily maintained and successful.

Working with Paraprofessionals

If paraprofessionals are part of the team's recommended support plan for a student, then they usually confer with classroom teachers about the student's progress during the day. As part of the student's support plan, paraprofessionals need corresponding preparation, follow-up, and feedback to ensure they are skilled with delivering the supports in the way intended. Researchers found that paraprofessionals spent a significant amount of time managing student behavior, instructing, and teaching social skills (Liston, Nevin, & Malian, 2009). The paraprofessionals need to have regular, planned opportunities to interact with the special education teacher to whom they report. If predictable exchanges or trust between them are lacking, then this link will be weak; however, this arrangement is beneficial when team trust and consensus exist. Although some paraprofessionals' views of a student's progress or problems may lack the expertise of other professional team members, paraprofessionals' perspectives are usually rich in valuable detail. In addition, paraprofessionals may be asked to supplement their verbal descriptions of a student's progress or problems with clarifying demonstrations ("Show me what Molly did when you had her add") or may be directly observed ("Just continue, and I will watch").

In situations where paraprofessionals interact more directly with specific students and general educators and have more information about what occurs on a day-to-day basis, the paraprofessional should not be the sole link of communication between the special educator and the classroom teachers. This communication gap sometimes occurs when special educators are heavily booked in resource teaching, have too many classroom teachers to link to, or choose to rely primarily on the paraprofessionals' perspectives. Some special educators supervise between 3.5 and 12 paraprofessionals, indicating both a wide range and a large quantity of time needed for appropriate supervision (Suter & Giangreco, 2009). It is critical that paraprofessionals be appropriately prepared to carry out responsibilities designated within the student's support plan (Fisher & Pleasants, 2012; Howard & Ford, 2007), and the support plan's design must also keep in mind the need for direct communication between the special educator and general educator, via both on-the-fly exchanges and more formal team meetings. Absent this direct communication, the special educator 1) does not know what is happening in the general education classroom and cannot provide resource support that is relevant, 2) does not know if students transfer their skills back to the classroom, 3) lacks a picture of student behavior in the classroom, and 4) is not present to support students in the classroom or monitor the paraprofessional. The special educator must have both an ongoing direct line of communication with the classroom teachers and a predictable presence in the classroom (Snell, 2002; Snell & Macfarland, 2001).

4

Problem Solving and Action Planning

FOCUSING QUESTIONS

- What sorts of issues, concerns, and problems do teams address?
- What problem-solving steps do teams use to organize the team's discussions?
- What are components for action plans?
- How are data used throughout the problem-solving and action-planning processes?
- In what kinds of solutions is it important to monitor the fidelity of implementation?

 ## Team Snapshot

Han's core team, including his parents, convened to discuss his progress at the midpoint of sixth grade. He was in general education science, math, and language arts. He receives some accommodations for reading, which is the main area for his learning disability, and his school day includes one study skills class in which he receives specialized reading instruction, particularly on decoding multisyllable words, comprehension skills, and specialized writing instruction. The meeting's purpose is to identify his progress and areas in which there are concerns. The core team will sequence through a problem-solving process and decide what to do for the concerns that are mentioned, depending on the issues that arise.

Information was acquired from the three content-area teachers prior to the meeting. Han's special educator, who teaches the study skills class, is in attendance and has information from Han's elective classes. Han himself submitted a report about how he felt he was doing in each class. His parents had information to share, as did his speech-language pathologist. Maybe too much information! No one was quite sure where to start and how to make the most of their limited meeting time.

⟳ ACTIVITY: *How could Han's core team organize their initial discussion? As you get to the point of identifying concerns, describe the process you think the team should use to problem-solve. After you read this chapter, return to the problem-solving process you describe now. What refinements would you make in light of information in this chapter?*

One might assume that problem-solving methods, sometimes referred to as *team-based problem solving*, are already within the skill sets of teachers and other adults on teams. Yet, people are not necessarily familiar with effective and efficient ways to jointly solve problems and make decisions unless they have been prepared to do so (Bahr et al., 2006; Goltz, Hietapelto,

Reinsch, & Tyrell, 2008; Newton, Horner, Todd, Algozzine, & Algozzine, 2012). Solving problems as a member of a team is different from solving problems independently.

The effective interpersonal skills described in Chapter 3 (e.g., clear verbal communication, open nonverbal behaviors) are put to work while using the problem-solving methods described in this chapter. School personnel rate problem-solving teams as more acceptable when team members demonstrate effective interpersonal communication and collaboration (Yetter, 2010). Having effective interpersonal skills but not knowing problem-solving methods does not get the team to solutions (at least not efficiently)— just as knowing problem-solving methods but having ineffective interpersonal skills does not get the team to solutions (at least not in a pleasant manner).

COMMON PROBLEM-SOLVING ISSUES

The overall function of team meetings is to develop students' school programs and schedules in ways that address their educational priorities, ensure consistency in program implementation, and problem-solve any relevant issues or concerns that arise.

Initial Problem Solving to Start the School Year

Core teams start the school year focused on the student's daily schedule and how the student participates academically and socially throughout the day. The team begins by sharing information about the student (or students) and the classroom. The general education teacher needs to know the student's present levels of performance (what the student knows and can do now) with respect to the IEP goals (what the student will learn or learn how to do), the student's IEP accommodations and modifications, and the supports that have been successful for the student

in the past. The special educators must learn about the curricular goals and the typical classroom procedures that the student will experience—routine instructional activities, frequently used student tasks or responses, homework, texts and other materials, classroom teacher assistance, assessment and grading practices, classroom rules and norms, and organizational routines. Information about the student and the classes leads to specific starting points for building the student's daily schedule and determining how the student participates throughout the day. The team will problem-solve answers to questions such as the following:

- What parts of the school day can the student participate in with no supports or natural supports? (These tasks, activities, and routines will require minimal or no preparation for the teacher[s].)

- What parts of the day will require individualized supports? Which supports?

- Is there a need to plan routines, specialized instruction (e.g., intensive reading instruction, preteaching, additional practice), or other activities that must be completed apart from typical peers (e.g., personal care, community-based instruction)? If so, when, where, and with what support?

- Do we need to make accommodations or modifications to any of the classroom procedures?

- Do we need other supports to increase academic and social participation?

For students with high support needs, a detailed matrix, as described in the next Student Snapshot and corresponding Figure 4.1, plus observations of the student across the day allow team members to plan when and how that student's priority goals can be addressed within ongoing class activities and routines. If the student has goals for functional skills that are not typically addressed in the general curriculum, then the team needs to problem-solve how to mesh instruction of these functional goals with the classroom schedule and curriculum. If the student has needs for personal support (e.g., for positioning, mobility, hygiene), then the team also will need to determine who assists the student and when. The team works to problem-solve any needed adaptations. Corresponding support and instruction that matches the student's needs are identified. The adaptation planning process is addressed in detail in *Modifying Schoolwork* (Janney & Snell, 2013).

 ## Student Snapshot

Gerry is a fifth-grade student with high support needs, so her team begins the school year by having Gerry and her mother introduce themselves to all the school personnel who do not yet know Gerry. This allows everyone on the team, including the general education teacher, to acquire a better understanding of Gerry. Gerry's learning needs are clustered in communication, independence building, math, and language arts. Her team planned ways to integrate her goals into the daily schedule by constructing a matrix of Gerry's class schedule with her IEP goals (see Figure 4.1). Goals that can be addressed during each time block are checked; any needed support may also be indicated in each cell. For example, Gerry goes with her class to lunch and works on communication and functional goals—using *yes-no* and pointing to answer questions and indicate food choices, following the cafeteria routine, and watching for cues from peers.

⟳ ACTIVITY: *In what ways can a matrix of the school day and IEP content be used to identify opportunities for inclusion? Does your team have a different strategy for determining how students' IEP goals will be embedded in ongoing class activities?*

The program planning matrix can be adapted to suit a range of purposes. For example, students with fewer support needs often have IEPs that emphasize accommodations to general education along with supplementary curriculum goals for skills used across the day (e.g., organization, self-management, study skills). The team can construct a matrix to guide the specific ways those accommodations and supplementary goals will be addressed within various subject areas or classes. Figure 4.2 shows the matrix developed for Alissa, a fifth-grade student with learning disabilities that affected her reading, writing, and organizational skills. All three of Alissa's supplementary goal areas needed to be addressed in all subjects across her school day. The team needed to problem-solve several issues: 1) the specific ways Alissa's accommodations for her disabilities would be provided for each subject area; 2) when it made the most sense for Alissa to receive the intensive reading and writing instruction required by her IEP; and 3) how Alissa's supplementary reading, writing, and organizational skills would be addressed within the daily classroom schedule. Alissa's core team will monitor her progress as the year unfolds and continue to problem-solve ways to improve or fade the supports they provide.

Ongoing Problem Solving

Teams problem-solve and develop action plans to address new and recurring problems as the school year progresses. Common problem-solving issues involve required special education procedures (e.g., determining supplementary aids and services, developing behavior support plans) and general education issues (e.g., planning supports needed by students for successful participation in general education, evaluating and grading students, addressing problem behavior). The latter issues will be resolved in the context of RTI or SW-PBIS teams when students do not have IEPs or have IEPs with fewer support needs or as a part of grade-level or multigrade teams that address all students in need. These problem-solving issues are addressed in student-focused teams (e.g.,

Program Planning Matrix

Student: _Gerry_   Teachers: _Yeager (5th grade), Dunst (IEP)_   Date: _September 2014_

IEP goals (in a few words)	Arrival/morning work	Reading	Language skills	Specialty	Math	Lunch	Science/social studies	Recess	Shared reading	Departure
Communication and self-management										
Use words/gestures and pictures/symbols to communicate (e.g., greet/farewell, make choices, answer questions)	X	X	X	X	X	X	X	X	X	X
Follow directions (e.g., get materials, sit at desk/floor) from teacher cues and peer models	X	X	X	X	X	X	X	X	X	X
Functional skills and school participation										
Use picture/word schedule to begin and end activities	X	X	X	X	X	X	X	X	X	X
Participate in large and small groups (e.g., take turns, follow instructions, share materials)		X	X	X	X		X		X	
Increase participation in school routines: arrival/departure, lunch, classroom jobs	X				X					X
Math										
Recognize numerals 0–10 in a variety of contexts	X				X		X			
Count and compare objects to 10					X		X			
Use mouse/keyboard to navigate computer activities	X	X	X	X			X			
Reading and language arts										
Answer basic comprehension ("wh") questions about read-alouds		X							X	
Read/write high-frequency words and phrases	X	X					X			
Match pictures with words or initial consonants			X	X			X		X	
Participate in science activities: focus on animal/plant, living/nonliving, weather, safety							X			
Participate in social studies activities: focus on community, family, school, past/present							X			

Figure 4.1. Program planning matrix for Gerry. (Key: IEP, individualized education program.) (From Janney, R., & Snell, M.E. [2013]. *Teachers' guides to inclusive practices: Modifying schoolwork* [3rd ed., pp. 104–105]. Baltimore, MD: Paul H. Brookes Publishing Co.; adapted by permission.)

core teams) that meet more often when students have higher support needs. Good teaming practices and rules for problem solving still apply, regardless of the team context.

PROBLEM-SOLVING AND ACTION-PLANNING METHODS

Observations of collaborative teams in elementary schools revealed that

Student: Alissa K. Fifth-grade teacher: Mrs. Johnson			

Individualized
education
program goals →
 	
↓ Subjects
	Reading
	R1. Decode unfamiliar
	  multisyllable words
	R2. Summarize text with
	  multiple main ideas
	R3. Answer factual,
	  descriptive, and
	  inferential compre-
	  hension questions
		Writing
		W1. Write sentences
		  with varied structures
		W2. Use grade-
		  appropriate vocabu-
		  lary words in writing
		W3. Respond to ques-
		  tions from other sub-
		  ject areas in writing
			Organization
			O1. Create outlines for writing
			  narrative stories
			O2. Use graphic organizers for
			  notetaking, charting, and
			  summarizing activities
			O3. Use folders, dividers, color
			  coding, and notebooks to
			  organize material for each
			  subject

Small-group
reading/centers
	Direct instruction during
	  reading using texts
	  at independent
	  reading level
	Identify prefix, base
	  words, and suf-
	  fixes derived from
	  passages
		Answer recall and infer-
		  ential comprehension
		  questions in writing
		  using complete
		  sentences with varied
		  structures
			Organize New Words box, with
			  tabs labeled, of multisyl-
			  lable words with similar
			  prefixes, similar base words,
			  and similar suffixes

Whole-group
reading
	Listen to e-book or
	  audio of text read by
	  whole class
		Same as above	Use outline for story elements
			Organize sections in notebook
			  for synonyms, antonyms,
			  and homonyms as the
			  terms come up in reading
			  passages

Writing/spelling	Derive new words and
	  word patterns from
	  all content areas,
	  including reading
		Direct instruction during
		  writing using content
		  from other subjects
			Organize vocabulary from mul-
			  tiple subjects, with defini-
			  tions as needed (determine
			  best method per subject)

Math	Illustrate word problems
	  for comprehension,
	  then solve
	Develop vocabulary
	  list based on math
	  concepts and
	  terminology
		Write "How I solved the
		  problem" using com-
		  plete sentences
			Use divided notebook
			  with labels for warm-up
			  problems, computation
			  classwork assignments,
			  word problem classwork
			  assignments, and home-
			  work assignments

Social studies
and science
	Develop vocabulary list;
	  add to New Word
	  box
	Listen to e-book or
	  audio of textbook for
	  each class
		Use computer with
		  word-prediction
		  software and spell
		  check
		Dictate to a peer
		Use thesaurus and dic-
		  tionary as needed
			Identify textbooks' features,
			  organized to facilitate
			  comprehension
			Select corresponding graphic
			  organizer (e.g., time line,
			  cause and effect) for note-
			  taking or summarizing after
			  reading specific parts of text
			Organize, label, and color-code
			  vocabulary for social studies
			  and science; notetaking for
			  social studies and science

Figure 4.2.   Program planning matrix of Alissa's individualized education program reading, writing, and organization goals plotted with her fifth-grade subject schedule.

teachers' thinking processes followed a cycle of steps as they fashioned, tried out, and refined solutions to student concerns over time (Snell & Janney, 2000). The basic process involved repeating a cycle to reach and refine solutions. Teachers would focus on a problem, observe, talk, generate ideas, decide what to try, and try it out. They repeated this process to reach real solutions, restating the problem as the solution was refined or as the problem changed. The process was not cut and dried but required the teams to make decisions based on the information before them at the time and then to improve their decisions as additional information became available. Hence, problem solving is actually more of an evolutionary cycle than a rigidly sequenced series of steps.

Problem-solving methods range from simple to complex. Some variations use the same essential sequence of steps, stages, or phases but use different terminology to name the steps or break the steps down into smaller substeps. IGNITE is a mnemonic to guide teams through the six generic steps of problem solving (see Figure 4.3):

1. **I**dentify the problem

2. **G**enerate possible solutions

3. **N**ote pros and cons of the possible solutions

4. **I**dentify a solution

5. **T**arget an action plan

6. **E**valuate the plan and make needed changes

The following sections provide guidelines for solving concerns teams have about students using IGNITE as a framework.

Identify the Problem

Teams need to take time to explore, define, and reach agreement on the problem (the terms *problem, issue,* and *concern* are used interchangeably throughout this chapter) before they search for solutions. Concerns about students in inclusive schools have been found to fall into one of three categories (Casale-Giannola, 2012; Deshler et al., 2008; King-Sears & Bowman-Kruhm, 2011; Snell & Janney, 2000; Stufft, Bauman, & Ohlsen, 2009):

1. *Student goals and abilities:* "What is this student capable of learning?" "What is reasonable, functional, and important to teach this student?" "Where shall we begin instruction?" The focus for secondary students shifts slightly to vocational, career, and other postsecondary goals. "Is the student being adequately prepared for postsecondary opportunities?" "Which careers are good matches?" "Is the student in the right courses now for the high school diploma he or she desires?"

2. *Participation in instructional activities and routines, and in state assessments:* "How will this student take part in class activities and school routines with classmates?" "How will this student learn his or her IEP goals in this class?" "What assistive technology might be necessary?" "Is the student being appropriately prepared for participation in state assessments?" "Are skills acquired during specialized

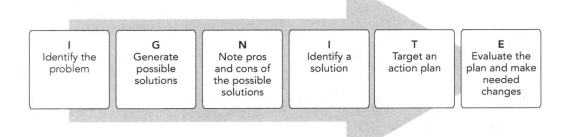

Figure 4.3.   IGNITE as a problem-solving method.

instruction generalizing and transferring to other contexts?"

3. *Classroom community and belonging:* "How can we improve this student's membership in the class?" "How can we give the student unobtrusive support to interact with peers?" "In what ways can we facilitate a range of authentic, positive interactions between students with and without disabilities?"

Student Snapshot

Jonah's IEP team met at the beginning of the school year to ensure that all of his teachers were familiar with Jonah's abilities, behavioral and academic goals, and general support needs. Clearing up these issues beforehand allows the core team to focus on Jonah's meaningful participation in his classes. Jonah's English and special education teachers later met informally to problem-solve three participation issues—gaining access to reading materials, reducing the amount and complexity of written assignments, and keeping Jonah's attention focused. They also discussed strategies to enhance Jonah's peer relationships, which included both formal peer support strategies used during certain instructional activities and more informal strategies to increase social interactions with classmates before and after class.

⟳ ACTIVITY: *How is information about students with IEPs shared at the beginning of the school year at your school? Compare processes used at your school with that of others. Discuss benefits of sharing information early on in the school year.*

To identify a problem to be resolved, a team needs to agree on what issues are problems, what problems need immediate attention, and a specific statement describing the problems. Reaching agreement in these areas can be accomplished in several ways.

- *Take a divergent/convergent approach:* List all of the visible problems and activities of concern (divergent). Converge on one problem or a combination of problems.

- *Prioritizing:* List an array of concerns and rank them from high to moderate to low in an effort to identify the top one or two to resolve.

- *Rewrite the problem in observable language:* Write down team members' views of the problem; without discussing solutions, identify and redefine imprecise terms, and seek to condense and identify the problem's focus the group agrees on. It is also easier to know what data to collect to document changes in the problem.

- *Categorizing:* Determine the type or category of problem (e.g., goal or ability, participation, membership, academic, behavior) and decide whether other types of problems exist in the same category. Add these to the problem statement to fully define the concern.

- *Apply consensus-reaching methods:* Compare the identified problems with actual student data; when there seems to be some agreement, ask the team if everyone feels comfortable addressing the problem. Or set a time limit for discussion, then ask for consensus.

If the step of clarifying the problem on which to focus is skipped or hurried, then the resultant problem-solving efforts might be misguided. For this reason, some problem-solving experts recommend using a two-phase, divergent/convergent process that involves using divergent thinking to expand the problem list prior to using convergent thinking to define or limit it (Cropley, 2006; Gressgord, 2012). Figure 4.4 suggests ways to divergently explore and generate ideas about the problems, issues, or concerns. Divergent thinking can be particularly fruitful for transdisciplinary teams because perspectives from multiple fields are shared (including related services professionals and the family's perspectives). No judgments are made about the ideas being identified during the brisk period when divergent thinking and sharing are occurring. Once either sufficient or depleted options are contributed, then the team focuses convergently to narrow the definition of the problem that will then be addressed throughout the problem-solving process (Cropley, 2006). Teams may find that the divergent/convergent approach shifts their focus from the original problem to one that is more relevant to the student or situation, is a higher priority, is more comprehensive, or needs to be resolved first.

 ### Team Snapshot

Chandler's core team, including his parents, was confounded for what would motivate him to complete his homework. He got the warm-up problems accurate each day, so they believed it was a motivational issue, not an instructional issue. Missing homework scores were affecting his grade in the class.

The team engaged in several minutes of spirited discussion, identifying everything they could think of that he might find reinforcing. After people seemed to slow down with generating ideas, they examined all they had before them. Now, what did they want to prioritize to use as reinforcers?

↻ ACTIVITY: *Identify situations in which divergent thinking would be helpful for generating a list of ideas, followed by convergent thinking to narrow the choices.*

Teams often will need to gather information to help them better understand the problem before moving ahead to the next step of the process. For example, the team may need to gather data to document the extent to which the problem occurs. For example, if the problem is that the student

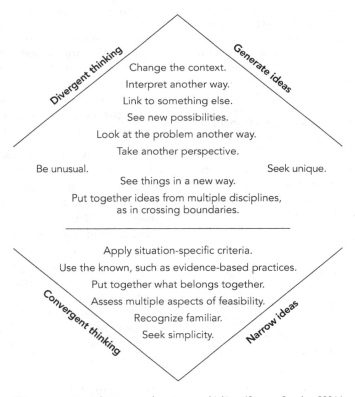

Figure 4.4. Using divergent and convergent thinking. (*Source:* Cropley, 2006.)

is not completing math homework, then the team should gather baseline data to show how often homework is missing or incomplete and whether there are any circumstances under which the student does complete homework assignments. If the problem is that the student has few interactions with classmates, then the team should collect information about the current frequency of peer interactions as well as information about the conditions that seem to make peer interactions more or less likely.

When a problem is significant enough to warrant an intervention—a concerted plan to achieve a particular academic outcome or behavior change—and/or it is related to an IEP goal, data should be acquired to quantify the extent of the concern or magnitude of the problem. These data continue to be gathered when the team's action plan is implemented so that the impact of the solution can be determined.

There are times when quantifiable data do not need to be collected. For example, if the problem is that the student needs different writing paper because the lines are too narrow on the sheet he or she has, then providing options of paper is a relatively straightforward solution. The nature of the problem needs to be identified, and the team should take note of the student's response to the new options provided, but formal collection of data for this type of problem is not necessary.

In some cases, the team will directly move from problem identification to solution finding because an immediate response to the problem is required. For example, if a field trip to a nearby community college for Career Day is scheduled for the day after tomorrow, then the team will want to leave the meeting with a plan to ensure that a student who uses a wheelchair or one who has severe anxieties about schedule changes will be supported during the trip. In many cases, however, team members may need to gather and analyze additional information about the problem before moving to the solution-finding phase. Indeed, the next step may be to determine 1) what kind of information needs to be gathered, 2) who gathers which type of information, and 3) when the team will reconvene to discuss the concern in light of the additional information gathered.

Generate Possible Solutions

Although team members certainly begin thinking of possible actions or solutions when they first see or hear of a concern, team ground rules generally dictate that the team waits to have all information before generating potential solutions. Ideas are only generated in this step of the cycle, not evaluated or selected. There are a number of ways to go about generating possible solutions; the team should explicitly decide which method it will use. The fragmented dialogue that may occur without a structured process is an inefficient use of team time and can lead to overlooking important aspects of the problem or its possible solutions.

Brainstorming is often suggested as the best and most creative approach for generating potential solutions when educational teams problem-solve. Brainstorming involves generating as many alternative ideas as possible within a short period of time while withholding discussion and judgment until all ideas have been expressed. Freewheeling brainstorming, during which team members state their ideas as quickly as possible without taking turns, however, has some possible pitfalls, especially when applied to making complex educational decisions: 1) less assertive members may hesitate to contribute, 2) the process may actually lead to conformity of ideas rather than creativity and variety (Goldenberg & Wiley, 2011), and 3) many of the problems being addressed by educational teams call for analytical judgment, not necessarily for creativity.

Brainstorming variations and other idea-generating approaches that avoid some of these pitfalls include the following:

- *Round robin:* Team members take turns stating their ideas in an around-the-circle fashion. If a team member cannot or does not want to contribute an idea, then that member passes, and the next person in the circle takes a turn. The session concludes once each consecutive participant has passed. This method is most useful when some team members dominate and others are hesitant to participate.

- *Nominal group technique (or the slip method):* Members anonymously write their ideas on slips of paper instead of offering them orally. A facilitator collects the slips, and a recorder writes them on a whiteboard or chart paper for the entire team to see. This method is useful when the problem is controversial, although it is slower than the first method.

- *Brainwriting:* Similar to the nominal group technique, team members write several ideas on a page; place it in a pile at the middle of the team table; select another member's list, read it, and add any new ideas they think of; and then repeat the process until no new ideas result (Friend & Cook, 2003). This approach promotes creative spring-boarding but is slower than the first two methods.

The process of generating potential solutions follows a divergent/convergent process: The team lengthens its list of ideas (diverge) and then separates out those that are most promising (converge). Generating ideas takes time. Logistical challenges (e.g., not enough time, key team members missing, pressure to act) have been shown to interfere with this step. When these barriers occur, teams select simple, quick, and satisfactory solutions, rather than working to seek optimal solutions that come from

Steps 2 (generate possible solutions) and 3 (evaluate possible solutions) or the carefully weighing of alternative solutions (Snell & Janney, 2000).

Note Pros and Cons of the Possible Solutions

Evaluating the ideas generated helps teams narrow their ideas down to those that will make the best solution. Teams naturally evaluate solutions when they allow time for it. A special educator described it this way:

> You just keep talking about it until you arrive at the next idea. I think that [what] we've experienced in our little round table discussions [is that] one person will say, "I don't think that will work, but if you take that idea and do a little something different to it, it might work." (Snell & Janney, 2000, p. 485)

When you think back on how you have decided what solution has the best chance of working, you can recall some common sense criteria most people automatically apply:

- *Feasibility:* "That sounds possible" versus "That is not feasible in my class!"

- *Team consensus:* "I think his parents would really approve" versus "That will not work for his parents."

- *Peer approval, nonstigmatizing:* "That is something that the kids would help with" versus "The kids will laugh."

- *Cost:* "We have all the materials we need to use that idea" versus "Where will we get the money to pay for the materials, the staff time, and so forth?"

Bahr and colleagues (2006) suggested additional criteria:

- *Evidence-based practice:* "There is research to support the technique."

- *Intervention builds on the student's strengths:* This criterion highlights the importance of building from what the student already knows and can do. It is also a reminder that the student brings strengths to the learning environment (i.e., all that is done for the student is not solely deficit driven).

As with most of the problem-solving steps, evaluation also involves a divergent and a convergent phase. In the divergent phase, team members generate the criteria they will use to evaluate their ideas. In the convergent phase, team members systematically compare each idea against the criteria and judge its acceptability. Teams who work together for a while often develop some standard criteria that match their shared values and the students they support. Even these teams, however, can benefit from reviewing their criteria list for possible omissions before evaluating possible solutions. Using a criteria worksheet can help teams be more systematic at this stage of problem solving. Figure 4.5 provides a form teams can use to evaluate their ideas according to a set of criteria. (A blank, photocopiable version is available in Appendix A and the forms download.) The team may decide to use some or all of the criteria listed; every criterion does not need to be used every time or for every idea, but the listing facilitates members' discussion of the pros and cons of ideas.

One team of researchers developed the Usage Rating Profile Intervention with the purpose of identifying potential facilitators or barriers to the use of an intervention (Briesch, Chafouleas, Neugebauer, & Riley-Tillman, 2013). Six categories of facilitators and barriers were rated for each potential intervention:

1. *Acceptability* applies both to the intervention's match for the student and to the reaction or response of team members who must implement the intervention. This is a measure of how well the intervention will fit the classroom context.

2. *Understanding* relates to team members' knowledge of the intervention and how it should be used.

3. *Feasibility* relates to the availability of adequate time and materials to implement the intervention.

4. *Family–school collaboration* refers to whether interaction with the student's family would be needed for effective implementation and also to the importance of designing culturally responsive solutions.

5. *System climate* refers to whether the intervention is philosophically compatible with team members' views, values, and ethics. This measure relates to the concept of social validity.

6. *System support* includes endorsement from administrators, colleagues, and parents for the intervention's use.

These facilitators and barriers can be used as criteria for noting pros and cons of solutions in conjunction with criteria noted in Figure 4.5. School teams should individualize the criteria for their context so that criteria most pertinent for their situation are used.

A team member serves as a recorder during the process of noting pros and cons of potential solutions, writing on chart paper or a whiteboard (be sure to take a photograph of the notes if the whiteboard is not interactive) or typing on a laptop that projects on a screen; this helps team members to ponder others' input and also serves to document the group's thinking. Using technology to enable the same content to be seen by all in real time is important, especially for team members who are not physically present at the meeting.

Identify a Solution

Given the pros and cons of the potential solutions generated, which solution emerges as having the most pros and the fewest cons? A convergent approach is exercised by the team in narrowing the solutions to the one that will be applied. Although team members select the "best

Pros and Cons of Possible Solutions

Criteria (Indicate yes or no for each criterion.)	Solution 1 *Create formal peer support network for Abby.*	Solution 2 *Create lunch bunch for Abby and several classmates.*	Solution 3 *Provide Abby and selected peers with booster sessions related to class social skills lessons.*	Solution 4 *Describe solution.*
1. Is the solution responsive to the student's needs?	Yes	Yes	Yes	
2. Are the resources available?	Yes	No	Yes	
3. Are there potential uses in other environments?	Yes	No	No	
4. Is it specific enough for data to be collected?	No	No	Yes	
5. Does the solution target evidence-based practices?	Yes	No	Yes	
6. Is the solution matched to the problem's severity?	Yes	No	Yes	
7. Does the solution promote participation in inclusive educational and/or community contexts?	Yes	Yes	Yes	
8. Is the solution manageable to implement?	Yes	No	Yes	
9. Is the solution acceptable to implementers?	Yes	No	Yes	
10. Does the solution hold team consensus?	Yes	No	Yes	
11. Does the solution promote the student's independence?	Yes	Yes	Yes	
12. Is the solution as nonintrusive as possible from the student's perspective?	Yes	No	Yes	
13. Does the solution relate to other valued life outcomes?	Yes	Yes	Yes	
14. Other criteria:				
15. Other criteria:				
The quantity of yes and no responses can help the team select the best-fit solution.[a]	Total yes _12_ Total no _1_	Total yes _4_ Total no _9_	Total yes _12_ Total no _1_	Total yes ___ Total no ___

[a]Some criteria may be more important to the team than others.

Figure 4.5. Criteria to consider when determining pros and cons of ideas, then selecting solution(s). (*Source:* Giangreco, Cloninger, Dennis, & Edelman, 1994.) (A blank, photocopiable version is available in Appendix A, and blank and filled-in versions are available in the forms download.)

bet" when they choose a solution, the solution should be viewed as only a tentative one until it proves workable. Also, teams may find several "winning" solutions that can be combined into a more comprehensive answer to the problem. Multiple solutions will be chosen when teams have time to address several problems in a session. The agenda needs to allot enough time for team members to examine the solutions to each problem and reach agreements by consensus (e.g., a quick check by the group facilitator, "Is everyone okay with this?") (Baron, 2008; Dulaney, 2013; Liu, Friedman, Barry, Gelfand, & Zhang, 2012). Attaining team consensus must not be sacrificed due to a lack of time, particularly if the team members not in agreement with the solution are those who will be the primary implementers of it. It may be better at times for teams to move forward with some solutions and delay others until agreement can be reached.

 ## Student Snapshot

Once Abby's team decided to focus on Abby's communication, especially her communication with peers, they agreed to gather 3 days of data on the communication interactions between Abby and her classmates. They created a simple data sheet to assess Abby's communication with her peers during activities when students are most likely to interact socially—classroom arrival, snack, activity centers, lunch, recess, and departure. Abby's first-grade teacher, her IEP manager, and a classroom paraprofessional divided the responsibility for recording observations. During each activity, the observer noted 1) who initiated an interaction, 2) what the initiator said and did, 3) what the responder said and did, and 4) whether the interaction was understood. It was clear from the observations that Abby wanted to interact with her peers, and they with her, but neither had the tools to make their interactions understood. The team then problem-solved ways to facilitate communication between Abby and her peers, such as using communication books and simple voice-output devices.

⟳ ACTIVITY: *Could Abby's team develop effective communication supports for Abby without collecting observational data? Why or why not?*

Target an Action Plan

Teams need to build enough time into their agendas to complete action plans. The primary elements of an action plan are

- *Problem or issue:* What is the problem or issue on which we need to take action? If the problem is one that involves a learning or behavior change goal, then operationally define the behavior.

- *Goal:* What is the desired level of behavior change or other hoped-for outcome of the plan?

- *Action:* What action step or steps do we agree to take to resolve this issue?

- *Fidelity:* Which actions need corresponding fidelity checks to ensure the plan is being used as intended?

- *Who is responsible:* Who will help develop or implement each task or action?

- *By when:* When will each planned action be implemented?

- *Logistics:* Date, team members present, date and time of next meeting

Action plans can be fairly brief as long as the team members who have responsibility for specific tasks understand how to carry out their respective tasks (see Figure 4.6). Teams are usually motivated by their results at this point in a session, and it usually is easy to reach consensus on each task planned for the identified solution if everyone has been participating. Consensus at this point of problem solving is just as important as at any other point because team members are deciding how their ideas or solutions will be implemented.

Teams may need to identify preparatory steps that need to be taken before an action plan can be fully developed or

Team meeting date: October 15	Team members present: Mr. Folkins, math teacher Mrs. Rogers, special educator Mrs. Schick, counselor Mrs. Ellen, behavior support specialist		
Issue being discussed: JS's behavior during math Outbursts by speaking loudly and saying he will not do the work, needs help, or the work is stupid	Next meeting date and time: November 12 at 2:30		
Action plan goal: Decrease the frequency of inappropriate behaviors exhibited by JS from 15 outbursts during the 45-minute math class to 0 outbursts by teaching JS to use self-management and replacement behaviors.			
Who	Does what?	By when?	Fidelity checklist
Mrs. Rogers (special educator)	Develops self-management device	October 22	
	Teaches JS how to use the self-management device (follows script of 10-step sequence)	October 29	Observe for 10-step sequence
	Arranges logistics for JS to use the self-management during math	October 29	
	Monitors JS's use of self-management during math	Intermittently until next team meeting	Observe JS's use of self-management
Mr. Folkins (math teacher)	Continues collecting data on JS's outbursts	Ongoing until the next team meeting	

Figure 4.6. Action plan.

implemented (e.g., conducting assessments, developing or acquiring materials). This step includes checking with team members or outsiders who were absent when the plan was discussed—but are nonetheless critical participants—so the plan reflects team consensus. If the action plan focuses on a specific intervention being used by one or more people, then it also should address how that intervention will be monitored (the fidelity) to ensure it is implemented as intended. Data collection that initially occurred to identify the problem continues because these data inform the team of the effect the targeted action plan is having on the problem.

Evaluate the Plan and Make Needed Changes

Once an action plan is made, the team will convene for a follow-up meeting to evaluate its implementation. (The follow-up meeting may simply be the next regular core team meeting if a set meeting schedule is already in place.) Team members often repeatedly touch base with each other informally as they implement the plan and observe its effects, sometimes even making quick refinements without needing to reconvene the team (Snell & Janney, 2000). These on-the-fly interactions help the plan get going more smoothly and allow team members to coordinate their efforts during initial implementation. Face-to-face discussion at team meetings allows teams to develop excellent plans, but it is usually through actual "field tests" and conversations on location that planned solutions can be refined through use.

If the solution works as intended, then the original issue or problem is abating. If the problem is not improving, then it is important to determine whether 1) the solution is faulty or 2) the solution has not been implemented the way the team envisioned.

When team members determine that an intervention is not having the desired effect, they must decide whether to refine the intervention, improve their application of the intervention, or find another solution. It is possible the team returns to earlier ideas generated, reviews the pros and cons in light of the new information (i.e., data about the implementation of the first solution), and targets another solution. The team has recycled through the problem-solving steps to Step 5 (target an action plan), and a revised plan is developed.

 ## Student Snapshot

Connor's team decided the point system used by his classroom teacher did not reward positive behavior frequently enough for him to make the connection between his appropriate behaviors and the reinforcement. The team put an action plan in place for Connor to receive points at specific intervals that coincided with natural breaks during the day, such as transitions between subjects. If he earned enough points, then he could select his reward at the end of the day, rather than only having a reward opportunity at the end of the week, as his classmates did.

Connor's classroom teacher often forgot to deliver points to Connor at the scheduled intervals, however, and several times did not allow enough time for Connor to select a reinforcer before his bus arrived. Connor's behavior did not change.

The team met 2 weeks later to review their action plan. Connor's teacher reported the plan was not working and that she could not keep up with the increased frequency of distributing points earned throughout the day. One of the team members realized that they really did not know whether the plan worked because it was not being implemented as intended. The team discussed ways the classroom teacher could be supported so she could remember to provide Connor's points throughout the day. One team member committed to getting to the classroom 10 minutes before the buses left to coordinate for Connor's selection of his daily reward. The team also decided to learn more about how to teach Connor self-management skills that would reduce his dependence on teacher-delivered rewards and phase him back into the classroom behavior management system.

⏱ ACTIVITY: *What ramifications might there have been for Connor and his team if no one on the team had considered that the point system was not being implemented as intended?*

Details matter for fidelity of implementation of the solution because if the solution works as intended, then the team needs to have confidence that changes actually are due to the solution. For example, if each team member leaves the meeting with different ways of operationalizing, for example, reinforcement, redirection, and nonverbal cues, then the action plan is not clear. Team members need to know the precise "who, what, when, and where" of the new intervention or support they are implementing. Fidelity measures should be discussed when the action plan is developed and monitored when the action plan is implemented.

Choosing When to Use IGNITE

IGNITE is a problem-solving framework that is robust enough for collaborative teams' use for a range of concerns, problems, issues, or tasks. For example, one student's core team may meet fairly regularly to ensure materials are in place in advance for participation in the general education curriculum, such as determining which materials are needed for the upcoming fifth-grade social studies unit and who does which adaptations. Other teams may be meeting less frequently or on an as-needed basis for specific students who have IEPs. Still other teams may have regularly scheduled times with agendas for individual students, a small group of students, or class issues.

Although problem solving is a primary focus of this chapter, collaborative teams convene for purposes other than solving what is typically considered a problem. The problem and corresponding solution may not need a comprehensive action plan at times. Some solutions may be more direct or obvious. For example, to meet the needs of a student with learning disabilities who has a testing accommodation on his or her IEP for extended time, the general educator may alert the school counselor that the student will come to his or her office to use a space there or arrange for use of a study carrel in the library. Alternatively, a core team who is discussing plans for the school field day may talk about the peer support and adaptive sports equipment that a student with multiple disabilities will need in order to participate.

Collaborative teams may find the details in each step more or less time consuming, depending on the complexity and quantity of issues being addressed. Collaborative teams who work together more repeatedly, or team members who are on several collaborative teams, may also find their experiences with examining issues, considering different solutions, and developing action plans expand their repertoire of contributions for subsequent teams. The transdisciplinary mindset of openness to ideas from other disciplines can be evident in that team members not only learn from but use ideas from different disciplines. Teams become familiar with the problem-solving steps over time and use them very naturally. The problem-solving process for parents of students with IEPs crosses years and teachers, and the emphasis on collaboration makes a tremendous difference to them as their child makes transitions across settings (see Figure 4.7).

CHALLENGES TO TEAM PROBLEM SOLVING AND ACTION PLANNING

Team problem solving and action-planning processes are subject to the

ongoing challenges teams face when doing any of their joint work, including finding time to meet, integrating the perspectives of generalists and specialists, and maintaining parity among team members. Collaborative team problem solving should result in action plans that reflect parity both in input and output. All team members help reach the team's decisions and responsibilities for completing action steps. Jameson (2009) described how individual team members can preempt authentic team discussions and decision making when they do the following:

- Rush the team through the problem-solving process

- Persuade others to concur with their idea

- Hold power over others who are too quickly silenced to share ideas

- Propose solutions without allowing time for clear problem identification

Jameson (2009) further noted that the team's desire for cohesiveness could inadvertently undermine its productivity. That is, if team members are uncomfortable with disagreeing with another team member who has differing ideas, then they may be acquiescing to ideas and solutions that are not the best solutions for students. New team members may be particularly prone to defer to others, either because they are not familiar with the collaborative problem-solving process or they lack experience using the interpersonal skills that enable team members to disagree and yet achieve consensus (see Chapter 3). Schools should ensure that there are processes in place for orienting new personnel to the collaborative teaming approach, including interpersonal skills and processes for problem solving and action planning (Hansen, Anderson, Munger, & Chizek, 2013).

Voices from the Classroom

January: I open my e-mail to find a frantic message from the parent of one of my students. She just got home from the transition meeting information session offered by the county's preschool specialists and has a few questions. When can we meet? Mrs. White's son, Jack, is 5 years old, has autism, is nonverbal, and is about to make the transition to kindergarten. We have talked about the transition process before, but it is a nerve-wracking experience for parents, and the closer we get to the spring, the more questions there are. I immediately write back. I am free after school a few days that week and would be happy to meet.

February: Parents begin trickling in. The four other preschool teachers at my school join me in welcoming them to our round table meeting, "Transition Experiences." We have invited parents of students we have taught before to share their observations of the transition process. They explain what went well with their child's transition and what could have gone better. Mrs. White is diligently taking notes, and I notice her nod when a parent mentions how difficult it was to think about sending her child off to a new school.

March: The coordination of Team Jack begins. I draft the individualized education program (IEP) goals and objectives based on Jack's current strengths and needs a week and a half before the IEP meeting, and I send it home with a note asking for questions and input from his parents. In addition, an agenda for the meeting and a blank document for the parents to fill in regarding their perception of Jack's school performance are in the packet. Three days later I get an e-mail with suggestions, changes, and questions from the draft IEP. This delights me—the parents are participating in the process.

April: It is a crowded table, the eight of us there to plan for Jack's transition to kindergarten, his best interests in the front of our mind. I sit with five other professionals—the kindergarten teacher from Jack's neighborhood school, the special education teacher from the kindergarten autism classroom (a similar program to the preschool autism class he currently attends), the speech-language pathologist, the occupational therapist, and the special education administrator. Jack's parents are there, quietly taking in the team. We start the meeting talking about Jack's strengths and weaknesses, and I take it slow, even though we have been through this before. The IEP draft is a fluid document, and we make changes as we discuss Jack's needs. The parents ask questions, team members make suggestions, and the IEP wording is adjusted. The meeting is over an hour and a half later.

The school personnel recommend that the school year begin with Jack in the regular kindergarten class so he can start the day with peers, attending the morning meeting and specials such as art, music, and physical education. He will also be with peers in lunch and recess, key times for him to have natural opportunities for social interactions, and activities at the end of the school day. The kindergarten autism program will be used for other academic programming and support, seeking opportunities throughout the school year to collaborate with the regular kindergarten program. The two kindergarten teachers have worked together for several years, and they reassure Jack's parents that they will monitor both his academic and social progress while maximizing natural situations for all kindergarten students to learn and play (which is part of the learning) together. His parents take the document home to look over; in agreement, they return it signed the next day. With the legal part finalized, we prepare for the actual transition.

May: Jack and his parents attend kindergarten orientation. They take a tour of the new school and meet the principal and therapists. Everyone seems welcoming and confident of Jack being included in kindergarten with peers, while emphasizing how his academic and social needs can be met with the blended approach. The school personnel are accustomed to maintaining close communication with the parents, particularly as the year begins. That also sounds reassuring to Jack's parents. Meanwhile, Jack is introduced to other students who will be in his classes in the coming year, and

Figure 4.7.   Parent involvement in team planning. (Contributed by Rachel Hamberger.)

(continued)

Figure 4.7.   *(continued)*

---

the children play together while the parents attend an information session about the academic content of kindergarten.

June: I put together a packet of data on Jack's IEP goals and his behavioral strategies, in addition to anecdotal notes about his favorite toys and activities. I send this off to his potential teachers for next year. I have also prepared a Social Story for Jack's transition. It has pictures of his new school and places he will visit, such as the library, the cafeteria, the gym, and, of course, the playground. This goes home for him to read with his parents. My eyes well up as I say good-bye on the last day of school.

5

Collaborative Consultation

FOCUSING QUESTIONS

- What is collaborative consultation?
- How is collaborative consultation different from traditional expert-driven consultation?
- Who uses collaborative consultation, and for what purposes?
- During what situations and contexts might team members or teams use 1) expert-driven consultation or 2) collaborative consultation?
- What are benefits of collaborative consultation for students, families, and school personnel?
- In what ways does collaborative consultation require use of effective interpersonal skills, problem-solving processes, and action plans?

 ## Student Snapshot

Abby, a first grader with multiple physical and intellectual disabilities, has several adaptations and supports that are used across the day to enable her to gain access to learning opportunities with her classmates, including augmentative and alternative communication (AAC) devices and systems (e.g., a Cheaptalk device, BIGMack and LITTLE Mack communicators, a communication book, a picture-word schedule system) and some adaptive seating and movement devices (e.g., a bolster seat, a walker). Abby also uses a variety of adapted books, writing tools, a computer mouse, and other materials that provide her with access to curriculum content and ways to demonstrate her learning. Abby's team has developed these supports through collaborative team problem solving, which sometimes occurs at regular meetings of the core team but other times involves collaborative consultation between one or both of her teachers and the physical therapist, speech-language pathologist, and severe disabilities consultant who are members of her IEP team. The team recently decided to request consultation with an AAC specialist at the nearby university-based technical assistance center because they were concerned about Abby's slow progress on her expressive communication goal (refer to Chapter 2, Figure 2.7).

⟳ ACTIVITY: *In what other ways might collaborative consultation be used by Abby's team or teams serving other students with disabilities? In what ways would the consultation among Abby's teachers and other members of her IEP team be different from the consultation her team requests from an AAC specialist from a technical assistance center?*

Collaborative consultation is a term used in diverse disciplines to describe activities conducted for a range of purposes; the term has a variety of definitions. A general definition that suits the way it is used in inclusive schools is this: "Collaborative consultation is an interactive process which enables people with diverse expertise to generate creative solutions to mutually defined problems" (Idol, Paolucci-Whitcomb, & Nevin, 1986, p. 1). It is one of the triumvirate of collaborative structures required to make inclusion work, along with collaborative teaming and collaborative teaching. The "mutually defined problems" addressed through consultative partnerships focus on meeting students' learning and behavioral needs, as defined by their IEPs, in ways that enhance their academic and social inclusion.

Collaborative consultation is an indirect service in most cases: A consultant interacts with another professional who then provides direct service to a student (see Figure 5.1). For example, a classroom teacher might turn to a special education teacher when a student with a learning disability suddenly stops completing homework and is not prepared for quizzes so that her once excellent grades are in jeopardy. Collaborative consultation in inclusive schools also can involve instances of direct service, however, in which a special educator or other specialist works directly with a student for a particular purpose for a period of time, such as when a speech-language pathologist assists a student to use a new communication device during class and then coaches a classroom teacher or special educator to use the device with the student. At its center, collaborative consultation in inclusive schools

> Is interaction in which school personnel and families confer, consult, and collaborate as a team to identify learning and behavioral needs, and to plan, implement, evaluate, and revise as needed the educational programs that are expected to serve those needs. (Dettmer, Thurston, & Dyck, 2005, p. 6)

RATIONALE FOR COLLABORATIVE CONSULTATION

The rationale for collaborative consultation is quite straightforward: No teacher has all the expertise needed to serve all

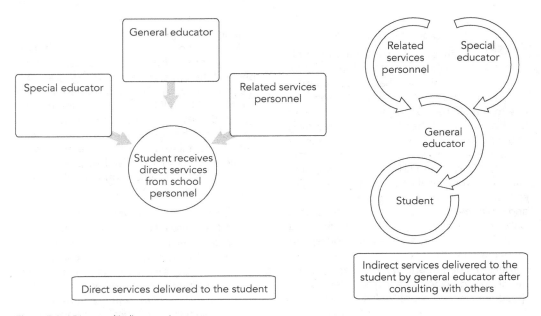

Direct services delivered to the student

Indirect services delivered to the student by general educator after consulting with others

Figure 5.1. Direct and indirect services.

students. Collaborative consultation is a way to bring expertise (which is portable) to the student, rather than burdening the student with having to travel to a different school or spend time making the transition back and forth between general education, special education, or clinical settings (which are not portable). Meeting the complex needs of students like Abby, as well as other students introduced in the Student Snapshots throughout this book, requires an educational team to assemble an array of services and supports and can only be accomplished through the joint work of personnel with various areas of expertise. The teams supporting these students do not want students' educational experiences to be isolated or fractionated, however. Abby's IEP (refer to Table 1.4 for a listing of Abby's special education and related services and to Figure 2.7 for Abby's Program-at-a-Glance) includes accommodations and modifications to general education, as well as specialized instruction, physical support, speech-language services, and physical therapy. If Abby were to receive all of those services directly from specialists, when would she get to be just a student? Collaborative consultation, along with teaming, collaborative teaching, and direct service from specialists, can ensure that Abby's educational and related needs are met without interfering with her class membership.

Teams apply the "only-as-special-as-necessary" criterion (introduced in Figure 1.2) in order to provide necessary services and supports in ways that do not interfere with membership and belonging. That is, their decision making about students' services and programming is guided by an effort to use natural supports, typical contexts, and methods that are as nonintrusive as possible, while at the same time providing services and supports that meet identified individual needs. Collaborative consultation assists teams to efficiently use a wide array of expertise while also building the team's capacity to support the focal student and the class as a whole.

Collaborative consultation has received impetus not only from inclusive education but also from other contemporary education improvement efforts that focus on building schoolwide systems to support the increasingly diverse student population. The IDEA and NCLB requirements that teachers be highly qualified in the subject areas they teach and schools be held accountable for instruction and assessment of all students have propelled secondary schools in particular to increase their use of collaborative service delivery in the form of collaborative consultation and collaborative teaching (see Chapter 6) (Carpenter & Dyad, 2007).

Notwithstanding this recent boost in popularity, consultation has been a prominent service delivery option for students with high-incidence disabilities since the early 1960s (e.g., Lilly, 1971). In addition, consultation has a long history within the fields of mental and behavioral health and school counseling, which have used consultative service delivery approaches long before inclusive education was a familiar concept (Dettmer et al., 2005). Figure 5.2 summarizes key research findings for special education consultation.

EXPERT-DRIVEN AND COLLABORATIVE CONSULTATION

What is different about contemporary applications of consultation for inclusive education is the shift in orientation away from the use of consultants and specialists to fill strictly expert roles to the use of a more collaborative orientation for consultation among members of transdisciplinary teams. Expert-driven consultation based on the traditional medical model used in mental health is prescriptive: A specialist who has been consulted by virtue of his or her specialized knowledge prescribes an intervention to address needs jointly targeted by the consultee and consultant. The consultant selects interventions, trains the consultee to implement

What the Research Says

The research base for consultation includes descriptive, how-to reports; studies that examine the skills and knowledge acquired by consultees; outcome studies that focus on improvements in students' academic and behavioral performance as a result of the teachers' implementation of interventions developed through consultation; and reports of improvements in systems-level measures (e.g., reductions in referral rates, fewer removals to more restrictive settings) influenced by consultative partnerships. Key findings include the following:

- Collaborative solutions to student needs generally are more successful than those developed individually. Consultation in special education showed favorable outcomes for targeted students or systems approximately three fourths of the time (Sheridan, Welch, & Orme, 1996). These improvements in students' learning and social skills are brought about by team members' enhanced skills and knowledge (Dettmer, Thurston, & Dyck, 2005).
- Specific outcomes of consultation for students include improved homework performance and grades (Theodore et al., 2009), reduced student disruptive behavior (Denton, Hasbrouck, & Sekaquaptewa, 2003), improved achievement of individualized education program objectives (Ruble, Dalrymple, & McGrew, 2010), and improved achievement in reading and mathematics (Schulte, Osborne, & McKinney, 1990).
- Collaborative consultation may increase team members' joint ownership of student learning and increase general education teachers' level of confidence and skill in teaching students with diverse learning needs (Sheridan et al., 1996).
- General education teachers tend to rate collaborative consultation as an acceptable service option. The majority view the experience positively and are willing to participate in future collaborative partnerships (Schulte et al., 1990; Sheridan et al., 1996).
- Interventions created and implemented through collaborative consultation (in contrast with traditional expert-driven consultation) are more likely to be culturally responsive, ecologically valid, and acceptable to consultees (Nastasi et al., 2000).
- Web-based consultation may be as effective as face-to-face consultation for preparing teachers to use evidence-based practices for students with autism (Ruble, McGrew, Toland, Dalrymple, & Jung, 2013).

Figure 5.2. Research base for special education consultation.

them, monitors the implementation, and provides feedback.

In contrast, collaborative consultation relies on a nonhierarchical relationship between consultant and consultee. It is a process-oriented approach based on shared responsibility for identifying and defining intervention targets, determining solutions, developing and implementing action plans, and monitoring the success of the intervention (Friend & Cook, 2007). The consultant may indeed bring both content and process expertise to the partnership but does not provide a diagnosis or prescribe an intervention. Instead, interventions are based on pooled knowledge of evidence-based practices, along with the consultee's knowledge of

the feasibility of implementing those practices in inclusive contexts. In traditional expert-driven consultation, the consultant says, "Here's what you need to do." In collaborative consultation, the consultant says, "Let's figure this out together."

Collaborative teams in inclusive schools will likely have occasion to use expert-driven consultation for specific purposes. For example, if a student with a serious medical condition moves into the school, then the student's team would want to get an effective support plan in place as soon as possible. Consulting an expert is appropriate when efficiency counts and highly specialized knowledge is not immediately available within the team or the school. When an expert-driven consultation approach is initially used, however, it can evolve into a more collaborative partnership over time as team members gain skills and the consultant is able to release the role of expert. Collaborative, process-oriented consultation will be used on an ongoing basis by teams whose goal is to ensure that all students achieve and belong. Figure 5.3 summarizes the characteristics of collaborative consultation in inclusive schools.

WHO USES COLLABORATIVE CONSULTATION, AND FOR WHAT PURPOSES?

Any number of school teams, including teacher assistance teams, PBS teams, grade-level and departmental teams, IEP teams, core teams, and co-teaching teams, may utilize collaborative consultation. The primary focus in this chapter is on collaborative consultation as it is used by IEP, core, and co-teaching teams. Because reciprocity characterizes collaborative consultation, any member of the team may act as consultant or consultee at different times.

Who Uses Collaborative Consultation?

Many special educators and other specialists have job titles or position descriptions that specifically task them to provide consultative services. It is important to distinguish, however, between collaborative consultation as a service delivery approach and the roles filled by school personnel whose position descriptions include providing consultative services. As previously noted, any team member may act as a consultant or consultee at different times. The following is not an exhaustive catalogue of personnel who are designated to provide consultative services in inclusive schools, but it covers the most common sources:

- *Special educators who are designated as consulting teachers.* Job titles and position descriptions vary widely from one state and/or school system to another (e.g., inclusion facilitator, inclusion support teacher) (Jorgensen, Schuh, & Nisbet, 2006), but these educators provide indirect services for students through their consultative interactions with other team members. The general education

---

Consultation in schools with an inclusive, collaborative culture typically evidences these characteristics:

- *Process-driven, collaborative consultation orientation that is supplemented by expert-driven consultation when necessary and appropriate.*
- *Focus on shared goals:* As a transdisciplinary team, members of a student's individualized education program (IEP) team do not write separate goals according to their disciplines (e.g., the general educator writes the academic goals, the special educator writes the functional skill goals, the physical therapist writes motor goals, the parents write social goals) and then staple the pages together. The IEP team instead develops integrated goals to enhance the student's academic, social, physical growth and well-being, and creates support plans to maximize achievement of those goals within inclusive contexts. Likewise, the members of a student's core team establish shared goals for their ongoing problem solving to more effectively include students (see Chapter 4).
- *Reciprocity:* The roles of consultant and consultee are interchangeable. All team members may fill either role at various times, depending on the situation and the type of expertise required.
- *Parity:* Participants in the consultative interaction (whether a dyad or a larger team) are equal partners with diverse but equally valued expertise. The knowledge and skill base of the specialists on the team is valued but does not elevate them to a higher status than teachers and parents or allow them to dictate what students' goals will be or how they will be addressed.
- *Formal and informal uses:* A formal approach is used when an individual or team identifies the need for additional knowledge or skill, identifies a consultant, arranges a preplanned meeting, and takes specific action steps to implement agreed-on supports. An informal approach is used when team members interact on the fly, in the hall, during lunch, or after a faculty meeting to touch base or check in with one another about a new or ongoing issue.

Figure 5.3.   Characteristics of collaborative consultation in inclusive schools.

teacher is the most likely team member to fill the role of consultee, although parents, paraprofessionals, other team members, and even other school personnel might also be involved. In some school systems, larger schools might have a full-time, dedicated consulting teacher, whereas in smaller schools, a position might be partitioned (i.e., part-time consulting and part-time teaching) or itinerant. In many cases, consulting teachers perform administrative functions, such as serving as the principal designee for eligibility and IEP teams.

Special educators may be designated as resource/consulting teachers in some localities. This is a specific program model developed by Idol, Paolucci, Whitcomb, and Nevin (1986), although numerous other iterations of the role have been devised. Resource/consulting teachers fill dual roles of 1) providing specialized instruction to individual or small groups of students (direct service through resource or tutorials) and 2) providing consultative services to general education teachers and other team members (indirect services). Although many special educators must learn consulting skills through in-service professional development, pre-service teacher education programs for resource/consulting teachers intentionally provide preparation for both direct and indirect service delivery.

Teachers of students with very low-incidence disabilities (e.g., deaf and hard of hearing, deafblind, blind) often fill itinerant positions, so they essentially function as consultants to classroom teachers and other special educators in multiple schools. Figure 5.4 provides a look at the way one itinerant special educator collaborates and consults with general educators.

School systems and individual schools vary greatly in how carefully they distinguish between direct and indirect services from a consulting special educator. Roles are flexibly

interpreted in some localities, whereas others strictly govern time by the actual minutes of service dictated by students' IEPs. Balancing the demands of providing direct and indirect services is a major challenge of this dual role.

- *Related services personnel (e.g., physical therapists, occupational therapists, speech-language pathologists, school psychologists) often fill dual roles as direct and indirect service providers.* In accordance with students' IEPs, related services may be provided 1) through direct service to the student and/or 2) through indirect, consultative services to an individual educator (general education teacher, special education teacher, or even consulting teacher) or to a student's core or IEP team.

- *Other specialists (e.g., behavior support specialists, assistive technology specialists, orientation and mobility specialists, vocational counselors, transition specialists), as well as technical assistance providers from technical assistance centers or universities, provide consultative services.* These specialists may consult with individual team members but are more likely to consult with IEP, core, and co-teaching teams to assist them in developing and implementing intervention and support plans. These specialists are members of individual students' whole or core teams in many cases, though they attend team meetings only when their particular expertise is required. In other cases, a specialist might consult with a larger team, such as a grade-level or departmental team (see Figure 5.5).

What Are Some Uses of Collaborative Consultation?

Collaborative consultation in inclusive schools is used for two broad purposes: 1) to deliver IEP services and supports (IEP-based consultation) and 2) to address incidental or persistent concerns about

Voices from the Classroom

Ms. Nelson is an itinerant teacher of students with visual impairments who serves 14 students across 11 schools in her district. She maintains a collaborative relationship with each of her students' classroom teachers through regularly or intermittently scheduled appointments, spontaneous brief check-ins (i.e., on the fly), and communication through e-mail.

At the beginning of the school year, Ms. Nelson met with classroom teachers to discuss students' accommodations. For example, some students require large print or braille and tactile graphics. Ms. Nelson asked teachers to provide lesson plans and work in advance because of the time it takes to make these accommodations. She also instructed some teachers on how to enlarge work for certain students. For example, the students with low vision need tests and other written materials printed in 24-point sans-serif fonts. Most of the teachers create exams electronically, so they can change the font size and print a copy for their student with a visual impairment.

Next week, two students will need graphic organizers in different classes. Ahmed, a student with low vision, will work with a graphic organizer in ancient civilizations. Sarah, who is almost totally blind, will use one for planning the writing process. Both students will receive models of completed organizers from their classroom teachers, and both will have to create their own.

Ahmed's history teacher e-mailed Ms. Nelson the organizer, which was made through an online mapping tool, a week in advance; Sarah's teacher placed her example in Ms. Nelson's school mailbox. Sarah's organizer contains shapes and connecting lines with handwritten notes filling each shape. Both Ahmed's and Sarah's classroom teachers expressed concern over the students' ability to gain access to the lessons with their sighted peers. Ms. Nelson assured the teachers that both can benefit from accommodations and participate equally.

Ms. Nelson frequently engages Ahmed and Sarah in selecting the most appropriate accommodations for their vision-related needs, which promotes self-advocacy and their ability to self-accommodate. Ms. Nelson talks with Ahmed and his history teacher about possible options for Ahmed's graphic organizer for history class. One option would be to enlarge the graphic organizer, but it would have to be printed on several large pieces of paper and then taped together to make it large enough for Ahmed to read it. Another option is to provide Ahmed with an electronic copy of the graphic organizer on either a school touch-tablet, where he can see the layout of the organizer and zoom in on each item, or on a classroom computer with a screen enlargement program. The team agrees Ahmed will use the same web site the teacher used for the example to create his own graphic organizer. Ms. Nelson asks Ahmed to e-mail his final product to her to determine if this suited his needs and for the teacher and Ahmed to promptly relay any concerns to her.

Sarah, who primarily uses braille, will be given an adapted version of the teacher's example in tactile format. Sarah has not had much exposure to graphic organizers, so Ms. Nelson decides this is an opportunity to support Sarah's understanding of the way organizers work. Ms. Nelson has several options for adapting this assignment for Sarah. She may braille the handwritten notes onto adhesive braille labels and connect them with yarn or WikkiStix. Or, Ms. Nelson can take a high-tech approach and use a variety of tactile graphics programs and hardware. Ms. Nelson consults with the classroom teacher, who clarifies the graphic organizer will be referred to throughout the school year. Ms. Nelson chooses to make the graphic out of the more durable materials from a tactile graphic machine in her district. Ms. Nelson models for Sarah's teacher specific language to use when presenting the example to the class, such as precise spatial directions such as, "the next circle on the right" or "the large rectangle in the center." The explicit language facilitates Sarah's ability to follow along, whereas Sarah would have problems if the teacher just pointed and said "this one" or "over there." Ms. Nelson also provides braille labels and the templates for Sarah's upcoming work with the organizers. She also informs the teacher that Sarah may choose to use an outline format for her writing plans. Ms. Nelson

Figure 5.4.   Expert-driven consultation for students with visual impairments becomes collaborative. (Contributed by Kim Avila.)

(continued)

Figure 5.4. *(continued)*

> explains that Sarah's access to the tactile graphics will equip her with the concepts of the organizers, but some students who use braille work better with outlining. Ms. Nelson asks Sarah and the classroom teacher to follow up with her via e-mail. Ms. Nelson also checks in with the teacher shortly after the example was presented to the class to determine any further concerns or feedback.
>
> Collaboration and planning facilitated Ahmed and Sarah's access to general education lessons that required adaptations and consultation with the teacher of students with visual impairments. Every lesson will be different for each student who is blind or has visual impairments; however, open forms of communication and forward thinking are essential to promoting the most effective consult scenarios.

students' participation and progress (concern-based consultation).

Consultation can be a service listed on a student's IEP as part of his or her free appropriate public education (FAPE). Special education instruction and related services may be provided completely or in part through consultation. Special educators and related services providers acting in consulting roles engage in activities including the following:

- Confer, problem-solve, and plan with teachers, parents, and/or other team members

- Conduct observations to assess classroom activities and/or student needs and to evaluate progress

- Conduct curriculum-based assessments

- Train and supervise cross-age peer tutors or members of a peer support network

- Demonstrate instructional, therapeutic, and other supportive techniques with the student

- Demonstrate the use of adaptive equipment, assistive technology, and AAC systems with the student

- Observe and coach a teacher or paraprofessional as he or she uses a new technique or support

- Locate and share resources with other team members

- Provide in-service professional development for classroom teachers, paraprofessionals, other team members, or the broader school community

- Provide episodic or intermittent co-teaching for a specific purpose, but typically not for an extended period of time

 Student Snapshot

Jonah, a bright, articulate eighth grader with Asperger syndrome, has some considerable difficulties when it comes to frustration tolerance and peer relationships. Therefore, he has a PBS plan, and his IEP includes consultative services from Mrs. Walsh, the school psychologist, and Ms. Park, a special educator who is the school's behavior support specialist. Jonah's team, with input from Jonah and his parents, develops a plan to support Jonah's relationships with peers. First, Mrs. Walsh facilitates the team to conduct a thorough assessment of Jonah's current peer network—which peers he associates with and interacts with on a regular basis, both in and outside of school. The team uses the curriculum from *Skillstreaming the Adolescent* (McGinnis, 2012) to assess Jonah's present levels of performance on basic social interaction skills. Ms. Park involves Jonah in a social skills group that meets twice a week for 3 weeks during the teacher advisory period. Ms. Park has extensive experience using the skillstreaming approach, which is backed by a strong research base. After initial instruction in the skills targeted for the group (e.g., listening, starting a conversation, introducing yourself), Ms. Park involves other members of Jonah's team in learning the transfer-of-training techniques that will help Jonah use the targeted

Voices from the Classroom

My role as a behavior support specialist recently led me to embark on a collaborative effort on behalf of an entire grade-level team. I worked with five first-grade teachers, two special educators, and an English for speakers of other languages (ESOL) teacher. The school experienced a midyear change in administration, and the transition caused a notable disruption in the delivery of staffwide professional developments as well as some staff resignations. As a result, my objective was to bring the team together, work with team members to jointly develop teacher and classroom goals, and provide appropriate training and coaching to ensure consistent implementation of programs. Issues ranged from two first-year teachers struggling with basic classroom management, to a veteran teacher facing difficulty implementing individual positive behavior support plans and collecting behavioral data for the first time. In addition, this was the first year that two teachers had taught in inclusive classrooms, and they were not yet comfortable or familiar with the ongoing collaboration and communication required with special educators to ensure proper delivery of instruction.

I began the process of providing purposeful, organized collaboration by attending one of the weekly collaborative learning team meetings that consisted of the first-grade general and special educators, along with the interim principal. We set up a model for collaboration at this initial meeting in which each teacher voiced concerns, and a series of observations were scheduled over 2 weeks. My objective was to understand the full scope of each situation from multiple perspectives. Anecdotal notes, behavioral data, and (when permissions allowed) video data were used for the purposes of informing intervention planning. Interventions were carefully designed, with much consideration given to the time needed for teacher implementation. A series of short, hands-on type of trainings occurred following intervention drafting in which all of the teachers practiced strategies they would eventually use in the classroom. They also learned how to use data collection procedures. These trainings generally spanned the course of a week, with built-in time for discussions.

After this initial training, my role transferred to that of an in-class coach. I conducted a series of regularly scheduled follow-up coaching sessions with each teacher. Coaching sessions allowed me to become an active participant in their classroom and provide immediate and detailed feedback regarding the teachers' strengths and areas for improvement. The final stage of implementation relates to the data, which is compiled, analyzed, and visually displayed at the weekly collaborative learning team meeting. The teachers received practice reading and interpreting these data and were coached on how to use this information to guide their interventions. My role was systematically faded out over time, paring down the frequency of coaching sessions and, finally, formally dismissing myself from active participation. I always ensured that teams with whom I work have my contact information so they can be in touch with me for similar or different situations in the future.

Figure 5.5.   Classroom behavior support through collaborative consultation. (Contributed by Colleen Barry.)

skills, with gradually decreasing support, in his classes and other activities. Although Mrs. Walsh and Ms. Parks initially had more input into the social skills intervention than other team members because of their expertise, they gradually release responsibility to other team members, whose new knowledge and skills will help them to support not only Jonah but also other students.

(↻) ACTIVITY: *What characteristics of collaborative consultation are evident in this Student Snapshot about Jonah and his team?*

Collaborative consultation also is used to address incidental and persistent concerns about students' academic and social participation and progress. This problem-focused consultation can involve only IEP or core team members, or it can involve expert consultants from the school, school district, or professional community. Many, if not most, teachers have had the experience of feeling that they have tried everything with a student and are now so frustrated that the call for help begins with the phrase, "I am at my wit's end." The problem might be a recurring concern about the student's academic performance, behavioral needs, or social relationships. A student with extensive, complex support needs may present physical, health, or sensory issues with which no one on the team has much experience. A practiced team may be able to rally and draw on its own resources to problem-solve and generate a new action plan in cases such as these (see Chapter 4). Or, the individual or team may decide that a more expert-oriented consultation is needed.

Teachers and other members of collaborative teams who value the parity, reciprocity, trust, and shared responsibility that typify their work together may sometimes hesitate to seek help from specialists who have an expert-driven orientation to consultation (Walther-Thomas, Korinek, McLaghlin, & Williams, 2000). Team members should remember that no one is expected to know it all and that their goal is to improve outcomes for students. Furthermore, their knowledge of the differences between expert-driven and collaborative consultation can help them to understand how the specialist's orientation and training differ from their own. In addition, as educated consumers of the consultant's expertise, they can help ensure a positive experience by being prepared for the consultation, specifically articulating their expectations for the consultation, and actively participating in the problem-solving process.

 Student Snapshot

Mr. Bacci, a regional specialist on autism, periodically participates on Liam's team. Because he serves several school districts, Mr. Bacci is only available to meet once every 6 weeks. The first couple of times he met with Liam's team, Mr. Bacci was careful to learn all he could about Liam, his second-grade classroom, and the supports that already were in place. The team now keeps a running list of "questions for Mr. B."

Mr. Bacci asks what questions the team has for him when he is available to meet and joins in the problem solving with other team members. He contributes valuable information on autism to the core team members and suggests new strategies to their support plans for Liam. Ms. Jarvis, Liam's IEP manager, regularly e-mails Mr. Bacci with team meeting updates on Liam.

⟳ ACTIVITY: *What experiences have you had with expert-driven consultation? How were they similar to and different from the experience Liam's team had with Mr. Bacci?*

RELATED SERVICES DELIVERED THROUGH COLLABORATIVE CONSULTATION

Collaborative consultation is used to deliver related services (e.g., physical therapy, occupational therapy, speech-language therapy) due to best practice guidelines as well as issues of practicality. Therefore, the topic merits a special note. An integrated, transdisciplinary approach to related services allows students to receive necessary services largely within inclusive contexts. Transdisciplinary teams share decision-making and teaching roles instead of having some team members make recommendations as experts. An integrated approach means that assessment and implementation of speech-language, physical, or other therapies occurs during natural opportunities throughout the day (Cloninger, 2004). The rationale for this approach is that students need to use motor, speech-language, and other related skills throughout the day, not during motor skills class or speech class. Therefore, skill instruction should be embedded into natural contexts throughout the day. This means that skills cannot be taught only by related services providers but must be supported by general and special education teachers and other school personnel— who learn these support strategies through collaborative consultation with specialists. This integrated therapy model has been effective for student learning, may facilitate better skill generalization, and is preferred by teachers and related services staff (Huang, Peyton, Faota, & Pascua, 2011; Paul-Brown & Caperton, 2001; Shasby & Schneck, 2011; Woods, Wilcox, Friedman, & Murch, 2011). In keeping with this model and the IDEA definition, related services are provided to enable the student to participate in the classroom and benefit from the curriculum.

 ## Student Snapshot

Olivia, a fifth-grade student who has a learning disability and a degenerative neuromuscular disorder, has an IEP that calls for consultation services for occupational and physical therapy. Team members already have identified their major concern: Olivia lacks the muscle strength and coordination to use a writing implement or manipulate a computer mouse for any length of time, so she is not fully participating in writing and computer tasks. After meeting with Olivia's classroom teacher and her IEP manager to determine which class activities pose the biggest challenges for Olivia, the two therapists observed Olivia during those activities and worked directly with Olivia to get a better understanding of her capabilities. When the occupational therapist and physical therapist complete their observations and assessments, they meet again with Olivia's two teachers and her mother to generate an action plan. The physical therapist will teach the two teachers and part-time classroom paraprofessional several quick exercises that they will do four times a day with Olivia to help prevent her from losing more hand and arm strength. The occupational therapist will bring several low-tech assistive devices that can help Olivia with handwriting and computer use. She will test these devices with Olivia—first in private and then in the classroom, with Olivia's consent. The team will meet again in 2 weeks to report on actions completed, on Olivia's progress, and to do further problem solving if needed.

ⓘ ACTIVITY: *Which aspects of this Student Snapshot evidence expert-driven consultation? Which aspects evidence collaborative consultation? How does collaborative consultation support Olivia's fuller participation in the fifth grade?*

Chapter 4 noted that the potential solutions to an issue or problem being addressed by the team should be evaluated against several criteria, including acceptability (it matches the student's needs and the values of the implementers and other stakeholders on the team and is feasible to implement given the resources available) and efficacy (the evidence base suggests it will produce the desired outcome). These criteria apply to the interventions suggested by related services professionals and other consultants, regardless of their status as experts. Therapists must understand the demands of the classroom environment and the perspectives of the teachers and others who must integrate interventions into the classroom schedule and implement them. Interventions are implemented with a greater degree of fidelity when a collaborative approach rather than a traditional expert consultation approach is used to deliver related services (Kelleher, Riley-Tillman, & Power, 2013).

CHALLENGES OF ROLE DEFINITION AND LOGISTICS

Educators who provide special education services through a combination of direct and indirect services (e.g., consulting teachers, resource or consulting teachers) experience some predictable challenges. Providing answers to these challenges is beyond the scope of this book, but a quick glance at some key issues is in order.

Role definition is one issue. How, exactly, is their role defined?

> Until educators become comfortable with the concepts of consultation, collaboration, and educational teams, ambiguous feelings about it all may persist. Teachers and school staff sometimes are not sure why there are consulting teachers or what these people are supposed to be doing. (Dettmer et al., 2005, p. 14)

It is crucial that school districts provide consulting teacher job descriptions to clarify the role and delineate the activities that comprise the job. In addition, any change in educators' roles needs professional development to help all stakeholders understand the rationale for the change and how it will benefit students.

Managing workload is another issue. Special educators who provide consultative services to a dozen or more general educators and also have a caseload of students who require direct service face many logistical challenges, including scheduling their time, managing paperwork and materials, and maintaining communication flow for each student and/or team they serve. Eisenman, Pleet, Wandry, and McGinley (2011) studied the perspectives of high school special educators who shifted from providing direct services in a resource teacher role to providing a combination of direct and indirect services in a collaborative consultation role. The researchers noted that the teachers were required to "cultivate and negotiate multiple, instructional relationships with teachers and students. [T]hey constantly navigated between voluntary interactions requested by teachers or students and mandated interactions such as progress monitoring and IEP development" (p. 101).

Special educators who fill full- or part-time consulting roles must develop skills and strategies to organize their time, resources, and student records. (Helpful resources on that topic can be found in Appendix B.) Other aspects of workload management for consulting teachers are contingent on structures and resources at the school or systems level. Collaborative teaming in inclusive schools needs administrative support for class composition, special educator caseload, and assigning special educators to a narrower band of ages and/or subjects (see Chapter 2). For example, assigning special educators to a grade-level or departmental team yields advantages for both special educators and general educators because they collaborate with fewer individuals. In addition, special educators can gain increased familiarity with curriculum content and

teaching techniques and develop long-lasting collaborative relationships (Eisenman et al., 2011).

RECOGNIZING EACH OTHER'S EXPERTISE

Being a skilled teacher or specialist for students does not automatically make someone a skilled partner in a consultative relationship. Professional skills and specialized content knowledge are certainly essential to positive outcomes for consultation, but effective collaborative consultation also requires skills to facilitate the consultative process.

Taken together, the members of an IEP team have a wide array of skills, knowledge, and experience. Even so, teams may need to supplement their pooled expertise to meet complex or confounding student needs. Team members, whether acting as consultants or consultees, should be aware of the areas of expertise represented on the IEP or core team, as well as the expertise available within the school, the school system, and the wider professional community. Most team members will be aware of the expertise of general education teachers, which includes knowledge of the general education curriculum content and the pedagogies used to teach and assess different types of content. The context of general education—the organization, typical activities, and social environment of the classroom—is another key area of general educators' expertise that is not always understood by specialists. Some team members may need a better understanding of the content expertise of special educators, which includes the learning needs and strengths of students with IEPs, curriculum adaptation, specialized teaching methods, peer interactions and supports, behavior interventions and supports, alternate assessments, data-based decision making, and developmental and corrective reading.

Specialists who are team members should make sure that other members are aware of what they do for students and what they bring to the team. Most team members will recognize that concerns about motor skills, positioning, and adaptive equipment can be addressed by physical therapists. Team members may not know, however, that a student's difficulties with handwriting, unfastening and fastening clothing when using the restroom, and completing other activities of daily living can be addressed by occupational therapists. When students are pulled out of the classroom for direct therapy services, and when specialists do not collaborate to determine shared goals and interventions, classroom teachers in particular are not likely to know what a specialist knows and is able to do or how to reinforce students' skill use in natural contexts (Huang et al., 2011).

Professionals whose job descriptions include serving in consulting roles clearly need highly developed communication and collaborative problem-solving skills (see Chapters 3 and 4). In addition, they may falter in their consultative relationships if they do not have values that foster the parity and shared responsibility essential to effective collaborative teaming. Other team members (e.g., special and general education teachers) who participate in consultative partnerships also can make those partnerships more fruitful if they are skilled in problem solving and therefore can truly collaborate as they work with consultants to address concerns.

COLLABORATIVE CONSULTATION PROCESS

Various models have been outlined for collaborative consultation in inclusive schools (Dettmer, Thurston, & Dyck, 2005; Musti-Rao, Hawkins, & Tan, 2011; Wesley & Buysse, 2004). Collaborative consultation typically is conducted using a problem-solving process with steps or stages very similar to those in the IGNITE framework presented in Chapter 4. Some

differences are called for, however, when the consultant is an outside expert, particularly if the consultee is a teacher who will be responsible for ongoing implementation of an intervention or support and the consultant must ensure the intervention is being implemented as planned.

A seven-stage collaborative consultation process incorporates essential aspects of the generic problem-solving steps along with the relationship-building and recursive dialogue that collaborative consultation requires. The substeps at each stage will vary, as will the amount of time required for each stage.

Stage 1: Prepare for the Consultation

The consultee assembles information to help explain his or her concerns and what has already been done to address them. Documents might include the student's Program-at-a-Glance (see Figure 2.7), individualized adaptations and support plans (creating these plans is detailed in a companion book, *Modifying Schoolwork* [Janney & Snell, 2013]), student work samples, and relevant team action plans. The consultant reviews any intake information already provided and documents any previous consultations regarding the student and the classroom.

Stage 2: Initiate the Consultation

The consultant begins to establish rapport once a time and meeting place have been determined. Consultants (e.g., related services providers, psychologists, assistive technology specialists) may not have had opportunities to establish trust and build relationships with other team members because they are typically not at any one school on a daily basis. As itinerant professionals with multiple schools, their time for sustained interactions is limited (Villeneuve & Hutchinson, 2012). Outside consultants might have no previous relationship with a consultee. To mitigate this, consultants must use effective interpersonal skills and monitor their interactions (see Chapter 3). They also must apply strategies to make meetings efficient and effective (see Chapter 2). Consultants can share a little about their expertise and the services they are able to provide and then establish that their intent is to collaborate to reach a good outcome for the student. If the consultant is an IEP team member, then answering the question "What do we each do for or with the student?" can help each member acquire a greater understanding of the other's role for service delivery.

Stage 3: Collect Information to Pinpoint the Problem

This stage begins at the first consultation meeting but often requires gathering additional information to share at subsequent meetings. It may take longer than it does when a core team is problem-solving because the consultant needs to gain a clear understanding of the student's strengths and needs, the classroom context, the specific issue or concern, and what has or has not worked in the past. The consultant may need to assist the consultee at this stage to focus more narrowly on the specific concerns that prompted the consultation. For example, a classroom teacher says, "Alissa will not do anything I tell her to do," and the consultant asks, "Tell me about yesterday: What were some instructions you gave Alissa that she did not follow? What, exactly, did she do?" Or, a special educator says, "Jonah has very limited social skills; he is in his own little world," and the consultant asks, "How does Jonah respond when you talk with him before or after school? What does he do when a classmate says 'hi' or asks about his weekend?"

Based on observations, data, student records, and discussion, a specific problem or concern must be identified as the focus of the consultation. There is no point in identifying a problem if it is not stated in terms of observable behavior that

can be measured to determine if the intervention plan was effective (see Chapter 4). For example, a general concern about Jonah's poor social skills is not measurable. One can measure the effectiveness of an intervention plan, however, if the behavior is pinpointed as, "When a classmate or teacher greets Jonah, he puts his hands over his ears and walks away."

Formulating a target or goal statement is the final substep of this stage. For example, if Jonah currently responds correctly to 1 out of 4 greetings from teachers or classmates, then what will his rate of correct responses be following a social skills intervention? The consultation target might be a benchmark or objective toward a more long-term goal for the student, particularly if the consultant is an outside expert whose availability is limited by time.

Stage 4: Generate Potential Solutions and Target the Best Solution(s)

This stage of the process is almost identical to collaborative problem solving by a core team; readers can refer to the full description of the processes for generating and evaluating potential solutions and developing action plans in Chapter 4. It is here, however, that a consultant needs to take care to maintain a collaborative approach. Consultants will share their knowledge of evidence-based practices but must guard against prescribing solutions, even if consultees seem to be out of ideas or resistant to the process. Consultants need to find ways to draw consultees in, such as by asking them to consider the feasibility and potential effectiveness of different solutions and ways practices can be modified to better fit the student and the classroom situation. Consultants might ask, "How does this sound to you?" "Does this solution seem like something that the student will be responsive to?" "Will these materials be acceptable to the student?" (MacSuga & Simonsen, 2011).

An intervention with poor contextual fit (i.e., impractical and not feasible within the context of the teacher's workload and the classroom environment) and no sense of ownership by consultees may not be used correctly (MacSuga & Simonsen, 2011; McLaren, Bausch, & Ault, 2007).

Stage 5: Develop an Action Plan

Consultants and consultees develop an action plan that spells out implementation responsibilities; methods, criteria, and dates for monitoring progress; review dates; and steps for involving other relevant team members in the plan. It is crucial that consultees have genuine input into action planning. Team members may be less likely to carry out their part of an action plan when they perceive that they are being given directives (Wesley & Buysse, 2004).

Although supports for implementation fidelity are important for any intervention plan, they are especially crucial when the consultant is not a regular member of the team and/or will be on-site infrequently. Action plans may include some or all of the following steps to ensure reliable implementation (Huang et al., 2011; MacSuga & Simonsen, 2011; Minor, Dubard, & Luiselli, 2014):

- Make sure teachers (or other implementers) understand the rationale for the intervention.

- Demonstrate the technique, device, or strategy, first outside the classroom, then in context.

- Incorporate collaboration and problem solving (rather than directives) into the feedback process when consultees are learning new techniques.

- Schedule classroom visits with respect for the schedule and traffic patterns of other specialists.

- Provide a written instructional plan or a checklist with the steps of the intervention.

- Provide a schedule or log sheet to be checked each time the intervention is used.

Stage 6: Implement and Evaluate the Plan

After the plan is implemented with the student, observations or other methods for evaluating student progress will determine whether the desired effect is occurring. If it is not, these data are used to guide additional problem solving. Conversation also includes whether there are implementation issues to address. The collaborative process itself also should be evaluated, if not formally, then by reflecting informally on what went well and what could be done differently in the future to improve the process.

Stage 7: Follow Up on the Consultation

Effective consultants provide follow-up support for 1) accurate implementation of the plan, 2) documentation of the student's progress toward the goal, and 3) adjustments to the plan if the student gains fall short of the goal. As consultees gain confidence in implementing the new or improved techniques, consultants have the opportunity to release more of their role. The partners determine together whether the original problem or issue has been sufficiently addressed, and there is closure to the consultative interaction.

 ### Student Snapshot

Anna is a fifth-grade student with learning disabilities in reading and writing, which affect her reading comprehension and ability to complete complex writing assignments. Anna receives pull-out reading instruction to improve her decoding, comprehension, and written composition skills. To address Anna's written language skills, the speech-language pathologist provides indirect services to Anna's fifth-grade and special education teachers. The speech-language pathologist and the two teachers meet early in the school year to discuss how Anna is doing so far, particularly with respect to the demanding state writing standards, which are assessed for the first time in fifth grade. The team is already acquainted, so the meeting begins with setting the agenda. The team decides to 1) identify the types of class assignments that challenge Anna, 2) analyze the specific skills and strategies with which Anna has difficulty, and 3) generate ideas about possible interventions. The classroom teacher has brought samples of Anna's written assignments and her plan book to the meeting, so the team is able to accomplish the first agenda item. The writing samples show that Anna falters with assignments that call for written responses to comprehension questions about material she has read. Writing a summary or book report also is problematic. The speech-language pathologist asks the two teachers probing questions to determine if Anna's problems with written English lie more in 1) understanding what she has read, 2) organizing her thoughts to generate a response, or 3) using the writing process to put her thoughts down on paper. Although the two teachers are eager to develop an intervention plan that will accelerate the development of Anna's writing skills, they also realize that they really do not have enough data to decide on a suitable intervention.

Therefore, the team begins to develop an action plan. The first steps include these items: 1) the speech-language pathologist and the special education teacher will each observe (at separate times) an English lesson that requires both reading aloud and writing, 2) the special education teacher will conduct a one-to-one pull-out reading and writing

session during which Anna will tell what she has read and then describe her thinking process as she tackles comprehension questions about the passage, and 3) the classroom teacher will have all students in the class complete a self-assessment of reading and writing skills. The team commits to completing these steps before their next meeting.

⏱ ACTIVITY: *Which steps of the collaborative consultation process has Anna's team completed so far? What did the speech-language pathologist do as the consultant that was different from what the two teachers did as consultees?*

CONCLUSION

Consultation has been used to deliver special education and related services for several decades. Its use has increased and evolved, however, in schools that seek to be more inclusive and responsive to all students and their families. Although numerous variations of consultative roles and structures exist, inclusionary schools tend to employ a collaborative approach to consultation. Team members pool their expertise and trade consultant and consultee roles depending on the student needs being addressed. A collaborative style of problem solving and action planning is evident, even when expert consultation is required. Teams accomplish some of their work through collaborative teaming and consultation, but, as described in Chapter 6, they also teach collaboratively. All three collaborative structures are needed to create balanced inclusive experiences for students.

6

Collaborative Teaching

FOCUSING QUESTIONS

- What is collaborative teaching?
- What are characteristics of effective collaborative teaching or co-teaching teams?
- What is the purpose for co-teaching?
- What are co-teaching models?
- In what ways can co-teachers plan?
- How do the team's structures, skills, and problem-solving processes look or feel the same or different for co-teaching?

As a partnership between professional peers with different types of expertise, co-teaching can be viewed as a reasonable response to the increasing difficulty of a single professional keeping up with all the knowledge and skills necessary to meet the instructional needs of the diverse student population attending public schools and the complexity of the problems they bring. (Friend et al., 2010, p. 11)

Collaborative teaching (co-teaching) is a teaching model that teams two or more professionals (e.g., general education classroom or content area teacher, special education teacher, related services provider) with the purpose of designing and delivering ongoing instruction to a diverse group of students, some of whom have disabilities (Friend, 2008). Co-teaching enriches instruction by blending the perspectives and expertise of two unique partners. "Co-teaching partnerships between regular and special educators can combine complementary teaching competencies in core curriculum and instructional

methodology, respectively, to work toward a common goal for all students" (Beamish, Bryer, & Davies, 2006, p. 4). Individualized learning targets for students whose IEPs require them can also be addressed through co-teaching.

Co-teaching is a way to provide services to students with IEPs within general education classrooms and with typical peers. When special educators are members of co-teaching teams and co-teach on a regular basis, some or all of students' IEP content may be accomplished within the general education setting. When specialists, such as speech-language pathologists, occupational therapists, or physical therapists, function in roles of co-teachers, some or all of a student's related services goals can be met, although these specialists typically would not co-teach on a daily basis.

The instruction should be fundamentally different from what students would receive if there were only one teacher in the class in order for them to benefit from co-teaching. Indeed, administrators have a responsibility to make certain that when personnel are involved in what looks like a co-teaching arrangement, what they are doing can legitimately be described as co-teaching.

> By definition, co-teaching involves having two credentialed teachers in the same classroom rather than one teacher alone or a teacher and a paraprofessional. Thus, administrators have the right to ensure that teachers are engaged in something that is substantively different from that of more traditional approaches. Indeed, they have the responsibility to ensure that co-teachers are engaged in those collaborative activities that distinguish co-teaching from the type of traditional instruction that has not been effective in meeting student needs in the past. (Murawski & Lochner, 2011, p. 175)

RATIONALE FOR CO-TEACHING

The primary rationale for co-teaching is to help "meet the educational needs of students with diverse learning abilities" in inclusive classrooms (Friend & Cook, 2003, p. 176). Co-teaching has indeed provided more students with disabilities access to the general education curriculum and classroom (Bouck, 2007; Mastropieri et al., 2005; Murawski, 2006). For example, co-teachers who voluntarily co-taught middle school science classes noted that students with disabilities in their classes were "destined for more restrictive placements due to their low reading achievement and/or behavioral issues" (Brusca-Vega, Brown, & Yasutake, 2011, p. 29) had they not been co-teaching.

Having a specialist plan and teach alongside a generalist means better instruction of a diverse group of learners. Co-teaching makes sense logistically because it provides a platform to efficiently pair teams of professionals with different but complementary skill sets. Not only does co-teaching avoid pulling students with disabilities out of the classroom for instruction, which can be disruptive to

teaching and learning, but the pedagogies in effective co-taught classes are also responsive to the learning needs of students without disabilities. Co-teaching eliminates the stigma of being segregated in school, allows membership in general education classrooms, and helps provide opportunities for friendships and other positive relationships to develop between students with and without disabilities. There are multiple benefits for co-teachers and students when co-teaching is used, many of which would be unavailable in a solo-taught class.

Co-teaching is not a new teaching model that has been developed specifically for inclusive schools. Its appeal for meeting the needs of diverse students has been bolstered, however, by several requirements of NCLB. NCLB requires that 1) all students with disabilities have access to the general education curriculum; 2) teachers instructing students with disabilities be highly qualified in the subject matter they teach; and 3) students with disabilities be included in state assessments, with the scores disaggregated for both students completing alternate assessments and those completing the same assessments as typical students. Many special educators were teaching content (e.g., U.S. history, algebra, chemistry) for which they had little to no formal preparation prior to the NCLB's requirements for students with and without disabilities to receive instruction from teachers who are highly qualified in their subject matter (see Figure 6.1). The NCLB's establishment of the highly qualified mandate may have set the stage for some school systems to partner special educators with general educators in co-teaching arrangements merely to meet the letter of the law; other schools and school systems have authentically embraced co-teaching, especially at the high school level, as a way to enhance both teachers' skills and students' learning.

Voices from the Classroom

It is a few minutes until the bell rings, and students are clamoring in, taking their seats. One asks a question about homework, and another has a question about a lab assignment. Both get their answers right away because there are two teachers in this class—a general education chemistry teacher and a special education teacher. Several students with specific learning disabilities or other health impairments, such as attention-deficit/hyperactivity disorder, are included in the class. As the students get settled, the two teachers talk briefly about the plan for the day, which was discussed at the end of the last class. A quick decision is made that one will check homework while the other goes over questions from the homework on the board. The bell rings, and class begins with both teachers standing at the front, equal partners in teaching the lesson. Examples of their teaming follow.

- After one talks, the other interjects with an afterthought or clarification.
- When they go over some guided practice, one works up on the board getting students to actively participate while the other grades the quizzes so feedback can be given by the end of class.
- As the students work independently, both teachers circulate and answer students' questions.
- One teacher provides help to students before school, and the other assists students after the school day ends.

When class ends, the teachers quickly and briefly reflect about how the day went, particularly honing in on whether, or which, students understood the material. Their brief reflection enables the co-teachers to make decisions about the next class and which teacher will do what during the next lesson. If there is not enough time to talk, then e-mails go back and forth. Their teaming involves a continuous cycle of decision making, reflection, and feedback—bouncing ideas off each other in order to come to the best possible solution.

Although this is a first year co-teaching team, the teachers already work well together. Both had unsuccessful co-teaching experiences in the past, but that did not ruin the dream of making co-teaching work. When co-teachers are equal partners, their jobs become much easier, and all students receive the best possible education. The two teachers' complementary skills and knowledge—chemistry and special education—help ensure that all students have access to the curriculum as well as the individualized support they need. Their collaboration allows them to come up with ideas that they would not have thought of individually, such as a wacky way to teach a difficult concept or funny mnemonic devices for students to remember important details. Their personalities are slightly different as well, which allows students to "click" with one teacher better than the other.

Are these two co-teachers always successful? No. The teachers realize that ensuring all students are adequately supported yet appropriately challenged is an area in which they need to work. There are success stories, however. The co-teachers are reaching students who not only seek help and guidance but also participate and show a true interest in the class. They both truly believe that their students are successful because of the co-taught environment.

Although co-teaching makes differentiating instruction easier, it still is not an easy task. It takes a pair of teachers that are both willing to be flexible and open to suggestions. Both teachers need to give up a little bit of power to convey to the students that both teachers share authority in the classroom.

Figure 6.1. Co-teaching a high school chemistry class: The benefits of partnership. (Contributed by Julia Renberg and Michelle Dunaway.)

WHAT ARE THE CHARACTERISTICS OF EFFECTIVE CO-TEACHING?

Co-teaching is more complex than simply having two teachers teaching in a classroom at the same time. It also involves the following:

- Designing teaching roles to reflect the expertise and interests of both teachers

- Preserving regular time periods to plan together

- Expanding teacher roles and skills to enhance student outcomes

- Assessing and considering both the student and teacher outcomes of the collaborative partnership and exploring improvements

- Communicating and resolving conflicts together

- Using some process that helps teachers work together cooperatively (e.g., regular feedback and planning, peer coaching, role release)

Teaching teams clearly need to be good collaborators. They apply the skills for effective communication, problem solving, and action planning described in Chapters 3 and 4. In addition to their well-honed generic collaborative skills, effective co-teaching teams also demonstrate the following five characteristics (Beamish et al., 2006; Friend & Cook, 2007; Friend et al., 2010; Murawski & Lochner, 2011; Walther-Thomas, 1997; Zigmond & Magiera, 2001):

1. *Co-teachers are partners:* They work in tandem, sharing physical space and all major responsibilities with one another while sharing their pedagogical knowledge and skills with the students. Co-teachers co-plan, co-instruct, and co-assess. In addition, they share and pool resources, including textbooks and teachers' manuals, paper and other supplies, technologies, and paraprofessional support.

2. *Co-teachers are professional peers:* They demonstrate collegiality, seek professional growth, and have a positive outlook toward their students and the value of their efforts to include all students in the social and instructional life of their classrooms.

3. *Co-teachers use complementary skills and techniques:* They contribute content knowledge, pedagogical skills, knowledge of student growth and development, skills for teaching students how to learn and study, skills for developing students' self-control, and so forth. They achieve together what each may not have achieved alone.

4. *Co-teachers have shared goals for students with diverse learning needs and abilities:* They view providing responsive instruction for students with and without disabilities as the primary reason for co-teaching.

5. *Co-teachers evidence parity:* Each teacher has equal status. One teacher is not a helper or administrative support for the other. Both teachers are in charge, and the students are aware of this. Roles and responsibilities are evenly distributed. Symbols of professional status also are shared. For example, both teachers have desks and space for their belongings, and both names are on the classroom door, report cards, and correspondence with families. If the general educator leads instruction on a regular basis and students identify the general educator as the "real" teacher, then the special educator is not perceived as having equal authority, which diminishes his or her capacity to effectively teach all students (King-Sears, Brawand, Jenkins, & Preston-Smith, 2014; Ornelles, Cook, & Jenkins, 2007).

Operationalizing co-teaching for an effective instructional experience for students with and without disabilities is complicated and challenging. Not surprising, co-teaching can be inconsistently and poorly implemented (Murawski, 2006; Solis, Vaughn, Swanson, & McCulley, 2012). Table 6.1 contrasts characteristics of effective and ineffective co-teaching. Co-teachers need to figure out their roles and build their relationships. Due to changes in roles, along with concerns about skills for co-teaching, co-teachers may experience tensions as they determine what compromises they need to make and how instruction should occur. On the contrary, role changes can be good opportunities to learn from each other. Co-teaching means giving up autonomy in one sense, which can be difficult for some teachers (Bouck, 2007). If one teacher remains autonomous, however, then the other is not experiencing parity or partnership.

There can be an undesirable impact on student outcomes when the characteristics of effective co-teaching are missing or compromised (Murawski, 2006). High-quality instruction also affects student learning, whether in co-taught or other types of settings. Murawski also noted that if co-teachers are using primarily whole-group instruction, then the benefit of having another teacher

present is not realized. Although varying instructional approaches should be evident in co-taught settings, the expertise of one co-teacher is insufficiently used when the other co-teacher's pedagogical style or preference is prioritized and used as the major way to deliver instruction. "When this occurs, teachers are forced to accept one way of teaching as better or more important, rather than accepting both as meaningful instructional practices that could be incorporated to provide students with a more comprehensive instructional program" (Kim, Woodruff, Klein, & Vaughn, 2006, p. 284).

 ## Co-teacher Snapshot

Mr. Salter, a science teacher, and Mr. Ortiz, a special educator, are co-teaching eighth-grade earth science. This is their first time teaching together, although they have each previously co-taught. Five students with IEPs are in the class—three students have learning disabilities, one student has multiple disabilities, and another student has a cognitive disability. The principal arranged to provide the two teachers with a stipend to begin planning for 2 days in the summer.

First, they briefly discussed how they had worked with other co-teachers, then shared their own perspectives and philosophies on teaching. Second, they identified the roles and responsibilities each teacher would fill

Table 6.1. Characteristics of effective and ineffective co-taught classes

What you should see in effective co-taught classes	What you might see in ineffective co-taught classes
Each teacher is actively involved in designing and delivering instruction.	General educators take the lead for most instruction because it is their classroom and they are licensed in the subject area.
Co-planning is scheduled and occurs regularly.	There is no need for co-planning. The general educator teaches the same as usual. The special educator assists students with disabilities when they need it.
The teachers are perceived as equals; parity is evident.	It really does not matter that one teacher is perceived as the main teacher and the other teacher is seen as the support.
The teachers blend and share instructional methods and ways to modify the curriculum and flexibly group students.	One teacher's instruction predominates. Whole-group instruction mostly occurs.
The focus is on "our" students.	The focus is on "my students" and "your students."

in science class. Third, they discussed each student with an IEP. Mr. Ortiz gave Mr. Salter a copy of the Program-at-a-Glance for each student in the class with an IEP and reviewed the students' goals, accommodations, modifications, and learning strengths.

Fourth, Mr. Ortiz described how he typically structures units of instruction for earth science and the sorts of presentation and practice activities he uses most often. As he described how he usually taught the content, Mr. Salter interjected some questions: Would it be okay to use videos? Were there concrete materials or posters to illustrate the concepts? Which vocabulary did he feel was harder for students to learn? They ended this part of the discussion by talking about how Mr. Ortiz typically assessed students' performance. Mr. Salter pointed out which of the students with IEPs would need accommodations and modifications for assessments.

Given the students' characteristics, it became clearer which aspects of Mr. Ortiz's typical instruction would need to be altered and how accommodations and modifications could be woven into the lessons. Finally, the two teachers began generating ideas for ways they might actually teach as a team: "When you are telling about abstract concepts, I can provide visuals." "When we are doing lab activities, I can demonstrate the steps while you give the explanations." Perhaps most important was what they decided for the student with a cognitive disability: Mr. Ortiz would start off the school year actively engaged with the student, sending the message to the class that she belonged with them. This also gave Mr. Salter more lead responsibilities initially, again setting the tone for a united team.

⟳　ACTIVITY: *What characteristics of an effective co-teaching team do Mr. Salter and Mr. Ortiz demonstrate during their planning session? What key points did they cover? What key points are left to discuss?*

RESEARCH ON CO-TEACHING

The benefits and effects of collaborative teaching have been examined by a number of researchers (e.g., Austin, 2001; Hang & Rabren, 2009; Murawski & Swanson, 2001; Ornelles et al., 2007; Pugach

& Wesson, 1995; Rea, McLaughlin, & Walther-Thomas, 2002; Scruggs et al., 2007; Solis et al., 2012; Walther-Thomas, 1997). Most co-teaching research focuses on co-teachers' roles and relationships and the methods the teachers used to respond to diverse student needs, although more research examining the effect of co-teaching on students' achievement is emerging (Friend et al., 2010; Solis et al., 2012). What follows are brief summaries of research on the effects and benefits of teaching collaboratively for teachers and for students' academic and social outcomes.

Benefits and Challenges of Co-teaching for Teachers

Research reveals consistent patterns in the benefits and challenges of co-teaching for teachers. Co-teachers reported professional benefits, including mutual support; shared responsibilities; and, most important, opportunities to increase their repertoire of pedagogies, their content knowledge, and their classroom management skills (Austin, 2001; Hang & Rabren, 2009; Ornelles et al., 2007; Scruggs et al., 2007). Having higher expectations for students with disabilities was another important effect of co-teaching for general educators. For instance, the middle school general education co-teachers studied by Ornelles and colleagues "were surprised to find that many students with learning disabilities put forth a great deal of effort and were succeeding" (p. 148).

Co-teachers also reported that some challenges exist, many of which mirror the challenges of collaborative teams—having adequate planning time and administrative support; helping teachers get accustomed to working together; and providing appropriate training, mentoring, and sustained support (Austin, 2001; Friend et al., 2010; Scruggs et al., 2007). Another concern was that the co-teaching model used most often is one-teach, one-assist, with the special educator most often being in the subordinate role (Davis, Dieker, Pearl, & Kirkpatrick, 2012; Moin, Magiera, & Zigmond, 2009; Pugach & Wesson, 1995; Scruggs et al., 2007; Zigmond & Matta, 2004). Harbort and colleagues (2007) found that special educators presented material less than 1% of the time, even though they should have an active role for instruction. There clearly is a need for both co-teachers to find more equitable balances for instruction. For example, King-Sears and her colleagues (2014) found a high school science co-teacher led whole-group instruction 66% of the time when new content was presented, with the special education co-teacher leading the remaining time. Some co-teachers expressed support for co-teaching, however, in spite of the challenges encountered and perceived that its benefits for themselves and their students outweigh its challenges (Austin, 2001; Brusca-Vega et al., 2011; Hang & Rabren, 2009; Walther-Thomas, 1997).

Benefits and Effects of Co-teaching for Students

Because co-teaching has many variations and researchers have examined a range of approaches, it is difficult to draw simple conclusions about its effectiveness for students. Teachers and students in co-taught classes reported perceptions of gains in academic achievement and social competence, but few investigations have utilized objective pre- and postassessments of co-taught students that are compared with control groups or students taught using contrasting teaching approaches.

Murawski and Swanson conducted a meta-analysis of six quantitative research studies and concluded that "co-teaching is a moderately effective procedure for influencing student outcomes" (2001, p. 264), with good effect sizes for reading and language arts and moderate effect sizes for math. The authors urged cautious interpretation given the small amount of data.

Although the data they analyzed addressed both primary grades and high school and scores for reading and math, the data were not adequate to judge whether certain approaches had better outcomes for different ages, grades, disabilities, or curriculum areas.

Tremblay (2013) found mixed results when comparing achievement in reading, writing, and mathematics for elementary students with learning disabilities in co-taught versus solo-taught classes. Students in the co-taught class achieved significantly higher scores in reading and writing, but not in math. The achievement gap between students with learning disabilities and their same-age peers in the co-taught classes either reduced or stabilized by the second year of the study. In contrast, the achievement gap for students with learning disabilities in solo-taught classes compared with their typical peers "significantly and systematically increased" (p. 256). Researchers in another statewide study found elementary and middle school students with disabilities in co-taught classes narrowed their grade point average gap with their peers without disabilities (Pearl, Dieker, & Kirkpatrick, 2012).

Murawski (2006) conversely found no significant differences in achievement for students with learning disabilities who received instruction in co-taught classes, resource classes, or solo-taught general education classes. Observations of the co-taught classes, however, revealed that the co-teachers seemed to be inadequately prepared for co-teaching. It is possible that teachers' variable implementation of co-teaching accounts for the lack of statistical or empirical evidence that co-teaching consistently yields superior gains in student achievement over other service delivery models. Descriptions of what is happening in co-taught classes must be provided to ascertain whether effective co-teaching is occurring.

Social benefits for students that have been reported by teachers and/or by students themselves include increased cooperation among diverse students as well as increases in self-confidence, peer acceptance, friendship quality, self-concept, and social skills for students with disabilities (Hang & Rabren, 2009; Ornelles et al., 2007; Scruggs et al., 2007). Some of the co-teaching research focused on descriptive case studies of co-taught classrooms that can be valuable to teachers as sources of information about promising co-teaching practices and as examples of the transformative experiences that co-teaching can generate for teachers (e.g., Brusca-Vega et al., 2011; Case-Smith, Holland, Lane, & White, 2012; Dymond et al., 2006; King-Sears et al., 2014; Ornelles et al., 2007; Silverman, 2011; Walther-Thomas, 1997).

More research clearly is needed to examine how co-teachers can effectively ensure that all students benefit academically and socially. But co-teaching as a service delivery model is one option for students with disabilities to receive their special education services in the LRE alongside typical peers. Further research is needed, however, to establish how co-teachers can maximize benefits for students with and without disabilities. At the very least, research "clarifying minimal criteria that predict quality (that is, effectiveness) in such partnerships" (Friend et al., 2010, p. 19) as well as learning outcomes for students with and without disabilities is needed (King-Sears et al., 2014; Murawski, 2006).

 ### Co-teacher Snapshot

Mrs. Ho, the fourth-grade teacher, and Mr. Valdez, the special educator, are pleased so far with their co-teaching relationship. The students with and without disabilities are interacting well and appear to be benefiting from the variety of co-teaching arrangements and the multimodal, activity-based lessons the co-teachers are using. The co-teachers realize, however, that they need to be sure that their students are not only engaged but

also learning well. Mr. Valdez shares an article that he recently read about co-teachers and assessment with Mrs. Ho at their weekly planning session. Conderman and Hedin (2012) emphasized purposeful co-assessment, which occurs at four points:

1. Co-teaching teams that are forming discuss assessment philosophies and preferred practices. They determine grading requirements, particularly for students who need alternative grading criteria, and distinguish ongoing, or formative, assessment of learning from summative assessment, which determines grades.

2. Co-teachers conduct pretests (using predeveloped assessments if possible, constructing their own curriculum-based assessments if necessary) before lessons or units of study begin to determine what students already know about the unit content. They use a matrix to organize which students know what, a technique that can guide instructional groupings.

3. Co-teachers identify ways to conduct formative assessments of students' learning during instruction. For example, they might use *admit slips* (e.g., warm-ups at the beginning of class) to quickly determine students' recall of previously taught material. They might similarly use *exit slips* at the end of class. Admit and exit slips can be used to guide the groupings used for station teaching, parallel instruction, or alternative teaching (descriptions of these three models for co-teaching follow). Teachers can gauge individual students' understanding of content by providing all students with dry-erase boards, response cards, or clicker systems (if available), which allow each student to respond to each question posed to the class.

4. Teachers use admit and exit slips after instruction to determine retention of previously taught content. Teachers also can engage students in error analysis and goal setting so they acquire self-analysis behaviors. Rubrics, rating scales, projects, and quizzes are used

to determine students' grades, keeping any individualized accommodations and modifications in mind.

Mrs. Ho and Mr. Valdez are encouraged that several techniques they already use are described by the authors, and they acquire ideas for other assessments. They prioritize the new ones they will focus on first for their next unit of instruction.

⏱ ACTIVITY: *Have you brought professional journal articles or books to your colleagues' attention? Have you read about evidence-based or promising practices that you later incorporated into your teaching? What factors inhibit and facilitate teachers' use of research findings in their practice?*

CO-TEACHING MODELS

Teachers need to decide what kinds of organizational structures or co-teaching models they will use when they embark on a co-teaching relationship. Five of the co-teaching models found throughout the literature (Friend, 2008; Friend et al., 2010; Thousand, Villa, & Nevin, 2006) are featured in this chapter. (Figure 6.2 provides diagrams of classroom arrangements that suit the five co-teaching models. The teachers are labeled *A* and *B*.) Each of the models subsumes characteristics of other co-teaching models, illustrating the flexibility with which the model can be operationalized by co-teachers.

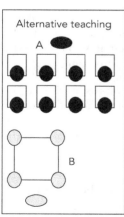
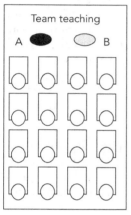
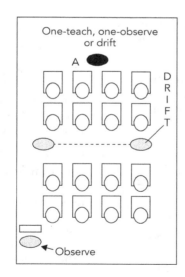
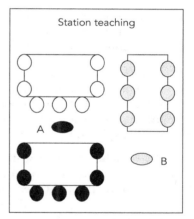
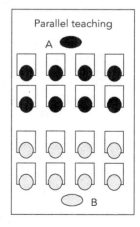

Figure 6.2. Five co-teaching models, showing Teacher A and Teacher B. (From *FRIEND, MARILYN; BURSUCK, WILLIAM D., INCLUDING STUDENTS WITH SPECIAL NEEDS: A PRACTICAL GUIDE FOR CLASSROOM TEACHERS, 5th Edition, © 2009. Adapted by permission of Pearson Education, Inc., Upper Saddle River, NJ.*)

Team Teaching

Team teaching involves two or more professionals (e.g., general educator, special educator, speech-language therapist, occupational therapist) who are actively sharing the instructional responsibilities, usually during whole-group instruction, in ways that are so seamless that it can be impossible for an observer to distinguish which teacher has which role. Friend and colleagues (2010) sometimes called this approach *teaming* to distinguish it from the team teaching that occurred in the 1990s, when team teaching referred to two general educators who taught two classes of students together. The term *team teaching* in this text is one general educator and either a special educator or a specialist teaching together. There are many ways each co-teacher can be active when teaching the whole class as a team.

- One teacher explains while the other teacher shows (e.g., through a demonstration, by showing a model, by writing terms on a whiteboard) what is being explained.

- One teacher presents while the other co-teacher models how to take notes; some students might use regular paper for notes, whereas other students might use guided note pages (student choice).

- Both teachers demonstrate, taking turns during the demonstration.

Parity has been achieved between the co-teachers when students respond to both teachers as their real teachers. The challenge of team teaching is that students must truly be shared by teachers who have developed mutual trust and respect. Co-teachers sometimes begin a lesson using team teaching to gain students' attention, generate motivation, and present new content and then use one of the other co-teaching models for the practice portion of the lesson.

One-Teach, One-Assist and One-Teach, One-Observe

One-teach, one-assist and one-teach, one-observe are sometimes referred to as two different co-teaching approaches, but they are referred to as one model in this text because the roles of "assist" and "observe" can be interchangeable (i.e., the co-teacher needs to observe to know when to assist). While one teacher leads the lesson, usually during whole-group instruction, the other teacher assists individual students or small groups of students who need help. The teacher who is assisting can stand to the side and watch for visual or verbal cues from students needing assistance. Or, the teacher who is assisting can "drift" or circulate among the students, while staying clear of students' sight line for the teacher leading instruction. Circulating among the students can also provide proximity control for students who benefit from this nonintrusive classroom management strategy. This co-teaching model can be used to students' advantage in several ways:

- One teacher teaches organizational skills to the whole class, and the other teacher observes who is having problems getting organized and assists those students.

- One teacher leads a class discussion about an assigned reading while the other teacher circulates to ensure students are on the right page.

- One teacher explains and demonstrates a math computation while the other teacher monitors students to ensure they are correctly copying the steps.

Likewise, when one teacher is leading whole-group instruction, the other teacher may be observing the entire class and gathering academic or social-behavioral data, whether for specific students or the whole class. Or, one teacher may be observing for specific antecedent cues that predict when one or more students' behaviors will go in a downward spiral so that the teacher can intervene (i.e., assist) as a preventative measure.

The one-teach, one-assist model has a significant potential drawback. If the same co-teacher, usually the special educator, functions in an assistive capacity most of the time, and if the students with disabilities are the primary recipients of assistance, then it can appear that the special educator "belongs" to the students with disabilities (and vice versa) and is there to assist only them and not all students. In turn, the general educator can essentially continue business as usual, making few changes to typical instruction and acquiring minimal ownership of the students with disabilities. Furthermore, students with disabilities can actually receive too much assistance and become dependent on it, rather than learning to be independent and self-directed. This model sometimes is used by default when co-teachers do not have co-planning time and the special educator must enter the classroom and "wing it" each class session.

Walther-Thomas, Korinek, McLaughlin, and Williams (2000) described *interactive teaching*—a co-teaching model designed to ensure parity in the roles filled by general and special educators. As a hybrid of the team-teaching model and the one-teach, one-assist model, interactive teaching alternates the instructional lead between the two teachers. The teachers trade lead and assist roles and maintain dialogue to assist and clarify one another's efforts throughout the lesson. For example, as one teacher leads, the other might ask clarifying questions, much like those a student might ask (e.g., "Mr. Valdez, I understand what the *mode* is, but I am still confused about the difference between *mean* and *median*. Would you please explain them again?"). The teacher who is assisting might demonstrate a math problem, how to take notes, or how to put on an art smock, just as would be done in team teaching. That teacher would assist for one aspect of the lesson but then switch to the lead teacher role.

Co-teachers should not rely on the one-teach, one-assist model as a frequently used co-teaching model. Co-teaching is meant to take advantage of having two professionals with complementary expertise in the same classroom. Teachers should have equal roles. One teacher should not fill a role that could be done by a paraprofessional.

Station Teaching

Station teaching is essentially the same as using learning centers in the classroom (King-Sears, 2005, 2007). Small groups of students can rotate through several centers where they work independently as a cooperative group or under the direction of a teacher or helper (e.g., peer tutor, volunteer, paraprofessional). When using station teaching, students still might rotate in and out of stations where they work independently or with a helper, and they can also participate in instruction simultaneously taught by the co-teachers. Each co-teacher typically instructs a small group of students while another group of students is independently completing activities at a station. Students at stations may be working on the same skill but at different skill levels, or the instructional focus could be on the same skill level but with smaller groups of students, different materials, or at a different pace.

Although small-group instruction with each co-teacher can be considered a station, the aspect that distinguishes station teaching from alternative or parallel teaching is that there are one or more separate stations or centers where the students work independently (or with a helper) and proficiently. That is, students who cannot work on their own and with a high degree of accuracy may be interrupting teachers (e.g., when seeking clarification on directions) or practicing errors (e.g., if the task is too difficult for independent proficiency).

Students working at the independent or helper-mediated stations may or may not switch stations with the students working with each co-teacher during a given class session. Some co-teachers use the same set of stations for more than one day, so a group of students might work at an independent or helper-mediated station one day and receive small-group teacher-directed instruction the following day.

Students assigned to the independent or helper-mediated stations must have projects, tasks, or activities that they can complete proficiently and independently (or with the helper's guidance) in order for station teaching to work. Those students may otherwise disrupt the small-group instruction occurring with each of the co-teachers. Stations offer excellent opportunities for students to have differentiated activities. Some teachers use computers as stations, being careful to use software or web sites that help students achieve specific learning outcomes, not simply to play games. Computer stations also can be used for students to work on writing assignments, using hardware and software that is individualized and adapted as necessary for individual students or groups of students.

When co-teachers plan for and manage learning stations, they need to consider not only the content and activities provided at each station but also logistical and structural elements. Students may need to practice making transitions if they are moving from one station to another. The stations should be arranged to minimize noisy distractions and unnecessary movements. Using study carrels as stations is also helpful, particularly for students working independently so they are not disrupted or distracted by peers. Designating stations in the media center may also be an option for smaller classrooms or settings with less technology.

When using independent or helper-directed stations, do the following:

- Arrange independent activities for students to complete at the station.

- Provide self-correcting materials so students can complete their work and then determine their performance.

- Individualize so that students who need accommodations and modifications have them.

- Differentiate so that all students are involved in the same station activity (e.g., writing, reading, doing math) on a level that is sufficiently challenging.

 ## Co-teacher Snapshot

Ms. Lee, a first-grade teacher, and Mrs. Ryan, a special education teacher, planned to use team teaching for their next lesson on "fewer, more, and equal." They had done a quick assessment the previous day to check students' understanding of the terms. Each student was given "yes" and "no" response cards. Ms. Lee projected pictures of sets of objects onto the whiteboard (e.g., a picture of four apples and one orange) and posed questions to the class (e.g., "Are there more apples than oranges?"). Mrs. Ryan observed the students' responses and noted who had mastered the concepts, who was gaining proficiency but was still inconsistent, and who was still acquiring the concepts. The two teachers decided that station teaching would help them to meet their students' needs better than team teaching and quickly made plans for three stations for students who were ready for independent practice.

Mrs. Ryan conducted small-group instruction for four students who needed reteaching. She provided sets of manipulatives and cards printed with the three terms, and she used direct instruction, prompting strategies, and repeated practice to ensure that each student could correctly use the terms by the end of the session. Ms. Lee used the class assessment materials (pictures of sets of objects, oral questions, and response cards) to conduct a review session for the five students who were inconsistent in using the terms. The other 11 students in the class who had mastered the concepts of "fewer, more, and equal" worked at three "on-your-own" stations. These stations also were available for all students in the class during free, independent work time.

(↻) ACTIVITY: *Station teaching can also be designated by students' interests versus their mastery of concepts. What are other ways teachers can determine who does what in a station teaching model?*

Alternative Teaching

Alternative teaching features one teacher working with a larger group of students and the other teacher working with a smaller group of students. It is important that the same students are not always in the smaller group with the same co-teacher; flexible grouping practices are used, and the general educator directly teaches students with disabilities (i.e., it is not only the special educator who teaches students with disabilities).

In addition, alternative teaching is one way the special educator can work with a small group of students with IEPs who need specialized reading instruction. The special educator may be working with the larger group of students other times and teaching mnemonic strategies for vocabulary terms and definitions (an evidence-based technique) or focusing on how to use textbook features as a study guide, while the general education teacher works with a small group of students who need a booster session before taking their math test the next day. Co-teachers co-plan for alternative teaching, as their teaching must be coordinated even if it is conducted separately. The larger and smaller groups may be working on the same or different concepts or skills, but all students in the class should be working in the same subject area and the same general topic or type of skill (e.g., the large group is working on word problems involving sums of money while the smaller group is working on counting sets of bills and coins).

Three common uses of alternative teaching are 1) to reteach (or review) a lesson that has already been presented to the entire class; 2) to preteach an aspect of an upcoming lesson, such as vocabulary; and 3) to extend (or enrich) a previously taught lesson. For example, while one teacher is reteaching a lesson on the phases of the moon to a small group, the other teacher reviews for tomorrow's unit test with the rest of the class. Or, while one teacher extends the poetry unit by teaching a form of poetry not required by the learning standards, the other preteaches vocabulary for the upcoming novel unit. Either teacher can provide reteaching, previewing, or enrichment activities. Alternative teaching is best characterized by the different sizes of the groups the teachers work with (one large, one small), but, once again, it is important that group membership and teacher assignments are dynamic, not static.

Parallel Teaching

Parallel teaching is similar to alternative teaching except the two student groups are approximately the same size. Again, each teacher leads one group, but both teachers may be teaching the same lesson. Co-planning determines who is grouped with whom and how the lesson and corresponding content are designed. Co-teachers intentionally set up opportunities for the general educator to work with students with disabilities so that flexible grouping occurs.

Group membership can be based on the exit slips completed by students. Students who demonstrated proficiency are in a group, and students who need more practice are in a group. Or, groupings might be determined by the results of a quiz or performance on an in-class independent practice activity. The two teachers may be conducting virtually identical lessons at times, and the primary purpose of dividing students into two groups is to give each student more opportunities for active responding and each teacher a better opportunity to monitor those responses. The lesson taught in both groups might address the same curricular content in some instances, but the students are provided different supports or accommodations for their learning (e.g., one group uses manipulatives to solve math problems, the other does not).

An obvious advantage of parallel teaching is that it lowers the student–teacher ratio. The challenges of this co-teaching model are that noise levels can be high, and the teachers must pace their lessons to end at the same time. In addition, both teachers need to know the content being taught and the methods used to teach it.

 ## Co-teacher Snapshot

Mr. Jonas, a special educator in middle school, is certified in both special education and middle school mathematics. He co-teaches with Mrs. Gonzalez three periods per day. Students with learning disabilities, emotional disabilities, and other health impairments are enrolled in the co-taught classes. Mr. Jonas and Mrs. Gonzalez are co-planning for the upcoming unit on probability and statistics. They know from previous experience that some math concepts are more difficult for students to learn when they are taught in a large-group setting. For example, mean, median, and mode are related but distinct terms, which Mrs. Gonzalez knows can initially be hard for students (both those with and without IEPs) to distinguish. The co-teachers decide to focus on mode first, which they connect to the word *most* for a mnemonic: *Mode* is the *most frequently occurring* number within a set of numbers. In discussing how to teach mode in ways that promote active student engagement, they develop six word problems for demonstration, some having to do with modal choices of pizza toppings and similar relevant examples for students. The co-teachers decide that one teacher will present the word problem orally while the other writes the information on the whiteboard. This team teaching model works well for presenting new content because each teacher has an active role. Students will work in small groups on other mode word problems after the presentations. The co-teachers plan to use the learning station approach for small-group work. Each teacher will work with a small group while another group works independently at a station.

The co-teaching models that Mr. Jonas and Mrs. Gonzales use each day depend on the complexity of the content and on the students' needs. They experimented with all the models when they initially co-taught. Although they used team teaching and station teaching models the most, they realized they also used alternative and parallel co-teaching models when they did not have a learning station and each had different-size groups.

⏱ ACTIVITY: *Describe how you as a co-teacher, or co-teachers you have seen, determine which co-teaching model to use.*

Choosing Co-teaching Models

Although teaching teams typically will favor some models over others, all of the models should be used on a regular basis (Murawski, 2006; Thousand et al., 2006; Walther-Thomas et al., 2000) (see Figure 6.3). Using all of the models (and variations thereof) enables teachers to maximize the heterogeneous instructional opportunities available to their students and takes maximum advantage of having two teachers in the classroom. It also helps ensure parity in the two teachers' instructional responsibilities and helps prevent stereotyping of either the teachers or the students (Walther-Thomas et al., 2000). The different co-teaching models are not designed to constrict service delivery but to broaden the ways in which co-teachers conceptualize, design, and deliver pedagogy responsive to all students.

Incorporating Evidence-Based Instructional Practices with Co-teaching

Effective co-teaching involves much more than deciding which co-teaching model

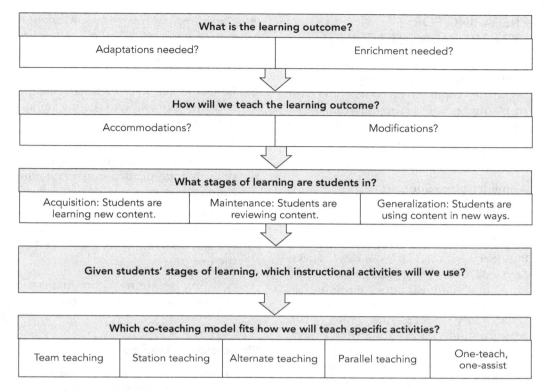

Figure 6.3. Decision making for co-teaching models.

to use. Co-teachers also need to consider all the aspects of evidence-based instructional design, delivery, and evaluation that they face when teaching alone. They must jointly determine what to teach and how to teach it so that all students learn what they need to learn. This entails targeting curriculum content, designing lesson routines, choosing (or adapting or creating) differentiated instructional materials, and selecting teaching methods. All of this is done in ways that incorporate any accommodations and modifications their students require.

Although co-teaching would seem to increase teachers' opportunities to incorporate evidence-based practices (because two heads are better than one and the student–teacher ratio is reduced), Scruggs and his colleagues (2007) found that instructional practices associated with improved student outcomes were rarely observed in the co-taught settings they

studied, which indicated that co-teachers were underutilizing opportunities to maximize students' success. The following are among the instructional practices they hoped to see co-teachers use more frequently:

- Effective instruction principles (e.g., explicit instruction using multiple modalities)

- Differentiated instruction

- Appropriate curriculum, including curriculum adjustments

- Mnemonic instruction

- Flexible grouping

- Reciprocal peer tutoring and classwide peer tutoring

- Cooperative learning

- Learning strategy instruction

PREPARING FOR COLLABORATIVE TEACHING

Preparing a school for co-teaching requires administrative support, professional development of co-teaching and co-planning skills, creating compatible co-teaching teams, appropriate scheduling for students and co-teachers, and collaborative planning.

Administrative Support

Administrative support is critical for initial preparation, ongoing implementation, and supervision of co-teaching (Friend et al., 2010; Scruggs et al., 2007; Van Hover, Hicks, & Sayeski, 2012). Friend and her colleagues noted that administrators are responsible for "situating co-teaching in a supportive, collaborative school culture" (2010, p. 10). Adequate time, cooperation from others, and workload have been listed as three primary obstacles to co-teaching (Bauwens, Hourcade, & Friend, 1989). Administrators need to be involved in creating ways to overcome these obstacles, such as the following (Thousand et al., 2006; Walther-Thomas, Bryant, & Land, 1996):

- Discussing the rationale for and characteristics of co-teaching with the whole school

- Identifying potential participants

- Assisting school personnel to understand the role changes required for co-teaching and assisting teaching partners to define their roles and responsibilities

- Addressing logistical factors (e.g., realistic class sizes, pragmatic special educator caseloads and distribution, options for mutual planning time, teaching resources)

- Creating classroom rosters that reflect heterogeneous groups, hand-scheduling students with special needs into classes, and not grouping students by test scores alone (Dawson, 1987)

- Providing parents with information regarding the planned changes, obtaining parent input, and addressing parent concerns

- Educating teachers about co-teaching and the approaches; creating opportunities to attend conferences and/or observe veteran co-teaching teams

- Ensuring that students' IEPs reflect skills that are needed in general education classrooms

- Exploring the use of one or several classrooms to pilot the approach chosen and make improvements based on the outcomes

- Assisting teachers to evaluate the effectiveness of their co-planning and co-teaching

Professional Development

Many teachers are still unprepared for co-teaching, even with the emergence of preservice preparation on co-teaching in special education (Pancsofar & Petroff, 2013). Many co-teachers in the current teaching force rely on attending conferences and professional development workshops provided by their school systems and reading professional journals and books to inform them about co-teaching (Friend et al., 2010). Some co-teachers learn how to co-teach by trial and error, which is seldom an efficient or reliable way to learn. Co-teachers who had more frequent opportunities to learn about co-teaching through professional development expressed more confidence in their practice, higher levels of interest in co-teaching, and more positive attitudes about co-teaching than teachers who received less professional development (Pancsofar & Petroff, 2013). Pancsofar and Petroff found that providing professional development also affected the willingness of general and special educators to volunteer to co-teach. Adequate professional development prior to co-teaching can minimize challenges and provide co-teachers a stronger foundation from which to design and deliver instruction to heterogeneous groups of students.

Identifying Co-teaching Teams

Many professional educators maintain that co-teaching should be voluntary (Friend, 2008; Scruggs et al., 2007). Why? Because teaching is hard, change is hard, and changing the way you teach is really hard. Teachers who display high levels of effort, flexibility, and compromise, as well as those who seek new opportunities for professional growth, are likely to volunteer. Enthusiasm can spread when teachers who volunteer demonstrate the benefits of co-teaching to their colleagues. Furthermore, building administrators who buy into co-teaching and initiate it in the school need to communicate co-teaching as a standard practice in which all teachers may be asked to participate. After all, even teachers who volunteer are not always able to self-select their teaching partners. Administrators must consider competency in content and assign teams based on subjects in which the general and/or special educator is highly qualified, particularly at the secondary level (Kamens, Susko, & Elliott, 2013). Student needs, course content, and school resources are usually the basis for arranging co-teaching teams.

In addition, compatibility is important for a healthy co-teaching relationship (see Figure 6.4). Compatibility does not mean that both teachers have identical skills, philosophies, personalities, teaching styles, and training (Friend et al., 2010; Kamens et al., 2013). Arbitrary pairing of teachers, however, may result in too many incompatibilities for the co-teaching to be successful. For example, Trent (1998) observed that incompatible teachers in a high school had differences in teaching styles, communication patterns, organization and operational methods, the amount of planning and preparation, and reliability or follow-through.

Teachers need to take several preparatory steps when they have an interest in learning about and applying a co-teaching approach and extending or supplementing pull-in services with co-teaching. Teachers should know themselves, their partners, their students, and their talents before they start a co-teaching partnership (Gately & Gately, 2001; Keefe, Moore, & Duff, 2004; Murawski & Dieker, 2004; Trent, 1998). The following are among the topics to be discussed, and sometimes resolved, prior to co-teaching (Friend, 2008; Solis et al., 2012; Walther-Thomas et al., 2000):

- Goals, expectations, and roles
- Classroom rules and consequences
- Classroom management techniques
- Tolerance for noise levels
- Teaching methods (for initial instruction, practice activities, and review)
- Types of tests, quizzes, and assignments; evaluation methods and modifications
- Planning processes and time lines
- Expectations for student participation during various parts of a lesson
- Classroom management and organizational routines (e.g., restroom use, homework procedures and policies, free time)
- Requirements for neatness and orderliness (for students and teachers)

Perfect agreement on all of these classroom practices and policies is not necessarily required. Co-teachers can and will disagree and still be effective co-teaching teams. It is important that 1) expectations be made explicit before the two teachers commit to co-teaching, and 2) differences that emerge after a commitment is made be

Voices from the Classroom

Relationships are growing, breathing partnerships. Most people can remember a time when they first entered the home of a new friend or acquaintance. The newness and uncertainty of the visit brought out their most polite and proper manners. Sometimes, over time, these new relationships grow and develop into friendships. We no longer hesitate to sit back, relax, and share our truest feelings, emotions, and opinions. Co-teaching is a perfect example of one of these relationships.

A classroom is a teacher's second home. Each teacher has unique strategies, philosophies, opinions, and individual ways of getting the job done. When two teachers are partnered in a co-taught classroom, these variables, combined with differences in personality, can make for a stressful start. Co-teachers need to navigate curriculum and classroom structure in a way that makes sense for them as a team much the way newly married couples need to leave behind "my way" and "your way" to make room for "our way."

After working together in a co-taught fourth-grade classroom for the last 8 years, we have long moved past the newness and uncertainty. Our relationship has grown both personally and professionally. We have a true understanding of each other's strengths and can plan to utilize them to teach the core curriculum and address individualized education program (IEP) goals in the most effective and efficient manner. Over time, we have developed a rhythm in the classroom that now seems natural. We can finish each other's sentences during the course of a lesson and "pass the baton" midlesson without skipping a beat. We are able to bring humor, fun, and enjoyment into our lessons. Each year, we take what we have done in the past and put our heads together to make it better.

The mutual respect and trust we have in each other's ability as professionals enables us to be flexible in how we deliver instruction to our students. We are comfortable enough with one another to utilize many different methods of co-teaching. We look at the core curriculum and discuss the individual needs of our students when we are deciding how to proceed in each subject area. We may use several different co-teaching models in any given day based on our discussions, anecdotal notes, student IEPs, and relationships with individual students. When introducing topics, we often utilize whole-group instruction, in which one of us teaches and the other assists. We sometimes parallel teach because we are fortunate enough to have two classrooms in which to work. This allows us to reduce distractions, reduce the student–teacher ratio, and deliver alternate forms of instruction to different groups when necessary.

With the exception of reading, we use flexible instructional groupings in most subject areas, which allows us to more easily differentiate instruction. We take time to recognize each student's comfort level with us as teachers, with the curriculum, and within cooperative partnerships. We discuss daily which students need additional reinforcement or revisiting of content, which students are able to move forward, and which students would benefit from more challenging higher level work. Though our co-teaching partnership was developed for the purpose of including students with disabilities in the general education setting, the use of flexible groupings truly makes it beneficial for students of all abilities.

Co-teaching is a partnership. Resources, responsibility, and accountability are shared. An effective partnership requires mutual respect, trust, and flexibility. Having the right partner and developing together as a team over time makes all the difference.

Figure 6.4.   Co-teachers' relationship evolves. (Contributed by Leighann Alt and Phil Yovino.)

handled using effective interpersonal and conflict-resolution skills (see Chapter 3). "Effective co-teaching depends, in part, on each teacher's interpersonal skills, willingness and ability to work collaboratively, and skills in successfully handling conflict" (Conderman, 2011, p. 222). Establishing ground rules for communication and discussing what it means to respect each other within a co-teaching situation is important (Van Hover et al., 2012). Co-teachers need to intentionally remind themselves to practice effective interpersonal skills so that clearer communication occurs (e.g., "We will ask for clarification when uncertain what the other means").

Potential co-teachers also should discuss how they will deal with the inevitable disagreements that arise. Will they use a particular problem-solving format; ask for assistance from an administrator, department chair, or lead teacher; or request additional professional development (Potts & Howard, 2011)? Unresolved conflict can result in unhappiness and even resentment; issues must be brought out and discussed, as uncomfortable as that may feel.

Finally, co-teachers need to have time to provide feedback to each other, reflect on the process, and decide what refinements they would like to target as part of their evaluation plan (Pearl et al., 2012; Thousand et al., 2006).

Scheduling of Specialists for Co-teaching

When special education teachers provide pull-in services and co-teach, they usually rotate among classrooms, rather than work with only one classroom. Some researchers and educators recommend concentrating students with disabilities in a smaller number of classes, thereby reducing the number of classrooms in which the special education teachers must co-teach. Although this approach may make the special education teacher's job logistically easier and more efficient, students with special needs should be assigned to classrooms with their peers without disabilities in proportions similar to their natural proportions in a neighborhood school.

Student Snapshot

Because 11% of students at Jonah's middle school have identified special needs, approximately 2 or 3 students in each class of 25 will have identified special needs; however, the proportion may be less in advanced courses. There are five students with IEPs in Mr. Adrian's basic science class, whereas there are two students with IEPs in his advanced science.

⟳ ACTIVITY: *Calculate the percentage of students with IEPs in co-taught classes at your school. What are some ways that schools with disproportionate placement of students with IEPs in co-taught classes can move toward more natural proportions?*

Scheduling classes so that students are enrolled in the courses they need while maintaining heterogeneous classroom groups can be particularly challenging in high schools. The school administrator must closely work with guidance counselors and special and general educators at each grade level to assess teachers' talent for and interest in co-teaching and to provide necessary training and support. Some administrators schedule students with disabilities into co-taught classes and their co-teachers' planning time first to increase the probability of shared planning time for co-teachers (Pearl et al., 2012). In addition, administrators who are supportive of co-teaching find ways to limit the teaming of general education teachers with whom the special educators co-teach or otherwise collaborate. For example, a special educator might serve students at a single grade level (e.g., one or more 10th-grade teams) or a high school department (e.g., mathematics, English).

The schedules of special education teachers and other support staff should reflect the needs of the students on their caseload, which can vary from intensive (e.g., one-to-one teaching for a period) to limited (e.g., monitoring during study hall). The following Co-teacher Snapshot illustrates the variety of teaching and support roles that high school special educators may need to fill.

Co-teacher Snapshot

Ms. Lopez, a high school special education teacher, begins her day with a planning period. She provides pull-in services during second period to Jonah, a student with Asperger syndrome, in Algebra 1 while monitoring two other students in the class who have learning disabilities. She goes to the academic lab during third period and checks on four students who often require assistance with studying or may need to complete tests for other classes. Ms. Lopez provides pull-in support during fourth period in a tenth-grade English class, which includes Melissa, who has a cognitive disability, and two students with learning disabilities. She co-teaches in English 9 during fifth and six periods. Therefore, Ms. Lopez's day consists of providing pull-in support during general education classes and academic lab and co-teaching for two of the six periods. Because she studied English literature (along with special education) in college, she was the logical person to support students in those classes and team with the English department. Ms. Lopez assessed classroom activities early in the year and then discussed needed accommodations and modifications with each teacher. Ms. Lopez touches base with the teachers of the two classes in which she provides pull-in support before school on Monday and after school on Thursday; she has access to both teachers' plans and all of the materials they share with students via the school's BlackBoard site for each class. Ms. Lopez co-plans with her English 9 co-teacher each Wednesday during their shared first period planning period.

(ᵗ) ACTIVITY: *What factors determine how Ms. Lopez spends her time? What factors might create changes in her schedule from one semester to the next or even midsemester?*

Collaborative Planning

Collaborative planning is essential to effective co-teaching, even though numerous obstacles can stand in its way (Bouck, 2007; Davis et al., 2012). Many teachers are used to planning alone, often at home; some have developed poor planning habits and either do not have written plans or do their planning on the fly. Naturally, co-teachers prefer co-planning time during school hours (Hang & Rabren, 2009). Therefore, collaborative planning requires teachers to change where, when, and with whom they plan. One co-teacher cannot make

last-minute plans or overnight changes to plans without informing the other co-teacher (Ornelles et al., 2007).

Co-teachers must structure their co-planning time and use it wisely (Bouck, 2007). Refer to Chapter 1 for specific techniques to acquire co-planning time. Teachers who repeatedly team have established planning routines (Solis et al., 2012; Walther-Thomas, 1997) and also have previously developed materials at their disposal, which can make their co-planning more efficient and propel them to focus more on shared responsibility (Ornelles et al., 2007). Experienced co-teachers who view themselves as effective planners 1) meet regularly, 2) prepare before the meeting, 3) use planning routines (i.e., sequences of steps and elements to consider), 4) design lessons and classroom environments that require active participation by themselves and their students, and 5) create written plans (Walther-Thomas, 1997). These experienced co-teachers think through their complementary roles for every lesson and make sure they distribute roles and responsibilities equitably (see Table 6.2).

Establishing predictable classroom routines and lesson formats is another practice common to experienced co-teaching teams (Solis et al., 2012). Having predictable organizational and management routines (e.g., ways of taking attendance, procedures for collecting and distributing assignments) makes it easier for the two teachers to rotate responsibilities. Using agreed-on teaching formats (e.g., certain games that are used for warm-up or review, learning stations that always use similar activities but with different content) helps reduce planning time and also facilitates switching roles.

For example, Van Hover and colleagues (2012) studied co-teachers in a ninth-grade world history class that included students with and without disabilities. The two teachers established structured teaching routines that made it easier to determine who did what, and they flexibly exchanged roles

Table 6.2. Distributing roles and responsibilities during a class session

Mathematics teacher	Special educator
Greets students at the door Reinforces students who bring in their homework and log it in to the homework file Reinforces students who begin the warm-up in their math notebook before the bell rings	
Circulates as students are solving the warm-up problem	Fills out attendance roster
Asks a student to explain how he or she solved the warm-up problem	Circulates to monitor which students accurately solved the warm-up problem
Provides advance organizer for the day's learning outcomes and activities	Organizes materials on the document camera or overhead projector for demonstrating fractions
Writes the abstract numbers on chart paper as each is demonstrated	Demonstrates two examples of adding mixed fractions with similar denominators by manipulating concrete objects and modeling by thinking aloud
Alerts students about why the numbers are being written and how the numbers go with what has just been demonstrated	Pauses as co-teacher alerts students
Tells students they will now be starting to write the numbers as the math teacher has been doing	
Cues students when to write Waits a few seconds before writing the correct information on the chart paper Asks students who wrote the same information to raise their hands	Continues with three more demonstrations with manipulatives Pauses as co-teacher cues and engages students at appropriate points in the demonstrations
Tells students they will now work with a partner to solve five problems by using manipulatives and writing out the numbers, which is the same process the teachers have just demonstrated	
Designates partners	Displays five problems on the SmartBoard Seeks assistance from three students to distribute manipulatives
Circulates and assists as partner teams are working on the five problems to ensure manipulatives are correctly used and number sentences are accurate Asks students to tell how they translated content from the word problem to manipulatives Asks students to explain their rationale for how they used manipulatives Asks students to describe how they translated the manipulatives to the number sentences Asks students to verbalize their solution using complete sentences Collects manipulatives at end of activity Conducts closure for activity: What was an important thing you learned from this activity? Makes the transition to demonstrations using illustrations instead of concrete objects	
Repeats demonstration sequence, except switches to the role of the special educator	Repeats demonstration sequence, except switches to the role of the general educator
Identifies homework assignment Elicits summary statements from students about what they learned today (closure activity)	
Reminds students of homework assignment	Circulates to ensure homework assignment is written in assignment book
Dismisses class when bell rings	

while conducting these routines. Some of the materials and activities routinely used by the two teachers included

- Guided notes, such as fill-in-the-blank notes to accompany slide presentations

- Graphic organizers

- Extension activities

- Charts and tables for students to synthesize information

The special educator provided note-taking cues and mnemonic strategies while the general educator led the whole-group instruction. The special educator modeled strategies for underlining and stressing critical information when he or she led a reading for the day's topic.

The success of co-teaching (Murawski, 2006) as well as the teachers' relationship (Ornelles et al., 2007) is jeopardized when teachers do not prepare for co-teaching and do not co-plan. Although useful as a supplement to focused co-planning, solely co-planning on the fly is insufficient (Solis et al., 2012). Teachers can use technology to facilitate co-planning when shared planning time is in short supply, whether communicating through e-mail or sharing a BlackBoard site.

Co-teachers' lesson plans specify who does what. Like all good lesson plans, the plan includes the learning targets, the teaching methods and strategies that will be used for each part of the lesson (e.g., advance organizer, presentation, guided practice), and provisions for any individualized adaptations needed by students in the class. In addition, the plan indicates what each of the two teachers will be doing to contribute to each part of the lesson.

Figure 6.5 shows an alternate form for planning lessons that occur over several days. There are, of course, numerous lesson planning formats available to teachers. Although having a jointly created, written plan is essential, collaborating teachers will determine the specific elements and the level of detail to include in their written plans (see Figure 6.6).

Modifying Schoolwork (Janney & Snell, 2013) explains in detail the planning of

General educator: *Harriett Golden*
Special educator: *Dean Gaines*
Class: *Basic science 7*

Date	Topic	Co-teaching approach	Specific tasks of both teachers	Materials	Evaluation of learning	Students who need follow-up
10/5	Roots and stems	Two or more groups, two teachers monitor/ teach; content varies	HG: Monitor the other groups DG: Work with one group	Celery stalks, carrots, colored water, lab notebook, short video	Completing lab report Following procedures	Raul: Have Raul paraphrase steps before beginning procedures
10/6	Photosynthesis	Two groups, two teachers teach same content	Each teacher works with one group of students	Various types of plants, library books on plants, colored transparencies	Weekly quiz Learning logs	John and Julie: Review vocabulary words one to one or with a partner Sarah: Reread library book to improve fluency Vanessa: More time on quiz in resource room
10/7	Leaves: Transpiration and water regulation	One group, one lead teacher; one teacher "teaching on purpose"	HG: Lead DG: Teach on purpose HG: Alternative information DG: Reteach	Textbook, broad-leaf plants, Vaseline, lab notebook, colors	KWL sheet Diagram of observation Lab report	Julie: Retype lab report on computer using spell-check to assist with handwriting and spelling

Figure 6.5.   Co-teaching daily lesson plans for seventh-grade basic science class. (*Key:* KWL, What we know, what we want to learn, and what we learned.) (From Vaughn, S., Schumm, J.S., & Arguelles, M.E. [1997]. The ABCDEs of co-teaching. *Teaching Exceptional Children, 30*[2], p. 6; adapted by permission of SAGE Publications.)

Voices from the Classroom

My most successful experience co-teaching came about suddenly and without warning. Our principal notified the general education math teacher and me 2 days before the start of the school year that we were going to be co-teaching an algebra and a geometry class. Did I mention we did not know each other? Did I mention we did not exactly volunteer to do this? Luckily, we were both seasoned teachers in our fields, but I did not find much comfort in this fact at the time. This was a directive coming from our district and one that is probably not unfamiliar for many educators.

Almost immediately, a mixed bag of commentary raced through my mind. "This is going to be interesting. They cannot force me to do this. Will we have enough time to plan? I am worried we will not get along." Even with concerns, I put on a smile and committed to trying to make this a positive experience. My co-teaching partner and I reflected on those initial times together years later, and he admitted that he also made a commitment for a positive co-teaching experience, although he had similar concerns.

Not that the experience was without its trials and tribulations. To start, my general education partner was quite direct about the fact that he was not sure how to proceed. I appreciated this confession because I shared his feelings. We discussed what was most important for each of us as we figured out how to deliver the content and create a positive environment for students. We honed in on two things. First, we wanted to ensure students consistently heard both of our voices. Second, we wanted to incorporate both of our ideas in our lessons. He labeled himself the content specialist, and I became the strategy specialist, although there was a lot of crossover in these two areas.

Flexibility is key to effective co-teaching. Participants must be willing to get out of their comfort zone, accept that there is never enough planning time, and be okay with the fact that the best laid plans do not always pan out. (This is the real world.) We found a great deal of humor in working through these challenges to our flexibility.

Creating a co-teaching lesson plan template was another key to our successful experience. I found this especially helpful because I did not know my co-teacher, and I was terrified of the content (math). This template enabled us to assign roles and responsibilities for each of us throughout the class period so that both teachers were equally involved. Students got used to hearing both of our voices. We gradually stopped using "I" and began using "we," which helped create a sense of unity in the class.

Did we get a chance to sit down together and plan every day? No. But we did commit to using this template in the beginning. We found that we could plan while conducting our duties, waiting for the copier, and eating lunch if we needed to. We also had a commitment to shared planning time at the beginning of each unit to create an overview and discuss strategies to differentiate based on the individual needs of students in the class.

As we became more comfortable working with each other, we agreed that a co-taught class should look and feel different from a solo-taught class. It essentially is an entirely separate class preparation and thus needs dedicated planning time, of which we had none. We modified our template to include the co-teaching models we would implement to meet particular needs. For example, we used alternative teaching when several students (with and without disabilities) needed more practice—one teacher worked with the smaller group of students, and the other teacher worked with the rest of the students. This planning process was initially a little tedious, but we found we could plan on the fly after we got used to the process, and there was no need to write things down all of the time (although keeping a written record may reduce planning time for future lessons).

We eventually did have official professional development, which fueled us with even more ideas and made us better co-teachers. That first year was quite memorable with many highs and a few lows. But we survived! We have now moved on to other schools, but we enjoyed our experience and still keep in touch. I still use that lesson plan template because, lo and behold, I have had to co-teach with

Figure 6.6. Volunteering is not always required for successful co-teaching, but commitment, flexibility, and effective planning are required. (Contributed by Catherine Morrison.)

(continued)

Figure 6.6. *(continued)*

> those I do not know, those who do not really want to, and those who are eager but have no experi-
> ence. The purpose of the template works like a charm. It starts the conversation and gives the teachers
> a voice that will ultimately affect the students.
>
> We conducted a survey of all students in co-taught classes after 2 years and bringing in 22 more
> teaching staff to co-teach. When asked about the biggest benefit of having two teachers in the class-
> room, one of students' top responses was getting help and feedback quickly. Students felt they mat-
> tered. Who does not want to be a part of that?

instruction for inclusive classes and spells out steps for creating individualized adaptations for students who need them.

EVALUATING OUTCOMES

Teachers who co-teach will want to evaluate their interpersonal effectiveness as a teaching team (e.g., communication, shared decision making, compatibility) and their impact on students (e.g., attitudes, knowledge and skills, behavior, friendship and group skills, referrals). Teachers should develop a plan and a regular schedule for evaluating their co-teaching. If problems do arise between teachers or with the success of co-teaching, then these evaluation plans will provide teachers with a previously determined opportunity to examine data and make modifications; it is awkward to suggest conducting an evaluation only after problems have already arisen.

Evaluating the Effects of Collaborative Teaching on Students

Co-teaching can be evaluated in many ways. Data can be gathered from students, teachers, and parents using a variety of methods (e.g., informal discussion, interviews, self-ratings, observation). In addition, school records can be examined before and after the use of co-teaching to assess its impact on student performance (e.g., attendance records, grades, office referrals). This information can be used to assess and improve the impact that a shift to co-teaching has had in a school.

 ## Student Snapshot

At the end of their first seventh-grade science unit in October, Harriet Golden (science teacher) and Dean Gaines (special education teacher) used a questionnaire to assess the effect that their collaborative teaching had on the class (see Student Feedback Form in Appendix A and the forms download). They read seven questions aloud and asked students to circle one of three ratings (e.g., *very helpful, helpful, not very helpful*) to rate the new teaching approaches they had used. After they collected the questionnaires (without student names on them), they held an open discussion regarding the questions and other issues that came up.

⟲ ACTIVITY: *Describe the kind of student feedback the teachers may receive. Discuss how the teachers might be responsive to that feedback.*

Processing Together Between Teachers

Similar to processing within collaborative teams (see Chapter 3), teachers who are involved in co-teaching should take a few minutes after each co-taught lesson to compare notes regarding their impressions of the session and explore ways they might improve less successful areas. The Co-teacher Feedback Form, available in Appendix A and the forms download, is a teacher reflection questionnaire; however, teachers can develop their own questionnaires based on the shared values and ground rules they developed with their collaborative team(s). They should also add items regarding the specific roles and responsibilities identified early in co-teaching to their list of interpersonal skills.

References

Alquraini, T., & Gut, D. (2012). Critical components of successful inclusion of students with severe disabilities: Literature review. *International Journal of Special Education, 27*(1), 42–59. doi:10.1177/0741932508327457

Andres, H. (2011). Collaborative technology and team-based problem solving. *Northeast Decision Sciences Institute Proceedings*, 872–877.

Andres, H.P., & Akan, O.H. (2010). Assessing team learning in technology-mediated collaboration: An experimental study. *Journal of Educational Technology Systems, 38*, 473–487.

Appl, D.J., Troha, C., & Rowell, J. (2001). Reflections of a first-year team: The growth of a collaborative partnership. *Teaching Exceptional Children, 33*(3), 4–8.

Austin, V.L. (2001). Teachers' beliefs about co-teaching. *Remedial and Special Education, 22*, 245–255.

Bahr, M.W., Walker, K., Hampton, E.M., Buddle, B.S., Freeman, T., Ruschman, N., . . . Littlejohn, W. (2006). Creative problem solving for general education intervention teams. *Remedial and Special Education, 27*, 27–41.

Bambara, L.M., Janney, R., & Snell, M.E. (2015). *Teachers' guides to inclusive practices: Behavior support* (3rd ed.). Baltimore, MD: Paul H. Brookes Publishing Co.

Baron, D. (2008). Consensus building: A key to school transformation. *Principal Leadership, 8*(6), 56–58.

Bauwens, J., Hourcade, J., & Friend, M. (1989). Cooperative teaching: A model for general and special education integration. *Remedial and Special Education, 10*(2), 17–22.

Beamish, W., Bryer, F., & Davies, M. (2006). Teacher reflections on co-teaching a unit of work. *International Journal of Whole Schooling, 2*(2), 3–19.

Bennett, M.S., Erchul, W.P., Young, H.L., & Bartel, C.M. (2012). Exploring relational communication patterns in prereferral intervention teams. *Journal of Educational and Psychological Consultation, 22*, 187–207. doi:10.1080/10474412.2012.706128

Billingsley, B. (2004). Special education teacher retention and attrition: A critical analysis of the research literature. *Journal of Special Education, 38*(1), 39–55.

Blue-Banning, M., Summers, J.A., Frankland, H.C., Nelson, L.L., & Beegle, G. (2004). Dimensions of family and professional partnerships: Constructive guidelines for collaboration. *Exceptional Children, 70*, 167–184.

Boe, E.E., & Cook, L.H. (2006). The chronic and increasing shortage of fully-certified teachers in special and general education. *Exceptional Children, 72*, 443–460.

Boerner, S., Schaffner, M., & Gebert, D. (2012). The complementarity of team meetings and cross-functional communication: Empirical evidence from new services development teams. *Journal of Leadership and Organizational Studies, 19*, 256–266.

Bouck, E.C. (2007). Co-teaching—Not just a textbook term: Implications for practice. *Preventing School Failure, 51*, 46–51.

Bradshaw, C.P., Koth, C.W., Bevans, K.B., Ialongo, N., & Leaf, P.J. (2008). The impact of school-wide positive behavioral interventions and supports (PBIS) on the organizational health of elementary schools. *School Psychology Quarterly, 23*, 462–473. doi:10.1037/a0012883

Briesch, A.M., Chafouleas, S.M., Neugebauer, S.R., & Riley-Tillman, T.C. (2013). Assessing influences on intervention use: Revision of the Usage Rating Profile. *Journal of School Psychology, 51*, 81–96.

Briggs, M.H. (1993). Team talk: Communication skills for early intervention teams. *Journal of Childhood Communication Disorders, 15*(1), 33–40.

Brownell, M.T., Yeager, E., Rennels, M.S., & Riley, T. (1997). Teachers working together: What teacher educators and researchers should know. *Teacher Education and Special Education, 20*, 340–359.

Bruder, M.B. (1994). Working with members of other disciplines: Collaboration for success. In M. Wolery & J.S. Wilbers (Eds.),

Including children with special needs in early childhood programs (pp. 45–70). Washington, DC: National Association for the Education of Young Children.

Brusca-Vega, R., Brown, K., & Yasutake, D. (2011). Science achievement of students in co-taught, inquiry-based classrooms. *Learning Disabilities: A Multidisciplinary Journal, 17,* 23–31.

Bumann, M., & Younkin, S. (2012). Applying self-efficacy theory to increase interpersonal effectiveness in teamwork. *Journal of Invitational Theory and Practice, 18,* 11–18.

Burke, M.M. (2013). Improving parental involvement: Training special education advocates. *Journal of Disability Policy Studies, 23,* 225–234. doi:10.1177/1044207311424910

Burns, M.K., Appleton, J.J., & Stehouwer, J.D. (2005). Meta-analytic review of responsiveness-to-intervention research: Examining field-based and research-implemented models. *Journal of Psychoeducational Assessment, 23,* 381–394.

Capper, C.A., & Frattura, E.M. (2009). *Meeting the needs of students with all abilities: How leaders go beyond inclusion* (2nd ed.). Thousand Oaks, CA: Corwin Press.

Caron, E., & McLaughlin, M.W. (2002). Indicators of beacons of excellence schools: What do they tell us about collaborative practices? *Journal of Educational and Psychological Consultation, 13,* 285–314.

Carpenter, L.B., & Dyad, A. (2007). Secondary inclusion: Strategies for implementing the consultative teacher model. *Education, 127,* 344–350.

Carpenter, S.L., King-Sears, M.E., & Keys, S.G. (1998). Counselors + educators + families as a transdisciplinary team = More effective inclusion for students with disabilities. *Professional School Counseling, 2*(1), 1–9.

Carroll, T. (2009). The next generation of learning teams. *Phi Delta Kappan, 91*(2), 8–13.

Carter, E.W., & Hughes, C. (2006). Including high school students with severe disabilities in general education classes: Perspectives of general and special educators, paraprofessionals, and administrators. *Research and Practice for Persons with Severe Disabilities, 31,* 174–185.

Carter, E.W., Hughes, C., Guth, C., & Copeland, S.R. (2005). Factors influencing social interactions among high school students with intellectual disabilities and their general education peers. *American Journal on Mental Retardation, 110,* 366–377.

Carter, E.W., Lane, K.L., Pierson, M.R., & Stang, K.K. (2008). Promoting self-determination for transition-age youth:

Views of high school general and special educators. *Exceptional Children, 75*(1), 55–70.

Carter, E.W., Sisco, L.G., Brown, L., Brickham, D., & Al-Khabbaz, Z.A. (2008). Peer interactions and academic engagement of youth with developmental disabilities in inclusive middle and high school classrooms. *American Journal on Mental Retardation, 113,* 479–494.

Carter, N., Prater, M.A., Jackson, A., & Marchant, M. (2009). Educators' perceptions of collaborative planning processes for students with disabilities. *Preventing School Failure, 54,* 60–70.

Casale-Giannola, D. (2012). Comparing inclusion in the secondary vocational and academic classrooms: Strengths, needs, and recommendations. *American Secondary Education, 40*(2), 26–42.

Case-Smith, J., Holland, T., Lane, A., & White, S. (2012). Effect of a coteaching handwriting program for first graders: One group pretest–posttest design. *American Journal of Occupational Therapy, 66,* 396–405. doi.org/10.5014/ajot.2012.004333

Causton-Theoharis, J., Theoharis, G., Bull, T., Cosier, M., & Dempt-Aldrich, K. (2011). Schools of promise: A school district–university partnership centered on inclusive school reform [Electronic version]. *Remedial and Special Education, 32,* 192–205.

Center for Applied Special Technology. (2010). *What is universal design for learning?* Retrieved from http://www.cast.org/research/udl/index.html

Cheatham, G.A., & Santos, R. (2011). Considering time and communication orientations. *YC: Young Children, 66*(5), 76–82.

Chen, Z., & Reigeluth, C.M. (2010). Communication in a leadership team for systemic change in a school district. *Contemporary Educational Technology, 1,* 233–254.

Clift, R.T., Houston, W.R., & Pugach, M.C. (Eds.). (1990). *Encouraging reflective practice in education.* New York, NY: Teachers College Press.

Cloninger, C.J. (2004). Designing collaborative educational services. In F.P. Orelove, D. Sobsey, & R.K. Silberman (Eds.), *Educating children with multiple disabilities: A collaborative approach* (4th ed., pp. 1–29). Baltimore, MD: Paul H. Brookes Publishing Co.

Coelli, M.B., & Green, D.A. (2012). Leadership effects: School principals and student outcomes. *Economics of Education Review, 31*(1), 92–109.

Conderman, G. (2011). Methods for addressing conflict in cotaught classrooms. *Intervention in School and Clinic, 46,* 221–229. doi:10.1177/1053451210389034

Conderman, G., & Hedin, L. (2012). Purposeful assessment practices for co-teachers. *Teaching Exceptional Children, 44*(4), 18–27.

Conroy, P. (2007). Paraprofessionals and students with visual impairments: Potential pitfalls and solutions. *Re:View, 39,* 43–56.

Conroy, P.W. (2012). Collaborating with cultural and linguistically diverse families of students in rural schools who receive special education services. *Rural Special Educational Quarterly, 31*(3), 20–24.

Cook, L., & Friend, M. (2010). The state of the art of collaboration on behalf of students with disabilities. *Journal of Educational and Psychological Consultation, 20,* 1–8. doi:10.1080/10474410903535398

Copeland, S.R., & Cosbey, J. (2008/2009). Making progress in the general curriculum: Rethinking effective instructional practices. *Research and Practice for Persons with Severe Disabilities, 33/34,* 214–227.

Cropley, A. (2006). In praise of convergent thinking. *Creativity Research Journal, 18,* 391–404.

Damore, S.J., & Murray, C. (2009). Urban elementary school teachers' perspectives regarding collaborative teaching practices. *Remedial and Special Education, 30,* 234–244. doi:10.1177/0741932508321007

Daniel R.R. v. State Board of Education, 874 F.2d 1036 (1989).

Darling-Hammond, L. (1997). *Doing what matters most: Investing in quality teaching.* New York, NY: National Commission on Teaching and America's Future.

Davis, K.E.B., Dieker, L., Pearl, C., & Kirkpatrick, R.M. (2012). Planning in the middle: Co-planning between general and special education. *Journal of Educational and Psychological Consultation, 22,* 208–226. doi:10.1080/10474412.2012.706561

Dawson, M.M. (1987). Beyond ability grouping: A review of the effectiveness of ability grouping and its alternatives. *School Psychology Review, 16,* 348–369.

DeBoer, A. (1995). *Working together: The art of consulting and communicating.* Longmont, CO: Sopris West Educational Services.

DeBoer, A., & Fister, S. (1995–1996). *Working together: Tools for collaborative teaching.* Longmont, CO: Sopris West Educational Services.

Dennis, A., Fuller, R.M., & Valacich, J.S. (2008). Media, tasks and communication processes: A theory of media synchronicity. *MIS Quarterly, 32,* 575–600.

Denton, C.A., Hasbrouck, J.E., & Sekaquaptewa, S. (2003). The consulting teacher: A descriptive study in responsive systems consultation. *Journal of Educational and Psychological Consultation, 14,* 41–73.

Deshler, D.D., Schumaker, J.B., Lenz, B.K., Bulgren, J.A., Hock, M.F., Knight, J., & Ehren, B.J. (2008). Ensuring content-area learning by secondary students with learning disabilities. *Journal of Education, 189,* 169–181.

Dettmer, P., Thurston, L.P., & Dyck, N.J. (2005). *Consultation, collaboration, and teamwork for students with special needs* (5th ed.). Upper Saddle River, NJ: Pearson.

Doll, B., Haack, K., Kosse, S., Osterloh, M., Siemers, E., & Pray, B. (2005). The dilemma of pragmatics: Why schools don't use quality team consultation practices. *Journal of Educational and Psychological Consultation, 16,* 127–155.

Doyle, M.B., York-Barr, J., & Kronberg, R.M. (Vol. Eds.) & York-Barr, J. (Series Ed.). (1996). *Creating inclusive school communities: A staff development series for general and special educators. Facilitator guide. Module 5. Collaboration: Providing support in the classroom.* Baltimore, MD: Paul H. Brookes Publishing Co.

Duhon, G.J., Mesmer, E.M., Gregerson, L., & Witt, J.C. (2009). Effects of public feedback during RTI team meetings on teacher implementation integrity and student academic performance. *Journal of School Psychology, 47,* 19–37.

Dulaney, S.K. (2012). A middle school's response-to-intervention journey: Building systematic processes of facilitation, collaboration, and implementation. *NASSP Bulletin, 97,* 53–77.

Dymond, S.K., Renzaglia, A., Rosenstein, A., Eul Jung, C., Banks, R.A., Niswander, V., & Gibson, C.L. (2006). Using a participatory action research approach to create a universally designed inclusive high school science course: A case study. *Research and Practice for Persons with Severe Disabilities, 31,* 293–308.

Education for All Handicapped Children Act of 1975, PL 94-142, 20 U.S.C. §§ 1400 *et seq.*

Eisenman, L.T., Pleet, A.M., Wandry, D., & McGinley, V. (2011). Voices of special education teachers in an inclusive high school: Redefining responsibilities. *Remedial and Special Education, 32,* 91–104. doi:10.1177/0741932510361248

Elliott, D., & McKenney, M. (1998). Four inclusion models that work. *Teaching Exceptional Children, 31*(4), 54–58.

Esquivel, S.L., Ryan, C.S., & Bonner, M. (2008). Involved parents' perceptions of their experiences in school-based team meetings. *Journal of Educational and Psychological Consultation, 18,* 234–258. doi:10.1080/10474410802022589

Falk-Ross, F., Watman, L., Kokesh, K., Iverson, M., Williams, E., & Wallace, A. (2009). Natural complements: Collaborative approaches for educators to support students with learning disabilities and literacy difficulties. *Reading and Writing Quarterly, 25,* 104–117. doi:10.1080/10573560802004530

Farrell, A.F., & Collier, M.A. (2010). School personnel's perceptions of family–school communication: A qualitative study. *Improving Schools, 13,* 4–20. doi:10.1177/1365480209352547

Fisher, M., & Pleasants, S.L. (2012). Roles, responsibilities, and concerns of paraeducators: Findings from a statewide survey. *Remedial and Special Education, 33,* 287–297.

Fleming, J.L., & Monda-Amaya, L.E. (2001). Process variables critical for team effectiveness: A Delphi study of wraparound team members. *Remedial and Special Education, 22,* 158–171.

Foley, R.M., & Lewis, J.A. (1999). Self-perceived competence in secondary school principals to serve as school leaders in collaborative-based educational delivery systems. *Remedial and Special Education, 20,* 233–243.

Ford, A., Davern, L., & Schnorr, R. (2001). Learners with significant disabilities: Curricular relevance in an era of standards-based reform. *Remedial and Special Education, 22,* 215–222.

Ford, A., Messenheimer-Young, T., Toshner, J., Fitzgerald, M.A., Dyer, C., Glodoski, J., & Laveck, J. (1995, July). *A team planning packet for inclusive education.* Milwaukee: Wisconsin School Inclusion Project.

Fortenberry, N.L. (2011). Teaching the practical skills. *Mechanical Engineering, 133*(12), 36–40.

Frankel, E.B. (2006). The knowledge, skills, and personal qualities of early childhood resource consultants as agents of change. *Exceptionality Education Canada, 16*(2/3), 35–58.

Frattura, E., & Capper, C.A. (2007). *Leading for social justice: Transforming schools for all learners.* Thousand Oaks, CA: Corwin Press.

Friend, M. (2000). Myths and misunderstandings about professional collaboration [Electronic version]. *Remedial and Special Education, 21,* 130–132.

Friend, M. (2008). *Special education: Contemporary perspectives for school professionals* (2nd ed.). Boston, MA: Allyn & Bacon.

Friend, M., & Cook, L. (2003). *Interactions: Collaboration skills for school professionals* (4th ed.). New York, NY: Longman.

Friend, M., & Cook, L. (2007). *Interactions: Collaboration skills for school professionals* (5th ed.). Upper Saddle River, NJ: Pearson/Merrill.

Friend, M., Cook, L., Hurley-Chamberlain, D., & Shamberger, C. (2010). Co-teaching: An illustration of the complexity of collaboration in special education. *Journal of Educational and Psychological Consultation, 20*(1), 9–27.

Fuchs, D., Fuchs, L.S., & Compton, D.L. (2012). Smart RTI: A next-generation approach to multilevel prevention. *Exceptional Children, 78,* 263–279.

Fullan, M. (2007). *The new meaning of educational change* (4th ed.). New York, NY: Teachers College Press.

Gately, S.E., & Gately, F.J. (2001). Understanding coteaching components. *Teaching Exceptional Children, 33*(4), 40–47.

Giangreco, M.F. (1996). *Vermont Interdependent Services Team Approach (VISTA): A guide to coordinating educational support services.* Baltimore, MD: Paul H. Brookes Publishing Co.

Giangreco, M.F. (2007). *Absurdities and realities of special education: The complete digital set (CD).* Thousand Oaks, CA: Corwin Press.

Giangreco, M.F., Broer, S.M., & Suter, J.C. (2011). Guidelines for selecting alternatives to overreliance on paraprofessionals: Field-testing in inclusion-oriented schools. *Remedial and Special Education, 32,* 22–38. doi:10.1177/0741932509355951

Giangreco, M.F., Cloninger, C.J., & Iverson, V.S. (2011). *Choosing Outcomes and Accommodations For CHildren (COACH): A guide to educational planning for students with disabilities* (3rd ed.). Baltimore. MD: Paul H. Brookes Publishing Co.

Giangreco, M.F., Dennis, R., Cloninger, C.J., Edelman, S., & Schattman, R. (1993). "I've counted Jon": Transformational experiences of teachers educating children with disabilities. *Exceptional Children, 59,* 359–372.

Giangreco, M.F., Dennis, R., Edelman, S., & Cloninger, C. (1994). Dressing your IEPs for the general education climate: Analysis of IEP goals and objectives for students with multiple disabilities. *Remedial and Special Education, 15,* 288–296.

Giangreco, M.F., Prelock, P.A., Reid, R.R., Dennis, R.E., & Edelman, S.W. (2000). Role of related services personnel in inclusive schools. In R.A. Villa & J.S. Thousand (Eds.), *Restructuring for caring and effective education: Piecing the puzzle together* (2nd ed., pp. 360–388). Baltimore, MD: Paul H. Brookes Publishing Co.

Goddard, Y., Goddard, R., & Tschannen-Moran, M. (2007). A theoretical and empirical investigation of teacher collaboration for school improvement and student achievement in public elementary schools. *Teachers College Record, 109,* 877–896.

Goldenberg, O., & Wiley, J. (2011). Quality, conformity, and conflict: Questioning the assumptions of Osborn's brainstorming technique. *Journal of Problem Solving, 3,* 118–141.

Goldsmith, B. (2008). Difficult conversations. *Cost Engineering, 50*(9), 20.

Goltz, S.M., Hietapelto, A.B., Reinsch, R.W., & Tyrell, S.K. (2008). Teaching teamwork and problem solving concurrently. *Journal of Management Education, 32,* 541–562. doi:10.1177/1052562907310739

Goodlad, J.L. (1984). *A place called school.* New York, NY: McGraw-Hill.

Greer v. Rome City School District, 950 F.2d 688 (1992).

Gressgord, L.J. (2012). Text-based collaborative work and innovation: Effects of communication media affordances on divergent and convergent thinking in group-based problem-solving. *Interdisciplinary Journal of Information, Knowledge, and Management, 7,* 151–174.

Gurgur, H., & Uzuner, Y. (2010). A phenomenological analysis of the views on co-teaching applications in the inclusion classroom. *Educational Sciences: Theory and Practice, 10,* 311–331.

Hagner, D., Kurtz, A., Cloutier, H., Arakelian, C., Brucker, D.L., & May, J. (2012). Outcomes of a family-centered transition process for students with autism spectrum disorders. *Focus on Autism and Other Developmental Disabilities, 27*(1), 42–50. doi:10.1177/1088357611430841

Hall, G.E., & Hord, S.M. (2011). *Implementing change: Patterns, principles, and potholes* (3rd ed.). Upper Saddle River, NJ: Pearson.

Hang, Q., & Rabren, K. (2009). An examination of co-teaching: Perspectives and efficacy indicators. *Remedial and Special Education, 30,* 259–268.

Hansen, D., Anderson, C., Munger, L., & Chizek, M. (2013). All aboard! In one Iowa school district, all teachers and principals are on the same journey. *Journal of Staff Development, 34*(2), 18–20, 22–23.

Harbort, G., Gunter, P.L., Hull, K., Brown, Q., Venn, M.L., Wiley, L.P., & Wiley, E.W. (2007). Behaviors of teachers in co-taught classes in a secondary school. *Teacher Education and Special Education, 30,* 13–23.

Harms, P.L., & Roebuck, D.B. (2010). Teaching the art and craft of giving and receiving feedback. *Business Communication Quarterly, 73,* 413–431. doi:10.1177/1080569910385565

Harry, B. (1992a). An ethnographic study of cross-cultural communication with Puerto Rican-American families in the

special education system. *American Educational Research Journal, 29,* 471–494.

Harry, B. (1992b). *Cultural diversity, families, and the special education system: Communication and empowerment.* New York, NY: Teachers College Press.

Harry, B. (1997). Leaning forward or bending over backwards: Cultural reciprocity in working with families. *Journal of Early Intervention, 23*(1), 62–72.

Harry, B. (2008). Collaboration with culturally and linguistically diverse families: Ideal versus reality. *Exceptional Children, 74,* 372–388.

Hong, S.B., & Reynolds-Keefer, L. (2013). Transdisciplinary team building: Strategies in creating early childhood educator and health care teams. *International Journal of Early Childhood Special Education, 5*(1), 30–44.

Howard, R., & Ford, J. (2007). The roles and responsibilities of teacher aides supporting students with special needs in secondary school settings. *Australasian Journal of Special Education, 31,* 25–43. doi:10.1080/10300110701268461

Huang, Y., Peyton, C.G., Hoffman, M., & Pascua, M. (2011). Teacher perspectives on collaboration with occupational therapists in inclusive classrooms: A pilot study. *Journal of Occupational Therapy, Schools, and Early Intervention, 4,* 71–89. doi:10.1080/19411243.2011.581018

Hunt, P., Soto, G., Maier, J., & Doering, K. (2003). Collaborative teaming to support students at risk and students with severe disabilities in general education classrooms. *Exceptional Children, 69,* 315–332.

Idol, L. (1997). Key questions related to building collaborative and inclusive schools. *Journal of Learning Disabilities, 30,* 384–394.

Idol, L. (2006). Toward inclusion of special education students in general education. *Remedial and Special Education, 27,* 77–94.

Idol, L., Paolucci-Whitcomb, P., & Nevin, A. (1986). *Collaborative consultation.* Austin, TX: PRO-ED.

Individuals with Disabilities Education Improvement Act (IDEA) of 2004, PL 108-446, 20 U.S.C. §§ 1400 *et seq.*

Jameson, D.A. (2009). What's the right answer? Team problem-solving in environments of uncertainty. *Business Communication Quarterly, 72,* 215–221. doi:10.1177/1080569909334558

Janney, R., & Snell, M.E. (2006). *Teachers' guides to inclusive practices: Social relationships and peer support* (2nd ed.). Baltimore, MD: Paul H. Brookes Publishing Co.

Janney, R., & Snell, M.E. (2013). *Teachers' guides to inclusive practices: Modifying schoolwork* (3rd ed.). Baltimore, MD: Paul H. Brookes Publishing Co.

Janney, R.E., Snell, M.E., Beers, M.K., & Raynes, M. (1995). Integrating students with moderate and severe disabilities into general education classes. *Exceptional Children, 61,* 425–439.

Johnson, D.W., & Johnson, F.P. (1997). *Joining together: Group theory and group skills* (6th ed.). Upper Saddle River, NJ: Pearson.

Johnson, D.W., & Johnson, F.P. (2000). *Joining together: Group theory and group skills* (7th ed.). Boston, MA: Allyn & Bacon.

Johnson, L.J., Zorn, D., Tam, B.K.Y., Lamontagne, M., & Johnson, S.A. (2003). Stakeholders: View of factors that impact successful interagency collaboration. *Exceptional Children, 69,* 195–209.

Jorgensen, C.M., Schuh, M.C., & Nisbet, J. (2006). *The inclusion facilitator's guide.* Baltimore, MD: Paul H. Brookes Publishing Co.

Kalyanpur, M., & Harry, B. (2012). *Cultural reciprocity in special education: Building family–professional relationships.* Baltimore, MD: Paul H. Brookes Publishing Co.

Kamens, M.W., Susko, J.P., & Elliott, J.S. (2013). Evaluation and supervision of co-teaching: A study of administrator practices in New Jersey. *NASSP Bulletin, 97,* 166–190. doi: 10.1177/0192636513476337

Kaniuka, T.S. (2012). Toward an understanding of how teachers change during school reform: Considerations for educational leadership and school improvement. *Journal of Educational Change, 13,* 327–346.

Katzenbach, J., & Smith, D. (1993). *The wisdom of teams.* Cambridge, MA: Harvard Business School Press.

Keefe, E.B., Moore, V., & Duff, F. (2004). The four "knows" of collaborative teaching. *Teaching Exceptional Children, 36*(5), 36–42.

Kelleher, C., Riley-Tillman, T.C., & Power, T.J. (2008). An initial comparison of collaborative and expert-driven consultation on treatment integrity. *Journal of Educational and Psychological Consultation, 18,* 294–324. doi: 10.1080/10474410802491040

Kim, A., Woodruff, A.L., Klein, C., & Vaughn, S. (2006). Facilitating co-teaching for literacy in general education classrooms through technology: Focus on students with learning disabilities. *Reading and Writing Quarterly, 22,* 269–291. doi:10.1080/10573560500455729

King-Sears, M.E. (2005). Scheduling for reading and writing small-group instruction using learning center designs. *Reading and Writing Quarterly, 21,* 401–405.

King-Sears, M.E. (2007). Designing and delivering learning center instruction. *Intervention in School and Clinic, 42,* 137–147.

King-Sears, M.E., & Bowman-Kruhm, M. (2011). Specialized reading instruction for adolescents with learning disabilities: What special education co-teachers say. *Learning Disabilities Research and Practice, 26,* 172–184.

King-Sears, M.E., Brawand, A.E., Jenkins, M., & Preston-Smith, S. (2014). Co-teaching perspectives from secondary science co-teachers and their students with disabilities. *Journal of Science Teacher Education, 25,* 65–68. doi:10.1007/s10972-014-9391-2

Klar, H.W., & Brewer, C.A. (2013). Successful leadership in high-needs schools: An examination of core leadership practices enacted in challenging contexts. *Educational Administration Quarterly, 49,* 768–808. doi:10.1177/0013161X13482577

Knackendoffel, E.A. (2007). Collaborative teaming in the secondary school. *Focus on Exceptional Children, 40*(4), 1–20.

Laframboise, K., Epanchin, B., Colucci, K., & Hocutt, A. (2004). Working together: Emerging roles of special and general educators in inclusive settings. *Action in Teacher Education, 26*(3), 29–43.

Lawson, J., & Berrick, J.D. (2013). Establishing CASA as an evidence-based practice. *Journal of Evidence-Based Social Work, 10,* 321–337. doi:10.1080/15433714.2012.663674

Leatherman, J. (2009). Teachers' voices concerning collaborative teams within an inclusive elementary school. *Teaching Education, 20,* 189–202. doi:10.1080/10476210902718104

Lee, G.V. (2009). From group to team. *Journal of Staff Development, 30*(5), 44–49.

Lilly, M.S. (1971). A training based model for special education. *Exceptional Children, 37,* 745–749.

Liston, A.G., Nevin, A., & Malian, I. (2009). What do paraeducators in inclusive classrooms say about their work? Analysis of national survey data and follow-up interviews in California. *Teaching Exceptional Children Plus, 5*(5), 2–17.

Litzelfelner, P. (2008). Consumer satisfaction with CASAs (Court Appointed Special Advocates). *Children and Youth Services Review, 30,* 173–186.

Liu, L., Friedman, R., Barry, B., Gelfand, M.J., & Zhang, Z. (2012). The dynamics of consensus building in intracultural and intercultural negotiations. *Administrative Science Quarterly, 57,* 269–304. doi:10.1177/0001839212453456

Losen, S.M., & Losen, J.G. (1994). Teamwork and the involvement of parents in special education programming, In H.G. Garner & F.P. Orelove (Eds.), *Teamwork in human services: Models and application across the life span* (pp. 117–141). Newton, MA: Butterworth-Heinemann.

Mackenzie, S. (2011). "Yes, but . . .": Rhetoric, reality and resistance in teaching assistants' experiences of inclusive education. *Support for Learning, 26,* 64–71. doi:10.1111/j.1467-9604.2011.01479.x

MacSuga, A.S., & Simonsen, B. (2011). Increasing teachers' use of evidence-based classroom management strategies through consultation: Overview and case studies. *Beyond Behavior, 20*(2), 4–12.

Malone, D.M., & Gallagher, P.A. (2010). Special education teachers' attitudes and perceptions of teamwork [Electronic version]. *Remedial and Special Education, 31,* 330–342.

Mardinos, M. (1989). Conception of childhood disability among Mexican-American parents. *Medical Anthropology, 12,* 55–68.

Mastropieri, M.A., Scruggs, T.E., Graetz, J., Norland, J., Gardizi, W., & McDuffie, K. (2005). Case studies in co-teaching in the content areas: Successes, failures and challenges. *Intervention in School and Clinic, 40,* 260–270.

Matzen, K., Ryndak, D., & Nakao, T. (2010). Middle school teams increasing access to general education for students with significant disabilities: Issues encountered and activities observed across contexts. *Remedial and Special Education, 31,* 287–304. doi:10.1177/0741932508327457

McGinnis, E. (2012). *Skillstreaming the adolescent* (3rd ed.). Champaign, IL: Research Press.

McLaren, E.M., Bausch, M.E., & Ault, M.J. (2007). Collaboration strategies reported by teachers providing assistive technology services. *Journal of Special Education Technology, 22*(4), 16–29.

Meleady, R., Hopthrow, T., & Crisp, R.J. (2013). The group discussion effect: Integrative processes and suggestions for implementation. *Personality and Social Psychology Review, 17,* 56–71. doi:10.1177/1088868312456744

Minor, L., DuBard, M., & Luiselli, J.K. (2014). Improving intervention integrity of direct-service practitioners through performance feedback and problem solving consultation. *Behavioral Interventions, 29,* 145–156. doi:10.1002/bin.1382

Moin, L.J., Magiera, K., & Zigmond, N. (2009). Instructional activities and group work in the U.S. inclusive high school co-taught science class. *International Journal of Science and Mathematics Education, 7,* 677–697. doi:10.1007/s10763-008-9133-z

Murawski, W.W. (2006). Student outcomes in co-taught secondary English classes: How can we improve? *Reading and Writing Quarterly, 22,* 227–247.

Murawski, W.W., & Dieker, L.A. (2004). Tips and strategies for co-teaching at the secondary level. *Teaching Exceptional Children, 36*(5), 52–58.

Murawski, W.W., & Lochner, W.W. (2011). Observing co-teaching: What to ask for, look for, and listen for. *Intervention in School and Clinic, 46,* 174–183. doi:10.1177/1053451210378165

Murawski, W.W., & Swanson, H. (2001). A meta-analysis of co-teaching research. *Remedial and Special Education, 22,* 258–267.

Musti-Rao, S., Hawkins, R.O., & Tan, S. (2011). A practitioner's guide to consultation and problem solving in inclusive settings. *Teaching Exceptional Children, 44*(1), 18–26.

Nastasi, B.K., Varjas, K., Schensul, S.L., Silva, K.T., Schensul, J.J., & Ratnayake, P. (2000). The participatory intervention model: A framework for conceptualizing and promoting intervention acceptability. *School Psychology Quarterly, 15,* 207–232.

National Center for Children and Youth with Disabilities (NICHCY). (July 1995). Planning for inclusion. *NICHCY News Digest, 5*(1), 1–31.

Newton, J.S., Horner, R.H., Todd, A.W., Algozzine, B., & Algozzine, K.M. (2012). A pilot study of a problem-solving model for team decision making. *Education and Treatment of Children, 35,* 25–49.

No Child Left Behind Act of 2001, PL 107-110, 115 Stat. 1425, 20 U.S.C. §§6301 *et seq.*

Noell, G.H., Witt, J.C., LaFleur, L.H., Mortenson, B.P., Rainer, D.D., & LeVelle, J. (2000). Increasing intervention implementation in general education following consultation: A comparison of two follow-up strategies. *Journal of Applied Behavior Analysis, 33,* 271–284.

Oberti v. the Board of Education of the Borough of Clementon School District, 995 F.2d (1993).

Olivos, E.M. (2009). Collaboration with Latino families: A critical perspective of home–school interactions. *Intervention in School and Clinic, 45,* 109–115. doi:10.1177/1053451209340220

Olivos, E.M., Gallagher, R.J., & Aguilar, J. (2010). Fostering collaboration with culturally and linguistically diverse families of children with moderate to severe disabilities. *Journal of Educational and Psychological Consultation, 20,* 28–40. doi:10.1080/10474410903535372

Olson, J., & Murphy, C.L. (1999). Self-assessment: A key process of successful team development. *Young Exceptional Children, 2*(3), 2–8.

Ornelles, C., Cook, L., & Jenkins, A. (2007). Middle school general education teachers' perspectives on including students with learning disabilities. *Learning Disabilities: A Multidisciplinary Journal, 14,* 145–154.

Pancsofar, N., & Petroff, J.G. (2013). Professional development experiences in co-teaching: Associations with teacher confidence, interests, and attitudes. *Teacher Education and Special Education, 36*(2), 83–96. doi:10.1177/0888406412474996

Park, Y. (2008). Transition services for high school students with disabilities: Perspectives of special education teachers. *Exceptional Education Canada, 18*(3), 95–111.

Parker, A., Alvarez-McHatton, P., & Allen, D.D. (2012). Elementary and special education pre-service teachers' understandings of collaboration and co-teaching. *Journal of Research in Education, 22,* 164–195.

Paul-Brown, D., & Caperton, C.J. (2001). Inclusive practices for preschool-age children with specific language impairment. In M.J. Guralnick (Ed.). *Early childhood inclusion: Focus on change* (pp. 433–464). Baltimore, MD: Paul H. Brookes Publishing Co.

Pearl, C., Dieker, L.A., & Kirkpatrick, R.M. (2012). A five-year retrospective on the Arkansas Department of Education co-teaching project. *Professional Development in Education, 38,* 571–587. doi:10.1080/194152 57.2012.668858

Piercey, D. (2010, September). Why don't teachers collaborate: A leadership conundrum. *Phi Delta Kappan, 92*(1), 54–56.

Polito, J.M. (2013). Effective communication during difficult conversations. *Neurodiagnostic Journal, 53,* 142–152.

Potts, E.A., & Howard, L.A. (2011). *How to co-teach: A guide for general and special educators.* Baltimore, MD: Paul H. Brookes Publishing Co.

Pugach, M.C., Blanton, L.P., Correa, V.I., McLeskey, J., & Langley, L.K. (2009). *The role of collaboration in supporting the induction and retention of new special education teachers* (NCIPP Doc. No. RS-2). Retrieved from http://www.ncipp.org/reports/rs_2.pdf

Pugach, M.C., & Johnson, L.J. (2002). *Collaborative practitioners: Collaborative schools* (2nd ed.). Denver, CO: Love Publishing.

Pugach, M.C., & Wesson, C.L. (1995). Teachers' and students' views of team teaching and general education and learning-disabled students in two fifth-grade classes. *Elementary School Journal, 95,* 279–295.

Raforth, M.A., & Foriska, T. (2006). Administrator participation in promoting effective problem-solving teams. *Remedial and Special Education, 27,* 130–135. doi:10.1177/0741932 5060270030101

Rainforth, B., & England, J. (1997). Collaborations for inclusion. *Education and Treatment of Children, 20,* 85–104.

Rainforth, B., & York-Barr, J. (Eds.). (1997). *Collaborative teams for students with severe disabilities: Integrating therapy and educational services* (2nd ed.). Baltimore, MD: Paul H. Brookes Publishing Co.

Ratcliffe, M.J.A., & Harts, M.L. (2011). *Schools that make the grade: What successful schools do to improve student achievement.* Baltimore, MD: Paul H. Brookes Publishing Co.

Rea, P.J., McLaughlin, V.L., & Walther-Thomas, C. (2002). Outcomes for students with learning disabilities in inclusive and pullout programs. *Exceptional Children, 68,* 203–222.

Reinke, W.M., Lewis-Palmer, T., & Martin, E. (2007). The effect of visual performance feedback on teacher use of behavior-specific praise. *Behavior Modification, 31,* 247–263. doi:10.1177/0145445506288967

Roach, V. (1995, May). *Winning ways: Creating inclusive schools, classroom, and communities.* Alexandria, VA: National Association of State Boards of Education.

Ruble, L.A., Dalrymple, N.J., & McGrew, J.H. (2010). The effects of consultation on individualized education program outcomes for young children with autism: The collaborative model for promoting competence and success. *Journal of Early Intervention, 32,* 286–301. doi:10.1177/1053815110382973

Ruble, L.A., McGrew, J.H., Toland, M.D., Dalrymple, N.J., & Jung, L.A. (2013). A randomized controlled trial of COMPASS web-based and face-to-face teacher coaching in autism. *Journal of Consulting and Clinical Psychology, 81,* 566–572. doi:10.1037/a0032003

Russ, S., Chiang, B., Rylance, B.J., & Bongers, J. (2001). Caseload in special education: An integration of research findings. *Exceptional Children, 67,* 161–172.

Sacramento City Unified School District Board of Education v. Rachel H., 14 F.3d 1398 (1994).

Sailor, W., & Roger, B. (2005, March). Rethinking inclusion: Schoolwide applications. *Phi Delta Kappan,* 503–509.

Sailor, W., Zuna, N., Choi, J., Thomas, J., McCart, A., & Blair, R. (2006). Anchoring schoolwide positive behavior support in structural school reform. *Research and Practice for Persons with Severe Disabilities, 31,* 18–30.

Salisbury, C.L., & Dunst, C.J. (1997). Home, school, and community partnerships: Building inclusive teams. In B. Rainforth & J. York-Barr (Eds.), *Collaborative teams for students with severe disabilities: Integrating therapy and educational services* (2nd ed., pp. 57–87). Baltimore, MD: Paul H. Brookes Publishing Co.

Salisbury, C.L., & McGregor, G. (2002). The administrative climate and context of inclusive elementary schools. *Exceptional Children, 68,* 259–274.

Sanger, D., Friedli, C., Brunken, C., Snow, P., & Ritzman, M. (2012). Educators' year long reactions to the implementation of a response to intervention (RTI) model. *Journal of Ethnographic and Qualitative Research, 7,* 98–107.

Santoli, S., Sachs, J., Romey, E.A., & McClurg, S. (2008). A successful formula for middle school inclusion: Collaboration, time, and administrative support. *Research in Middle Level Education Online, 32*(2), 1–13.

Sargeant, J., Loney, E., & Murphy, G. (2008). Effective interprofessional teams: "Contact is not enough" to build a team. *Journal of Continuing Education in the Health Professions, 28,* 228–234. doi:10.10020chp.189

Scheeler, M.C., Congdon, M., & Stansbery, S. (2010). Providing immediate feedback to co-teachers through bug-in-ear technology: An effective method of peer coaching in inclusion classrooms. *Teacher Education and Special Education, 33,* 83–96. doi:10.1177/0888406409357013

Schnorr, R.F. (1997). From enrollment to membership: Belonging in middle and high school classes. *Journal of The Association for Persons with Severe Handicaps, 22,* 1–15.

Schoorman, D., Zainuddin, H., & Sena, S. (2011). The politics of a child study team advocating for immigrant families. *Multicultural Education, 18*(4), 31–38.

Schulte, A., Osborne, S., & McKinney, J. (1990). Academic outcomes for students with learning disabilities in consultation and resource programs. *Exceptional Children, 57,* 162–172.

Scruggs, T.E., Mastropieri, M.A., & McDuffie, K.A. (2007). Co-teaching in inclusive classrooms: A meta-synthesis of qualitative research. *Exceptional Children, 73,* 392–416.

Selvalakshmi, M. (2012). Probing: An effective tool of communication. *The IUP Journal of Soft Skills, 6*(3), 55–58.

Senge, P., Roberts, C., Ross, R., Smith, B., & Kleiner, A. (1994). *Learning to work together: The fifth discipline fieldbook.* New York, NY: Doubleday.

Sethi, D., & Seth, M. (2009). Interpersonal communication: Lifeblood of an organization. *IUP Journal of Soft Skills, 3*(3), 32–40.

Shasby, S., & Schneck, C. (2011). Commentary on collaboration in school-based practice: Positives and pitfalls. *Journal of Occupational Therapy, Schools, and Early Intervention, 4,* 22–33. doi:10.1080/19411243.2011.573243

Sheridan, S., Welch, M., & Orme, S. (1996). Is consultation effective? A review of outcome research. *Remedial and Special Education, 17,* 341–354.

Sileo, T.W., Sileo, A.P., & Prater, M.A. (1996). Parent and professional partnerships in special education: Multicultural considerations. *Intervention in School and Clinic, 31,* 145–153.

Silverman, F. (2011). Promoting inclusion with occupational therapy: A coteaching model. *Journal of Occupational Therapy, Schools, and Early Intervention, 4,* 100–107. doi:10.1080/19411243.2011.595308

Smith, R., & Leonard, P. (2005). Collaboration for inclusion: Practitioner perspectives. *Equity and Excellence in Education, 38,* 269–179.

Snell, M.E. (2002, May). *Inclusion of children with high and low support needs in upper elementary classrooms.* Paper presented at the meeting of the American Association on Mental Retardation, Orlando, FL.

Snell, M.E., & Brown, F. (2011). Selecting teaching strategies and arranging educational environments. In M.E. Snell & F. Brown (Eds.), *Instruction of students with severe disabilities* (7th ed., pp. 122–185). Upper Saddle River, NJ: Merrill/Prentice Hall.

Snell, M.E., & Janney, R.E. (2000). Teachers' problem solving about young children with moderate and severe disabilities in elementary classrooms. *Exceptional Children, 66,* 472–490.

Snell, M.E., & Janney, R. (2005). *Teachers' guides to inclusive practices: Collaborative teaming* (2nd ed.). Baltimore, MD: Paul H. Brookes Publishing Co.

Snell, M.E., & Macfarland, C.A. (2001, November). *Inclusion in upper elementary classrooms: "A lot of it falls apart without the planning."* Paper presented at the meeting of The Association for Persons with Severe Handicaps, Anaheim, CA.

Snell, M.E., Raynes, M., Byrd, J.O., Colley, K.M., Gilley, C., Pitonyak, C., . . . Willis, C.J. (1995). Changing roles in inclusive schools: Staff perspectives at Gilbert Linkous Elementary. *Kappa Delta Pi Record, 31,* 104–109.

Solis, M., Vaughn, S., Swanson, E., & McCulley, L. (2012). Collaborative models of instruction: The empirical foundations of inclusion and co-teaching. *Psychology in the Schools, 49,* 498–510. doi:10.1002/pits.21606

Stufft, D.L., Bauman, D., & Ohlsen, M. (2009). Preferences and attitudes toward accommodations of traditional assessment in secondary social studies classrooms. *Social Studies Research and Practice, 4*(2), 87–98.

Suter, J.C., & Giangreco, M.F. (2009). Numbers that count: Exploring special education and paraprofessional service delivery in inclusion-oriented schools. *Journal of Special Education, 43*, 81–93. doi:10.1177/0022466907313353

Symeou, L., Roussounidou, E., & Michaelides, M. (2012). "I feel much more confident now to talk with parents": An evaluation of in-service training on teacher-parent communication. *School Community Journal, 22*(1), 65–87.

Theodore, L.A., Dioguardi, R.J., Hughes, T.L., Aloiso, D., Carlo, M., & Eccles, D. (2009). A class-wide intervention for improving homework performance. *Journal of Educational and Psychological Consultation, 19*, 275–299.

Theoharis, G., & O'Toole, J. (2011). Leading inclusive ELL: Social justice leadership for English language learners. *Educational Administration Quarterly, 47*, 646–688. doi:10.1177/0013161X11401616

Thomas, C.C., Correa, V.I., & Morsink, C.V. (1995). *Interactive teaming: Consultation and collaboration in special education.* Upper Saddle River, NJ: Prentice Hall.

Thomson, C. (2013). Collaborative consultation to promote inclusion: Voices from the classroom. *International Journal of Inclusive Education, 17*, 882–894. doi:10.1080/13603116.2011.602535

Thousand, J.S., & Villa, R.A. (2000). Collaborative teaming: A powerful tool in school restructuring. In R.A. Villa & J.S. Thousand (Eds.), *Restructuring for caring and effective education: Piecing the puzzle together* (2nd ed., pp. 254–293). Baltimore: Paul H. Brookes Publishing Co.

Thousand, J.S., & Villa, R.A. (2005). Organizational supports for change toward inclusive schooling. In R.A. Villa & J.S. Thousand (Eds.), *Creating an inclusive school* (2nd ed., pp. 32–44). Alexandria, VA: Association for Supervision and Curriculum Development.

Thousand, J.S., Villa, R.A., & Nevin, A.I. (2006). The many faces of collaborative planning and teaching, *Theory into Practice, 45*, 239–248.

Toson, A.L., Burrello, L.C., & Knollman, G. (2013). Educational justice for all: The capability approach and inclusive education leadership. *International Journal of Inclusive Education, 17*, 490–506. doi:10.1080/13603116.2012.687015

Trainor, A.A. (2010). Educators' expectations of parent participation: The role of cultural and social capital. *Multiple Voices for Ethnically Diverse Exceptional Learners, 12*(2), 33–50.

Tremblay, P. (2013). Comparative outcomes of two instructional models for students with learning disabilities: Inclusion with

co-teaching and solo-taught special education. *Journal of Research in Special Educational Needs, 13*, 251–258. doi:10.1111/j.1471-3802.2012.01270.x

Trent, S. (1998). False starts and other dilemmas of a secondary general education collaborative teacher: A case study. *Journal of Learning Disabilities, 31*, 503–513.

Turnbull, A.P., & Turnbull, H.R. (2000). Fostering family–professional partnerships. In M.E. Snell & F. Brown (Eds.), *Instruction of students with severe disabilities* (5th ed., pp. 31–66). Upper Saddle River, NJ: Merrill/Prentice Hall.

Turnbull, A.P., Turnbull, H.R., Erwin, E., & Soodak, L. (2006). *Professionals, families, and exceptionality: Outcomes through partnerships and trust* (5th ed.). Upper Saddle River, NJ: Merrill/Prentice Hall.

Valle, J.W. (2011). Down the rabbit hole: A commentary about research on parents and special education. *Learning Disability Quarterly, 34*, 183–190. doi:10.1 177/0731948711417555

Van Hover, S., Hicks, D., & Sayeski, K. (2012). A case study of co-teaching in an inclusive secondary high-stakes World History I classroom. *Theory and Research in Social Education, 40*, 260–291. doi:10.1080/00933104.2012.705162

Vaughn, S., Schumm, J.S., & Arguelles, M.E. (1997). The ABCDEs of co-teaching. *Teaching Exceptional Children, 30*(2), 4–10.

Villa, R.A., & Thousand, J.S. (Eds.). (2000). *Restructuring for caring and effective education: Piecing the puzzle together* (2nd ed.). Baltimore, MD: Paul H. Brookes Publishing Co.

Villa, R.A., Thousand, J.S., Meyers, H., & Nevin, A. (1996). Teacher and administrator perceptions of heterogeneous education. *Exceptional Children, 63*, 29–45.

Villeneuve, M., & Hutchinson, N.L. (2012). Enabling outcomes for students with developmental disabilities through collaborative consultation. *The Qualitative Report, 17*, 1–29.

Waldron, N.L., & McLeskey, J. (2010). Establishing a collaborative school culture through comprehensive school reform [Electronic version]. *Journal of Educational and Psychological Consultation, 20*, 58–74.

Wallace, T., Anderson, A.R., & Bartholomay, T. (2002). Collaboration: An element associated with the success of four inclusive high schools: *Journal of Educational and Psychological Consultation, 13*, 349–381.

Walther-Thomas, C.S. (1997). Co-teaching experiences: The benefits and problems that teachers and principals report over time [Electronic version]. *Journal of Learning Disabilities, 30*, 395–407.

Walther-Thomas, C.S., Bryant, M., & Land, S. (1996). Planning for effective co-teaching: The key to successful inclusion. *Remedial and Special Education, 17*, 255–265.

Walther-Thomas, C., Korinek, L., McLaughlin, V.L., & Williams, B.T. (2000*). Collaboration for inclusive education: Developing successful programs*. Boston, MA: Allyn & Bacon.

Wesley, P.W., & Buysse, V. (2004). Consultation as a framework for productive collaboration in early intervention. *Journal of Educational and Psychological Consultation, 15*, 127–150. doi:10.1207/s1532768xjepc1502_2

West, J.F., & Idol, L. (1990). Collaborative consultation and the education of mildly handicapped and at-risk students. *Remedial and Special Education, 11*(1), 22–31.

Williams, E.R., & Baber, C. (2007). Part I: Advancing the conversation: Building trust through culturally reciprocal home-school-community collaboration from the perspective of African-American parents. *Multicultural Perspectives, 9*(2), 3–9. doi:10.1080/15210960701386228

Williams, R.B. (2006). Leadership for school reform: Do principal decision-making styles reflect a collaborative approach? *Canadian Journal of Educational Administration and Policy, 53*, 1–22.

Wodak, R., Kwon, W., & Clarke, I. (2011). "Getting people on board": Discursive leadership for consensus building in team meetings. *Discourse and Society, 22*, 592–644. doi:10.1177/0957926511405410

Wood, M. (1998). Whose job is it anyway? Educational roles in inclusion. *Exceptional Children, 64*(1), 181–195.

Woods, J.J., Wilcox, M.J., Friedman, M., & Murch, T. (2011). Collaborative consultation in natural environments: Strategies to enhance family-centered supports and services. *Language, Speech, and Hearing Services in Schools, 42*, 379–392.

Yetter, G. (2010). Assessing the acceptability of problem-solving procedures by school teams: Preliminary development of the Pre-Referral Intervention Team Inventory. *Journal of Educational and Psychological Consultation, 20*, 139–168.

York-Barr, J. (Series Ed.). (1996). *Creating inclusive school communities: A staff development series for general and special educators. Facilitator guide. Modules 1–5*. Baltimore, MD: Paul H. Brookes Publishing Co.

York, J., Doyle, M.B., & Kronberg, R. (1992). A curriculum development process for inclusive classrooms. *Focus on Exceptional Children, 25*(4), 1–16.

Zigmond, N., & Magiera, K. (2001). Current practice alerts: A focus on co-teaching: Use with caution. *Alerts, 6*, 1–4.

Zigmond, N., & Matta, D. (2004). Value added of the special education teacher on secondary school co-taught classes. In T.E. Scruggs & M.A. Mastropieri (Eds.), *Research in secondary schools: Advances in learning and behavioral disabilities* (Vol. 17, pp. 55–76). Oxford, UK: Elsevier Science/JAI.

APPENDIX A

Blank Forms

How Can We Stay in Touch?

Family member: _____   Teacher: _____   Date: _____

_____ I would like to come to the school to meet with you. Days and times that work best are:
_____ Monday   _____ Tuesday   _____ Wednesday   _____ Thursday   _____ Friday
Times: _____

_____ I would like you to come visit at our house.

_____ I would like to write in and read a notebook that travels in my child's backpack.

_____ I would like to write notes back and forth.

_____ I would like telephone calls at home between the hours of _____ and _____
(phone number: _____).

_____ I would like telephone calls at work between the hours of _____ and _____
(phone number: _____).

_____ I would like to use e-mail; my address is: _____.

_____ I would like to talk when I drop off or pick up my child on M T W R F (circle one) at _____.

_____ I would like to meet before _____ after _____ PTA meetings.

_____ I would like to have a school/class open house and meet there.

_____ I would like to observe in the classroom and talk afterward.

_____ I would like to receive school and classroom newsletters.

_____ I would like to participate in my child's individualized education program (IEP) meeting.

_____ I would like to bring a friend or other family members to meetings with me.

_____ I would like to talk and plan before the IEP meeting.

_____ I would like to talk and plan via Skype.

_____ I would like to talk and plan with multiple people via speakerphone.

_____ Another way: _____

Program-at-a-Glance

Student: _____ Date: _____

IEP goals (in a few words)	IEP accommodations and modifications
	Academic, social, and physical supports

Key: IEP, individualized education program.

Team Roles and Responsibilities Checklist

Student: _____   Date: _____

Teaching and support team members

Teachers: _____   Paraprofessional(s): _____

_____   Others: _____

Key:

P = Primary responsibility

I = Input into implementation and/or decision making

Roles and responsibilities	Who is responsible?			
	Classroom teacher	Special educator	Paraprofes-sionals	Others
1. Developing lesson and unit plans				
2. Developing individualized adaptations and support plans				
3. Providing instruction (with accommodations and modifications; list subjects or other targeted goal areas):				
a.				
b.				
c.				
d.				
4. Adapting instructional materials				
5. Assigning grades/report card				
6. Monitoring progress on individualized education program (IEP) goals				
7. Assigning duties to and supervising paraprofessionals				
8. Training paraprofessionals				
9. Scheduling and facilitating team meetings				
10. Daily communication with parents				
11. Communication and coordination with related services				
12. Facilitating peer relationships and supports (modeling and prompting appropriate ways to interact, organizing formal peer supports)				
13. Assigning student to partners or cooperative groups				

From Ford, A., Messenheimer-Young, T., Toshner, J., Fitzgerald, M.A., Dyer, C., Glodoski, J., & Laveck, J. (1995, July). *A team planning packet for inclusive education.* Milwaukee: Wisconsin School Inclusion Project; adapted by permission.

In *Teachers' Guides to Inclusive Practices: Collaborative Teaming, Third Edition* by Margaret E. King-Sears, Rachel Janney, and Martha E. Snell. (2015, Paul H. Brookes Publishing Co.)

Generic Meeting Form

Meeting purpose: _____

Date: _____ Start time: _____ Next meeting date: _____ Next start time: _____

End time: _____ End time: _____

Members present

Name: _____ Position: _____

Name: _____ Position: _____

Name: _____ Position: _____

Name: _____ Position: _____

Agenda topics	Decisions
1. _____	1. _____
_____	_____
2. _____	2. _____
_____	_____
3. _____	3. _____
_____	_____

Action plan

Who	Does what	By when
1. _____	1. _____	1. _____
_____	_____	
_____	_____	
2. _____	2. _____	2. _____
_____	_____	
_____	_____	
3. _____	3. _____	3. _____
_____	_____	
_____	_____	

Teachers' Guides to Inclusive Practices: Collaborative Teaming, Third Edition
by Margaret E. King-Sears, Rachel Janney, and Martha E. Snell.
Copyright © 2015 by Paul H. Brookes Publishing Co., Inc. All rights reserved.

Pros and Cons of Possible Solutions

Criteria (Indicate yes or no for each criterion.)	Solution 1 (Describe solution.)	Solution 2 (Describe solution.)	Solution 3 (Describe solution.)	Solution 4 (Describe solution.)
1. Is the solution responsive to the student's needs?				
2. Are the resources available?				
3. Are there potential uses in other environments?				
4. Is it specific enough for data to be collected?				
5. Does the solution target evidence-based practices?				
6. Is the solution matched to the problem's severity?				
7. Does the solution promote participation in inclusive educational and/or community contexts?				
8. Is the solution manageable to implement?				
9. Is the solution acceptable to implementers?				
10. Does the solution hold team consensus?				
11. Does the solution promote the student's independence?				
12. Is the solution as nonintrusive as possible from the student's perspective?				
13. Does the solution relate to other valued life outcomes?				
14. Other criteria:				
15. Other criteria:				
The quantity of yes and no responses can help the team select the best-fit solution.[a]	Total yes _____ Total no _____	Total yes _____ Total no _____	Total yes _____ Total no _____	Total yes _____ Total no _____

[a]Some criteria may be more important to the team than others.

Source: Giangreco, Cloninger, Dennis, and Edelman (1994).

Student Feedback Form

Co-teachers: _____   Subject: _____

_____   Period: _____   Date: _____

Directions: Do not write your name on this paper. Your co-teachers would like information about how you feel about this co-taught class. Put an *X* in the box that best fits your response.

1. How helpful is it to have two teachers in the same classroom?	Not very helpful	Somewhat helpful	Very helpful
2. How successful are you as a learner because of two teachers in the classroom?	Not very successful	Somewhat successful	Very successful
3. How quickly do you get help because you have two teachers in the classroom?	Not too soon after asking	Very soon after asking	Immediately after asking
4. How likely are you to attend this class because it has two teachers?	Not very likely	Somewhat likely	Very likely
5. How satisfied are you with the quarter grade you received?	Not very satisfied	Somewhat satisfied	Very satisfied
6. How motivated are you to learn in this class because it has two teachers?	Not very motivated	Somewhat motivated	Very motivated
7. How much more do you think you learn in a class that has two teachers?	Not sure	A little more	A lot more

If you have other comments about co-teaching, then please write them here or on the back of this paper.

_____

_____

_____

_____

_____

_____

_____

_____

_____

_____

_____

_____

_____

Contributed by Catherine Morrison.

In *Teachers' Guides to Inclusive Practices: Collaborative Teaming, Third Edition*
by Margaret E. King-Sears, Rachel Janney, and Martha E. Snell.
Copyright © 2015 by Paul H. Brookes Publishing Co., Inc. All rights reserved.

Co-teacher Feedback Form

Rating Scale	1 Strongly disagree	2 Disagree	3 Agree	4 Strongly agree
Statements	My rating for this statement	My co-teacher's rating for this statement	Do we agree? Yes or No	Discuss? Yes or No
1. I am treated as an equal by my co-teacher.				
2. My co-teacher and I are adept at using all five co-teaching models.				
3. My co-teacher and I share a common understanding of what co-teaching involves.				
4. Our students perceive both co-teachers as having equal status.				
5. I am an equal partner in the decisions that are made.				
6. My time is used productively when co-teaching.				
7. Our communication is effective.				

Teachers' Guides to Inclusive Practices: Collaborative Teaming, Third Edition
by Margaret E. King-Sears, Rachel Janney, and Martha E. Snell.
Copyright © 2015 by Paul H. Brookes Publishing Co., Inc. All rights reserved.

Resources

TECHNOLOGY RESOURCES FOR COLLABORATIVE TEAMING

Purpose	Web site	Use for collaborative teams	Cost
Schedule meeting dates	http://doodle .com/?locale=en	Use the site to identify open dates and times for meetings. Then, send the information to team members. Their responses help designate when most or all members can attend.	Free
Conference calls	https://www.free conference.com	Use the site to send autogenerated e-mails, reminders, and brief agendas to team members. It has the capacity for small to large team meetings. Team members call in to participate.	Free for basic conference calls
Videoconference	https://appear.in	Use this site to videoconference for up to eight people for free. Create a "room," then send the link to team members.	Free
Videoconference	http://www.any meeting.com	Use the site to videoconference for up to 200 people for free. The site can also take polls (e.g., for determining consensus).	Free
Digital whiteboard	http://www.scriblink .com	Use this digital whiteboard to share online in real time. Notes and images can be typed or drawn, saved as a document, then e-mailed to participants.	Free
Whiteboard	https://realtime board.com	This site is a real-time whiteboard for use by multiple people.	Educators eligible for free version with extended features
Multiuser whiteboard	http://www.scribblar .com	This site is a real-time multiuser whiteboard.	Requires payment
Web-based meeting	http://www.webex .com	Use this site to invite team members to conferences. Users can interact with real-time audio and visuals and use documents from different locations.	Requires payment
Web-based meeting	http://www.twiddla .com	The site allows real-time collaboration with access to a whiteboard.	Free; upgrade requires payment

(continued)

TECHNOLOGY RESOURCES FOR COLLABORATIVE TEAMING *(continued)*

Purpose	Web site	Use for collaborative teams	Cost
Visual workspace for teams and individuals (e.g., co-planning)	http://vyew.com	This site allows real-time work and web conferencing. It offers a checklist for assignments and the ability to track tasks' status, add notes to documents, and assemble documents.	Free version for up to 10 people; upgrade requires payment
Co-teaching manual	http://www.schools.utah.gov/sars/DOCS/resources/coteach.aspx	This manual is used in Utah for state training.	Free
Co-teaching lesson plans and blank template	http://www.2teachllc.com/lessons.html	This site is by Dr. Wendy Murawski and Ilona Merrit of California State University, Northridge.	Free
Paraprofessionals	http://www.paracenter.org/library/	This site is from the PAR²A Center Resource Library.	Free

RESOURCES ON CREATING EFFECTIVE INCLUSIVE SCHOOLS AND COLLABORATIVE TEAMING FOR INCLUSIVE EDUCATION

School Restructuring and Improvement to Create Effective and Inclusive Schools

Fisher, D., & Frey, N. (Eds.). (2003). *Inclusive urban schools.* Baltimore, MD: Paul H. Brookes Publishing Co.

Hehir, T., & Katzman, L.I. (2012). *Effective inclusive schools: Designing successful schoolwide programs.* San Francisco, CA: Jossey-Bass.

Villa, R.A., & Thousand, J.S. (Eds.). (2005). *Creating an inclusive school* (2nd ed.). Alexandria, VA: Association for Supervision and Curriculum Development.

Collaborative Teaming for Inclusive Education

Cuaston-Theoharis, J. (2009). *The paraprofessional's handbook for effective support in inclusive classrooms.* Baltimore, MD: Paul H. Brookes Publishing Co.

Dettmer, P., Knackendoffel, A.P., & Thurston, L.P. (2013). *Collaboration, consultation, and teamwork for students with special needs* (7th ed.). Upper Saddle River, NJ: Pearson.

Friend, M., & Cook, L. (2013). *Interactions: Collaboration skills for school professionals* (7th ed.). Upper Saddle River, NJ: Pearson.

McDonnell, J., Johnson, J.W., & McQuivey, C. (2008). *Embedded instruction for students with developmental disabilities in general education classes.* Alexandria, VA: Council for Exceptional Children, Division of Developmental Disabilities.

Murawski, W.W. (2009). *Collaborative teaching at the secondary level: Making the co-teaching marriage work!* Thousand Oaks, CA: Corwin Press.

Murawski, W.W. (2010). *Collaborative teaching at the elementary level: Making the co-teaching marriage work!* Thousand Oaks, CA: Corwin Press.

Potts, E.A., & Howard, L.A. (2010). *How to co-teach: A guide for general and special educators.* Baltimore, MD: Paul H. Brookes Publishing Co.

Villa, R.A., Thousand, J.S., & Nevin, A.I. (2013). *A guide to co-teaching: New lessons and strategies to facilitate student learning* (3rd ed.). Thousand Oaks, CA: Corwin Press.

Collaboration with Families (Multicultural Sensitivity, Family-Centered Programs, and Ways to Provide Services that are Culturally Responsive)

Turnbull, A.P., Turnbull, H.R., Erwin, E.J., Soodak, L.C., & Shogren, K.A. (2015). *Professionals, families, and exceptionality: Positive outcomes through partnerships and trust* (7th ed.). Upper Saddle River, NJ: Pearson.

Peer Relationships and Supports

Carter, E.W., Cushing, L.S., & Kennedy, C.H. (2009). *Peer support strategies for improving all students' social lives and learning.* Baltimore, MD: Paul H. Brookes Publishing Co.

Hughes, C., & Carter, E.W. (2008). *Peer buddy programs for successful secondary inclusion.* Baltimore, MD: Paul H. Brookes Publishing Co.

Janney, R., & Snell, M.E. (2006). *Teachers' guides to inclusive practices: Social relationships and peer support* (2nd ed.). Baltimore, MD: Paul H. Brookes Publishing Co.

Inclusive Teaching Strategies

Hammeken, P.A. (2007). *The teacher's guide to inclusive education: 750 strategies for success.* Thousand Oaks, CA: Corwin Press.

Mastropieri, M.A., & Scruggs, T.E. (2014). *The inclusive classroom: Strategies for effective differentiated instruction* (5th ed.). Upper Saddle River, NJ: Pearson.

Index